On the Emergence and Understanding of Asian Global Leadership

On the Emergence and Understanding of Asian Global Leadership

Edited by
David De Cremer

DE GRUYTER

ISBN 978-3-11-067194-0
e-ISBN (PDF) 978-3-11-067198-8
e-ISBN (EPUB) 978-3-11-067206-0

Library of Congress Control Number: 2021933603

Bibliographic information published by the Deutsche Nationalbibliothek
The Deutsche Nationalbibliothek lists this publication in the Deutsche Nationalbibliografie;
detailed bibliographic data are available on the Internet at http://dnb.dnb.de.

Cover image: hrabar/iStock/Getty Images Plus und leonello/iStock/Getty Images Plus
Typesetting: Integra Software Services Pvt. Ltd.
Printing and binding: CPI books GmbH, Leck

www.degruyter.com

To Hannah – wishing her much success and fatherly love on her life journey navigating cross-cultural differences in a globalized world.

Advance Praise for *On the Emergence and Understanding of Asian Global Leadership*

To truly understand Asia, one needs to grasp not only its cultural dimensions, but also the organizational and societal contexts which provide a training ground and unique challenges and opportunities for Asian leaders. In this book, leading scholars share the latest thinking and scientific research on exactly these topics. Highly recommended for both novices and seasoned executives and scholars!

–Donald L. Ferrin, Ph.D.
Professor of Organisational Behaviour and Human Resources
Lee Kong Chian School of Business
Singapore Management University

While Asia's rapid economic growth has caught the attention of the world, the study of the leadership engine behind the growth has been scarce. This book fills the void by assembling a coherent group of insightful articles to explore and explicate how Asian business leadership is different yet also similar to Western business leadership. The similarity resides in the meaning of leadership, that is, the capacity to influence others to achieve a common goal, whereas the difference manifests in the means or styles to exert such influence. With better and deeper understandings of Asian business leadership, this book offers invaluable wisdom to bridge the gap between the East and West for a more prosperous future of all mankind.

–Xiao-Ping Chen
Philip M. Condit Endowed Chair Professor in Business Administration,
Editor-in-Chief of Management Insights and Incoming Editor-in-Chief of
Management and Organization Review
Department of Management and Organization
Foster School of Business
University of Washington

https://doi.org/10.1515/9783110671988-202

Contents

Part III: **Asian Global Leadership in Action**

David De Cremer

Introduction to the Emergence of Asian Global Leadership

For quite some time, the idea that the 21st century would be dominated by the Asian continent has been traveling around. Today, we can see that this expectation is taking real and firm shape. Long gone seem the days where, for example, China was only the factory of the world and engaged in a kind of copy-paste type of innovation. Today, China is leading in technological developments and is one of the fastest – if not the fastest – leaders employing these new technologies almost immediately in their society and organizations to power efficiency at all levels. However, at the same time, we do see that despite this new reality, it is interesting and challenging to see that old stereotypes about China specifically and Asia more generally are still dominating in the West. But, do not be fooled: the reality is that the Asian continent – being powered by China and India as the two places with the largest populations – is the place to be if one wants to see and benefit from economic growth. As the chief client officer (CCO) and managing director of the Center for Creative Leadership, Dr. Thomas Goh, notes: "Asia is the new center of the world!"

The Growing Power of Asia

If we look at the numbers, we see for example that Asia's economic growth puts the growth of the rest of the world in shadow. Indeed, as of 2020, Asia's GDP is bigger than the rest of the world combined (Brown, 2020). This exponential growth of the GDP in Asia is no surprise, as the International Monetary Fund (IMF) demonstrated that over the last ten years the GDP in Asia went up 160 percent, whereas the average global growth in that same period was only 30 percent (Ihara & Cho, 2019). This economic growth has significantly increased purchasing power. For example, according to LMC Automotive, since 2007, Asians have been buying more cars and trucks than people in any other region in the world. And today, spending in Asia is higher than in the rest of the world (Wang, 2019). This is no surprise as the size of the global middle-class has grown by about 1.5 billion in the last decade and Asia is almost entirely responsible for this growth (Yueh, 2013). All of this has led to a reality where Asian economies in 2020–2021 have for the first time since the 19th century become larger than the rest of the world's economies combined (Romei & Reed, 2019). Moreover, let's not forget that Asia's recent surge is more a return to a reality that once used to be the default. Indeed, Asia used to dominate the world economy for most of human history until the 19th century.

Together with this economic growth, the awareness of Asia being the place to be has grown among its leaders and institutes. For example, Narendra Modi, prime

https://doi.org/10.1515/9783110671988-204

minister of India, told his audience at the annual meeting of the Asian Infrastructure Investment Bank, "Now the continent finds itself at the centre of global economic activity. . . . It has become the main growth engine of the world. In fact, we are now living through what many have termed the 'Asian Century.'" Awareness is also there when it comes down to how Asia is able to create value for organizations and society from an intellectual point of view. Indeed, intellectual capital is also growing exponentially – almost every year, a higher number of Asian universities enter the top 100 of many higher education rankings. So intellectual promotion combined with economic growth means that an increasing number of multinationals are starting to realize that the Asian market will move center stage with respect to having more wealthy and better educated talents and customers, requiring a strategy where the top employees in those companies will also have to be based in Asia.

When we see such drastic economic and demographic changes happening, it is clear that a power shift is taking place. Even more so, it has become clear that not only does Asia have the biggest purchasing power, but it also harbors the largest pool of digital talents. Indeed, many Asian countries (e.g. China, Japan, Vietnam and Singapore) are countries that have grown rapidly or are currently in full expansion, and interestingly, they have as much or more technology focus as Silicon Valley. Asian countries harbor the largest number of technology startups, and – in my experience – its population seems less fearful than their Western counterparts to use technology in their daily lives and organizations. In an era where AI and automation are increasingly affecting how we shape and lead our societies and organizations (De Cremer, 2020), the question that becomes prevalent is whether the notion of global leadership is also shifting to become an Asian-inspired kind of leadership. Indeed, being a global leader today holds that one needs to know the main stakeholder, which is now Asia. In addition, most of the trade is taking place in Asia, so companies from around the globe will have to acquire a mindset to work and do business in this part of the world.

A Focus on Asian Global Leadership

While in the early days of globalization, Western companies were moving East and implementing their way of leading organizations and businesses (we can call this Globalization 1.0, where Asia had to adapt), today's picture shows that Western organizations will now be influenced in their ways of working by Asian ways of doing business (we can now speak of Globalization 2.0), where the West and East will have to be integrated. It is therefore no exaggeration to say that with the rise of Asia's influence, a transformation is about to happen: an initial Western-dominated kind of thinking on global leadership will have to shift to a more comprehensive perspective where global leadership is the focus. In fact, Asian management practices and values are becoming more influential and will thus also color approaches to how leaders act and decide at the global level. Despite this reality, this transformation process, in which the East starts influencing the West, also comes with many challenges. For example, it is still the case that Asian leaders in most multinationals are a minority in global leadership teams. Although an increasing number of regional HR heads at global companies are talking about the necessity for developing local talents into global leaders, there still seems to be a lack of commitment to this goal, as most senior leadership levels in those companies are still lacking diversity.

In this book, I aim to present a number of thought pieces that address the question of why and how Asian leaders will become global leaders, what challenges they will face in this transition, and what such transformation of the notion of a Western global leadership style to an Asian global leadership means in terms of behaviors and actions.

Structure of the Book

In Part I, the focus will be on clarifying more deeply what the notion of Asian Global Leadership stands for and how prior research and conceptual analyses can help us in this endeavor. In Chapter 2, Song and Ma argue that Asia is increasingly playing an important role at the world stage, but this also introduces the challenge for Asian firms to develop more effective leaders and demands for scholars to develop a better understanding of Asian leadership. This chapter reviews the cross-cultural leadership research out there, with a specific focus on East, South and Southeast Asian countries. In Chapter 3, Chong and Richards note that in the wake of increasing globalization and the growth in Asian markets, it is important to explore and understand the driving forces behind the momentum of Asian leaders. They do so by highlighting the Asian perspective by introducing Chinese philosophies and their influence on leadership. In addition, they identify four further essential qualities of global leaders that they believe are universally applicable – namely, revolutionary, flexible, disciplinary and strategic leadership. In Chapter 4, De Cremer, De Cremer and Zhang provide evidence that people from Eastern societies are more likely to engage in abstract processing, whereas those from Western societies are more inclined to engage in concrete processing. The authors argue that understanding information processing capacities is important to those who are in leadership positions as it allows them to become better able to take different perspectives and understand how people perceive reality. These authors specifically focus on how Asian ways of looking at the world will influence practices of global leadership.

In Part II, the focus will be on identifying a number of challenges that Asian leaders face in a globalized world. In Chapter 5, Chia and Wei note that although Asia is home to the world's wealthiest individuals, it is also socially and economically diverse by simultaneously being home to the world's poorest citizens, with 1.2 billion people in Asia living under the international poverty line of US$3.20 a day. These authors present a careful examination of the leadership of successful Asian social innovators who have tried to tackle this highly diverse economic challenge. They primarily focus on social innovation for health in Asia. In Chapter 6, Tjosvold and Wong argue that cooperative goals develop mutual benefit motivation and integrative conflict management that in turn induce open-mindedness that makes organizations perform better. According to these authors, Asian managers have the advantage of considerable experiences working in collectivist organizational cultures that emphasize the value of mutual, cooperative relationships. And it is these experiences that in their view can contribute to the leadership competence and development of Asian managers. In Chapter 7, Shamdasani argues that while Asian companies have increasingly demonstrated that they have the technologies, business models, leadership and ambition to drive growth and build strong brands in Asia and globally, they have largely underinvested in internal branding, which is key to building a high-performing and purpose-led organization ready to take on the world. He outlines how aligning internal branding with delivery of the brand promise to customers can elevate Asian companies from having impact at the regional level to the global level.

In Part III, the focus will be on what Asian Global Leadership can reveal in terms of the behaviors and actions leaders show in Asian societies specifically and the world more generally. In Chapter 8, Eyring and Eyring start from the assumption that sustained business growth is a key indicator of success and that achieving such growth requires new collective leadership capabilities that not only span functions across a business, but also across entire business ecosystems. For this reason, they argue that global perspectives on leading growth can be enriched by the emerging paradigm of collective leadership and the incorporation of Asian values and experiences. In Chapter 9, Yam, Gloor and Liu argue that humor plays an important role in leadership effectiveness, but that a divergent understanding of humor exists across cultures. Therefore, these authors highlight the culturally embedded attitudes toward humor, including how they can facilitate effective global leadership. In Chapter 10, Lim and Yao introduce the proposition that the prevalence of uncivil and disrespectful behaviors in the workplace is disturbing, leading to negative work and personal outcomes. Effective leadership is therefore needed to create a conducive social environment for employees in order to sustain the long-term growth and functionality of the organization. Unfortunately, according to these authors, incivility seems prevalent, not just in Western cultures where individual rights and freedom of expression are encouraged, but also in Asian societies where social harmony is valued. As such, guidance to global leaders in building a respectful and supportive workplace is needed.

In Chapter 11, Mai addresses the importance of creativity as an essential factor to facilitate economic growth and social reform at the macro level and enhance individual performance and competitiveness at the micro level. He argues that Asian countries are also starting to suffer diminishing returns from capital investment, cheap labor and natural resources. As a result, Asian companies therefore have to re-evaluate economic growth strategies and instead focus more on promoting individual creativity and fostering industry innovation. In Chapter 12, de Pater and Xun examine the challenging job components of leaders in Singapore. They argue that this is necessary because leadership in the 21st century has new and unique requirements for leadership effectiveness, and therefore we cannot base ourselves only on the experiences of successful executives in the West. They develop an overview demonstrating that – due to cultural differences – leading in the East requires different behaviors, skills, knowledge and abilities than leading in the West. In Chapter 13, Kim argues that in the 21st century, work is one of the most common contributors to life stress and that leadership is one of the most important factors in enabling people to deal with work-related stressors. In exploring leadership as an important source of influence on employees' work lives and performances, he takes a specific focus on Asia.

Conclusion

When it comes to global leadership roles, both the economic situation and the emerging number of local talents underscore the importance of Asian practices, perspectives and values to leading effectively. With this transformation from dominating Western views (Globalization 1.0) to the almost reversed situation where we need to try integrating the East and West (Globalization 2.0), it is clear that many challenges, opportunities and dilemmas will present themselves. It is my hope that this book will help you deepen your understanding of these emerging issues and prepare yourself for a truly globalized experience at the leadership level.

References

Brown, G.D. (2020). *XL: Asia: Exponential leadership in the Asian Century*. Published by Pikkal & Co.

De Cremer, D. (2020). *Leadership by Algorithm: Who Leads and Who Follows in the AI Era?* Harriman House (London).

Goh, T. (2018). The global Asian leader: From local star to global CXO. *Center for Creative Leadership*. Retrieved on 21 January 2021 from https:https://www.ccl.org/articles/research-reports/the-global-asian-leader-from-local-star-to-global-cxo/

Ihara, K. & Cho, Y. (2019). Asia is home to 50% of world's fastest growing companies. *Nikkei Asian Review*. Retrieved on 21 January 2021 from https://asia.nikkei.com/Business/Companies/Asia-is-home-to-50-of-world-s-fastest-growing-companies2.

Romei, V. & Reed, J. (2019). The Asian century is set to begin. *The Financial Times*. Retrieved on 21 January 2021 from https://www.ft.com/content/520cb6f6-2958-11e9-a5ab-ff8ef2b976c7.

Wang, H. (2019). In 2020, Asian economies will become larger than the rest of the world combined – here's how. *World Economic Forum*. Retrieved on 21 January 2021 from https://www.weforum.org/agenda/2019/07/the-dawn-of-the-asian-century/.

Yueh, L. (2013). The rise of the global middle class. *BBC News*. Retrieved on 21 January 2021 from https://www.bbc.com/news/business–22956470.

Part I: **Understanding Asian Leadership in a Global Setting**

Zhaoli Song and Yu Ma

Chapter 1
An Asian-Centric View of Cross-Culture Leadership Research

Introduction

Asia is a continent with rich and diverse traditions.[1] Mesopotamia, Ancient India and Ancient China were cradles of civilization. For most of thousand years of history prior to the Industrial Revolution, Asia was much more developed than the rest of the world by many indicators (Khanna, 2019). Besides its historical significance, about 60 percent of the world's current population lives in Asia, which also contributes to more than one third of the world's GDP. Given its highest GDP growth rate among all continents, Asia is expected to cast even larger influences over the rest of the world in the near future. Statements claiming that the 21st century is "the Asian Century" (Ishida & Park, 1985; Kishore, 2008) and claims that "the future is Asian" (Khanna, 2019) exemplify how Asia is viewed for its current and future significance to the world. However, the breakneck pace of economic growth in many Asian countries has created a double-edged sword – many countries formerly regarded negatively by some as "backward countries" have become engines of development in the new world economy in just several decades, while there is a huge pressure to forge Asia business leaders in a compressed timeframe (Bruning & Tung, 2013). Asia's increasingly important role on the world stage and the challenges confronting Asian firms to develop effective leaders demand a better understanding of Asian leadership.

This chapter will review the cross-culture leadership research, with a focus on East, South, and Southeast Asian countries. We will first review cross-culture leadership research frameworks, including those developed by Hofstede and from the GLOBE Project. Then we will provide country-specific historical, social, cultural and leadership research overviews of several important Asian countries, including China, Japan, India, Indonesia, and Thailand. Finally, we will summarize challenges and opportunities to develop the Asian-centric leadership research by integrating current cross-culture leadership research literature.

1 This book chapter was partially funded by Singapore Ministry of Education Social Science Research Thematic Grant R-311-000-029-119.

https://doi.org/10.1515/9783110671988-001

Existing Cross-Culture Leadership Frameworks

Management scholars hold different views on the influences of culture on leadership. Accordingly, researchers are either taking on perspective culture-universal or perspective culture-specific, with the former viewing leadership as consistent across cultures and the latter viewing leadership as unique to a particular culture (Bass, Stogdill & Bass, 2008). This dichotomization of cross-cultural leadership views corresponds to the distinction of "emic" for the culture-universal versus "etic" for the culture-specific research approaches respectively that originated in linguistic and anthropology (Dorfman et al., 1997). The culture-specific or emic research is also sometimes named an "indigenous approach" in leadership (Cheng et al., 2004) as well as in social psychology (Yang, 2000). It is worth noting that a group of scholars from Hong Kong and Taiwan, including Kuo-Shu Yang and Kwang-Kuo Hwang, have made significant contributions to the progress of indigenous psychology, particularly the establishment of the indigenous Chinese psychology (Leung, 2007). In general, both culture-universal and culture-specific approaches have received some empirical support (Dorfman et al., 1997).

Bird and Mendenhall (2016) reviewed the cross-culture management studies from the past half-century. They reviewed leadership research based on a cross-culture research typology, including unicultural, comparative, and intercultural types, that was originally proposed by Adler (1983). The unicultural approach is essentially the culture-specific view with the focus on leadership within the cultural context of a single country. The comparative method is to compare leadership in two or more countries. The intercultural research is the examination of interactions of people from different cultures or countries. After summarizing past cross-culture leadership research based on this typology, Bird and Mendenhall (2016) proposed a fourth category of global leadership, referring to the exploration of leadership in a global context.

The most well-known and influential cross-culture framework was developed by Geert Hofstede. According to Hofstede, national cultures can influence management and leadership in substantial ways. Based on his cross-national surveys collected in IBM from the late 1960s to the early 1970s, he developed the culture dimension theory (Hofstede, 1984, 2001) to explain national culture through evaluating values of individuals along six dimensions: power distance, individualism vs. collectivism, uncertainty avoidance, masculinity vs. femininity, long-term orientation vs. short-term orientation, and indulgence vs. restraint (Hofstede & Milosevic, 2011). Among these dimensions, the first four have been more extensively studied by cross-cultural scholars. A review of literature summarizing management research between 1980 to 2002 shows the application of the Hofstede framework to study leadership at the individual, the group, as well as the country levels (Kirkman, Lowe & Gibson, 2006). Although his framework has been challenged on both the theoretical and empirical aspects through heated exchanges (Hofstede, 2002; McSweeney, 2002a, 2002b; Williamson, 2002), meta-analysis studies have shown the validity of this framework and have even proposed some new directions for improvement (Steel & Taras, 2010; Taras, Kirkman & Steel, 2010).

The Global Leadership and Organizational Behaviour Effectiveness (GLOBE) research program provides another well-known framework of culture value. According to the GLOBE Project leader Robert House, the purpose of GLOBE is to help understand how culture influences leadership, organizational effectiveness, and societal-level outcomes such as economic competitiveness and human conditions, through a collaboration among 160 scholars in 62 different cultures (House et al., 2004). GLOBE quantifies cultural attributes along eight dimensions, including uncertainty avoidance, power distance, collectivism (including institutional collectivism and in-group collectivism), gender egalitarianism, assertiveness, future orientation, performance orientation, and humane orientation. Based on the culturally endorsed implicit leadership theory (CLT), the GLOBE Project also describes leadership along six dimensions: charismatic/value-based leadership, team-oriented leadership, participative leadership, humane-oriented leadership, autonomous leadership, and self-protective leadership. These six dimensions are further divided into 21 subscales in the Leader Attributes and Behavior Questionnaire. Compared to Hofstede's framework, GLOBE claims to be more theory-oriented. There have been comparisons of these two cultural models and debates on which one is more valid (Hofstede, 2010; Javidan et al., 2006; Smith, 2006; Venaik & Brewer, 2010). The existing meta-analysis on GLOBE dimensions is available but limited (Schneid et al., 2015). Table 1.1 provides a summary to compare the Hofstede and GLOBE models.

Table 1.1: Summaries of the Hofstede and GLOBE studies.

Differences	Hofstede Model	GLOBE Model
Time period	1967–1973	1994–1997
Respondents	Managers and non-managers	Managers
Organizations surveyed	IBM and its subsidiaries	951 organizations globally
Industries	Information technology	Financial services, food processing, telecommunications
Dimensions	Power distance, individualism vs. collectivism, uncertainty avoidance, masculinity vs. femininity, long-term orientation vs. short-term orientation, indulgence vs. restraint	Power distance, uncertainty avoidance, collectivism (including institutional collectivism and in-group collectivism), gender egalitarianism, assertiveness, future orientation, performance orientation, and humane orientation

With the space limitation, we can only select a handful of Asia's 48 countries to discuss. In the following section, we review leadership in five Asian countries: China, India, Japan, Indonesia and Thailand. These countries are from East Asia, South Asia, and Southeast Asia. Each of these countries has its unique historical and cultural background and has nurtured its own rich indigenous leadership traditions. There are also many contemporary leadership studies for us to review. For each country, we first introduce its historical and cultural background, its traditional culture and leadership, followed by the contemporary leadership research.

Among those contemporary leadership studies across these five countries, transformational, servant, ethical, and authentic leadership styles have been examined most frequently. Transformational leaders inspire, encourage, and lead subordinates to devote into change processes that are related to individuals, teams, and organizations (Bass & Riggio, 2006). Servant leaders are leaders who put followers' needs and interests above their own. They focus on followers' growth and provide support for followers to grow and succeed(Greenleaf, 2002). Ethical leaders are honest, caring, and guided by principles. Their decisions are characterized as fair and balanced (Brown & Treviño, 2006). Authentic leaders cultivate self-awareness and transparency, internalize moral perspectives, and take balanced views of different opinions (Walumbwa et al., 2008). These leadership perspectives reflect a need to respond to constant changes and echo the moral expectations attached to leaders in Asian societies, which may be reasons why they have been more often adopted and examined in empirical studies.

Leadership in China

Historical and Cultural Background

China is one of the world's oldest civilizations, with history continuously expanding for thousands of years. Chinese philosophies, political systems, and technologies had huge influences over other adjacent countries in East Asia, Southeast Asia, and Central Asia in ancient times. Chinese hegemony in East Asia began to decline in the 18th century. After the First Opium War in the 1840s, China began its painful transformation process toward modernization. Major political events included the ending of the imperial era and the founding of a republic in 1911, the Second Sino-Japanese War, the Chinese Civil War and the winning of Marxism in the establishment of the People's Republic of China in 1949, which was led by Mao Zedong. In 1978, after a long period of closed-door policy, China began a new era of reform, opening up, and socialist modernization, championed by Deng Xiaoping. Forty years of reform and opening up have created a miracle: China is an economic powerhouse with the second-highest national GDP in the world.

With drastic changes in modern history, Chinese culture also has undergone great changes over the years, and has become very rich, complex, and dynamic (Lin, 2010). Chinese culture is often thought to be dominated by Confucianism (Keller & Kronstedt, 2005). However, it has also been pointed out that Chinese culture is also a mix of Buddhism, Taoism and Legalism (Shenkar et al., 1998). Recently, research has shown that traditional, Western, and socialist cultures have collectively influenced the contemporary Chinese culture (Shenkar et al., 1998). The various traditional philosophies and cultural elements are important components of the modern cultural structure of China (Liu, 2017).

Traditional Culture and Leadership

In the following section, we review traditional philosophies that have shaped Chinese leadership thinking and practices, including Confucianism, Taoism, Legalism, and Sun Tzu's military strategy thought.

Confucianism and Leadership

Confucius (551–479 BC) was a great philosopher, politician, and educator who founded Confucianism, the school regarded as one of the most influential ideologies in China (Song & Beckett, 2013). Confucian main values include harmony, benevolence, morality, and hierarchy.

Confucian philosophies are partly reflected in current Chinese leadership practices. First of all, Confucian leaders are supposed to maintain harmonious relationships with their followers and achieve organizational goals in a harmonious way (Liu, 2017). Second, Confucian-inspired leaders are expected to act with benevolence, which means that leaders should treat their employees selflessly and give them love and support. Moreover, Confucian leaders express strong ethicality through their behaviors. They act as role models for employees in shaping their moral behaviors (Ma & Tsui, 2015). Finally, Confucian-inspired leaders pay attention to propriety and deal with relationships based on traditional social norms and hierarchies.

Taoism and Leadership

Lao Tzu (about 571 BC–?) was one of the greatest ancient philosophers in China. His book *Tao Te Ching* laid the ideological foundation for Taoism. Taoism is a method and theory explaining how people understand the relationship between the universe and human survival, and is also regarded as the source of wisdom for China's modernization (Bai & Roberts, 2011).

In terms of its influence on leadership thinking, first, Taoism advocates that leaders should avoid interfering with the environment excessively and that extreme behaviors (such as over-emphasizing a single goal or favoring a certain group) can break the balance of the "Tao," the fundamental principles that are determined by heaven. Secondly, Taoism pays attention to flexibility and reversion (Cheung & Chan, 2005). Song and Beckett (2013) asserted that flexibility, spontaneity, and relativism are reflected in Chinese leadership behaviors and can be traced back to Taoism. Finally, the core believes of Taoism also include harmony and sustainable balance, which may explain why a successful leader is expected to have a peaceful personality in China (Zhang & Foo, 2012).

Legalism and Leadership

The core idea of legalism was proposed by Han Fei (280–233 BC). After reviewing and integrating the thoughts of different scholars, he proposed three elements for governing a state: "Fa" (law), "Shi" (power), and "Shu" (management technique) (Liu, 2017).

Firstly, Legalism proposes that effective leaders are proficient in formulating and implementing strict rules to govern. Because the efficiency of an organization's operation depends on the implementation of "Fa" (law), its importance cannot be overlooked by leaders (Hwang, 2008). Secondly, top leaders must have the right to reward and punish subordinates. Decentralized power may hinder the implementation of laws and even affect the solid position of power. Finally, leaders should master a series of management skills that can help organizations achieve their goals. The basic characteristics of these skills are objectivity, enforceability, practicability, and universality. From the perspective of legalists, effective management should be the combination of "Fa," "Shi", and "Shu."

Sun Tzu's Thought and Leadership

Sun Tzu (or *Sun Wu*) (545–470 BC) was a military strategist and author of *The Art of War*. He proposed five critical military leadership attributes: wisdom, trustworthiness, benevolence, courage and firmness (Sun, Chen, & Zhang, 2008).

First, leaders are supposed to have extensive knowledge and wisdom to guide subordinates and help organizations envision the future, as well as to develop tactics according to circumstances. Second, leaders earn trust from others by demonstrating their own integrity and trustworthiness. Third, leaders need to treat followers with respect and kindness to win their hearts. Fourth, courage can help leaders make quick and difficult decisions, and lift the spirit of their subordinates to face challenges. Finally, leaders are supposed to use the law strictly and handle things clearly (Liu, 2017).

Confucianism, Taoism, Legalism, and Sun Tzu's military strategy thought, among all traditional Chinese thinking, have the most significant influence over leadership in China. Other cultural traditions, such as Mohism and Buddhism, also have had important impacts on Chinese leaders. Moreover, culture is complex and dynamic. Traditional cultures, intertwined with Marxist ideology, socialist practices, and Western perspectives, have jointly shaped the leadership landscape of modern China.

Contemporary Leadership Research

The existing literature on Chinese leadership shows that the majority of research directly applies or verifies the existing Western leadership theories in China. For example, some scholars have verified the application of transformational leadership (Li, Zhao & Begley, 2015), authentic leadership (Lyu et al., 2019), servant leadership (Wang, Kwan & Zhou, 2017), empowering leadership (Li, He, Yam, & Long, 2015), ethical leadership (Ren & Chadee, 2017), charismatic leadership (Wu & Wang, 2012), humble leadership (Zhou & Wu, 2018), spiritual leadership (Wang et al., 2019), narcissistic leadership (Xiao et al., 2018), humorous leadership (Dai, Chin & Rafiq, 2019), and other leadership theories in Chinese organizations.

Some scholars have tried to develop Chinese characteristic leadership theories based on Western leadership theories by integrating Chinese culture, values, organizational characteristics, and other specific factors. For example, different from Western leadership research, Ling, Chen, and Wang (1987) and Ling, Chia, and Fang (2000) found a distinct factor of Chinese leadership – namely, personal morality in modeling leadership factors. Further, Li and Shi (2008) found that transformational leadership in China includes moral shaping, charm, vision shaping, and personalized thinking. According to these studies, Chinese leaders pay more attention to morality, which is consistent with traditional Chinese values that emphasize moral leaders (Wong, 2001). Moreover, Zhang et al. (2011) drawn upon Chinese Confucianism and the Western studies of aesthetic behavior in leadership to build and develop aesthetic leadership theory in a Chinese context.

Some scholars have also constructed indigenous theories of leadership. For example, Farh and Cheng (2000) identified three dimensions for paternalistic leadership: authoritarianism, mercy and moral leadership. Zheng (2006) defined differential leadership as a situation in which leaders treat subordinates differently according to whether they belong to a favored group. Based on Taoism and its key concepts of "Tao" (way), "Te" (virtue) and "Ho" (harmony), McElhatton and Jackson (2012) proposed a conceptual model of harmonious leadership to explain modern leadership in China. These studies emphasized the influence of culture on leadership, as well as distinctive leadership behavior and practice in Chinese culture.

Leadership in India

Historical and Cultural Background

The history of India began with the birth of the Indus Valley Civilization that dates back approximately to 3300 BC. From 1500 BC to 1200 BC, the *Vedas*, the Indian scriptures, were written and the caste system became formalized. Around 500 BC, two of India's most significant religions emerged: Buddhism and Jainism. In 321 BC, Chandragupta had annexed other states and built the Mauryan Empire, which was the first great Indian empire in Indian history (Smith, 1999). From the 8th century, the Islamic conquest had changed the cultural pattern of India tremendously. From the late 16th century, European influence and later colonization of India by British changed India dramatically. Mahatma Gandhi, through a non-violent movement of non-cooperation, helped establish the independent India after World War II (Chandra et al., 2016). After establishing independence, India's society had been influenced by nationalism, socialism, and protectionism, which restricted its economic development. Since the beginning of the 21st century, India has deepened its economic reform and has emerged as a fastest growing major economy in the world. India has a dual polity system, with the federal government at the center and 29 states at the periphery. Indian societies have salient diversities in terms of race, religion, and language.

Traditional Culture and Leadership

In the following section, we review traditional philosophies that have shaped Indian leadership thinking and practice, including religion and Indian ancient literature.

Religion and Leadership

Hinduism is the predominant religion in India and is one of the major religions of the world. Hinduism is a synthesis of Brahmanism, Buddhism, Jainism doctrine, Indian cultures, traditions, and philosophy.

The Hindu trinity consists of Brahma, Vishnu, and Shiva. They represent the three foundational powers of nature respectively: creation, destruction, and maintenance. Life in this world is the embodiment of the three powers. They are interrelated and they can't be separated. Low and Muniapan (2011) proposed that the thoughts of the Hindu trinity can be applied to explain organizational development and the organizational life cycle. Leaders play a crucial role in creating and maintaining effective cultures (Brahma), transforming cultures to adapt to uncertain environments (Vishnu), and organizing renewal (Shiva).

Indian Ancient Literature and Leadership

Valmiki's *Ramayana* is regarded as one of the most glorious Indian epics and the first written literature in India. The *Ramayana* constitutes the principal source of spiritual, cultural, sociological, political, and artistic inspiration for India and Southeast Asian countries. The *Ramayana* narrates the journey and adventure of the ideal hero Sri Rama. He is the embodiment of *dharma* (righteousness, occupational duty) and provides a model for all humans. This story shows that evil will be defeated by virtue, which provides lessons and wisdoms for human life. Muniapan and Satpathy (2010) maintained that the transformational leadership style has been demonstrated by Sri Rama in the *Ramayana* and that Sri Rama has exhibited the four dimensions of transformational leadership developed by Bass and Avolio (1993) – namely, inspirational motivation, idealized influence, intellectual stimulation, and individualized consideration.

The *Bhagavad Gita* (Song of God), a part of the ancient Indian epic *Mahabharata*, has been researched extensively in the management literature and especially in leadership. It has been considered as the source of contemporary management wisdom and translated into different languages. Many researchers have discussed its application in management practices (Muniapan, 2006, 2009). Satpathy and Muniapan (2008) pointed out that the concept of self-knowledge in the *Bhagavad Gita* can provide a theoretical foundation for human capital development. The *Bhagavad Gita* is also a philosophical foundation for understanding leadership issues and business practices (Natesan, Keeffe & Darling, 2009). By integrating the *Bhagavad Gita* and transformational leadership theory, Dhulla (2014) found that transformational leadership in an Indian context focuses on exploring the inner world of the self, which is different from the Western transformational leadership theory that focuses on the external world of matter and energy.

Contemporary Leadership Research

The existing literature on Indian leadership shows that the majority of research directly applies or verifies the existing Western leadership theories in India. For example, some scholars have verified the application of transformational leadership (Pradhan, Panda & Jena, 2017), paternalistic leadership (Rawat & Lyndon, 2016), servant leadership (Muthia & Krishnan, 2015), authentic leadership (Alok, 2014), and ethical leadership (Khuntia & Suar, 2004) in Indian organizations.

Some scholars try to adapt Western leadership theories to reflect Indian culture. For example, Singh and Krishnan (2005) identified and described specific attributes of Indian transformational leadership. Furthermore, they developed and validated a new scale to measure transformational leadership in an Indian context. They found that the culture-specific dimensions of Indian transformational leadership include nurturant, personal touch, expertise, simple-living-high-thinking (following a lifestyle marked by simple living and keeping calm in all situations), loyalty, self-sacrifice, and giving models of motivation.

Some Indian scholars have constructed indigenous models of leadership, including the Nurturant-Task Leadership Model (Sinha, 1980), the OCTAPACE Model

(Pareek, 1981), the Karta Model of Leadership (Singh & Bhandarker, 1990), the Four Steps Model of Enlightened Leadership (Sharma, 1995), the Yin-Trinity Model of Leadership (Sharma, 2007), the Mother Leadership Model (Banerjee, 1998), the Workship (i.e., work as worship) Model of Leadership (Chatterjee, 1998), the Wisdom Leadership Model (Chakrabarti, 1999), the Contribution Model of Leadership (Singh, 2000), the 24-hour Leader/Responsible Leadership (Bhatta, 2000), and the Rishi as Re-see Model (Sharma, 2001). These models describe various values and attributes of Indian leadership from different perspectives. For example, the Nurturant-Task Leadership Model, the Karta Model of Leadership, and the Mother Leadership Model all emphasize leader's paternalistic role. The 24-hour Leader/Responsible Leadership, the Workship Model of Leadership, and the Contribution Model of Leadership depict leaders' dedication and selflessness in the workplace. Other models describe leaders' different behavioral styles, such as openness, autonomy, and environmental sensitivity.

Furthermore, Alok (2017) proposed an indigenous leadership theory called *Sāttvika* Leadership. *Sāttvika* Leadership is related to many positive outcomes, such as ethical climate, psychological capital, psychological empowerment, and work engagement. *Sāttvika* is the cognate system of Yoga, which emerged from the *Vedas*, the most revered religious literature in India. *Sāttvika* Leadership refers to "a set of purposive leader actions comprising knowledge-driven cooperation that are initiated on the basis of positive and reasonably accurate assumptions and executed through morally responsible and sustainably fruitful means to secure the flourishing of followers and the collective" (Alok, 2017).

Leadership in Japan

Historical and Cultural Background

Japan is an economic superpower with huge global influence. To understand how it transformed itself into a modern superpower, tracing Japan's development and history is important. Japan was united as the Yamato state in the 4th century. During the Asuka period (538–710), Buddhism, Confucianism, and Taoism were introduced to Japan. In 645, a new government and administrative system based on the Chinese model was established through the Taika Reforms. During the Kamakura period (1185–1333), Zen, a school of Mahayana Buddhism, was introduced to Japan and was widely accepted among Samurais who were the leading social class (Suzuki, 2019). During the later period of the Tokugawa era, Japan formed some of its own philosophies (Sawada, 1998). Samurais developed a spirit of loyalty and devotion toward their country. Craftsmen cultivated a kind of professional spirit called Craftsman's spirit, which emphasizes completing work perfectly in order to create high-quality products and service. Ishida Baigan, a lecturer and philosopher who was influenced by the

Zhu Xi school of Neo-Confucianism of the Song dynasty in China, initiated the Shin-gaku movement (heart learning), which provided an ideological foundation for Japanese commercial capitalism. He argued the relationship between "Li" (moral principle) and profit. In 1868, the Meiji Restoration restored imperial power to the Empire of Japan. During the Restoration, Japan made rapid strides to industrialize by adopting Western thoughts and methods (Walker, 2015). By the beginning of the 20th century, the rise of extreme nationalism in Japan led to the outbreak of a series of expansionist wars. After suffering defeat in World War II, Japan rebuilt its economy, its social and political infrastructure and has since emerged as one of the largest economies in the world. By the 1950s, the Japanese economy had grown through close cooperation between the government and corporations, giving birth to the giants of modern organizations such as Toyota Motor Corporation and Sony Corporation (Walker, 2015).

Traditional Culture and Leadership

Religion and Leadership

Shinto and Buddhism are two major religions that have deeply influenced business practices in Japan and can help us better understand Japanese leadership styles.

Shinto is considered the indigenous religion of Japan, which means "the way of gods." The core idea of Shinto involves the concept of "Kami" (gods or spirits). Shinto is animistic and pantheistic, believing that supernatural entities exist in all things. The Japanese emperor is regarded as a descendant of their gods and has the same status as the gods. Shinto implies a logic of harmony that develops trust-building and a resonance of value between a leader and employees, which is important for improving teamwork and organizational commitment. This logic of harmony is reflected in resonant leadership, which is usually found in Japanese organizations (Shibata & Kodama, 2009).

Buddhism believes that all beings experience reincarnation – they are reborn as a new life after death. Shah (2010) pointed out that the six virtues of the Bodhisattva code – generosity, discipline, patience, joyous effort, meditation, and wisdom – are advocated by the Mahayana school and greatly influence the definition and application of leadership. Zen is a form of Buddhism that preaches that one can achieve spiritual enlightenment through meditation and self-discipline (Rarick, 1994). Zen masters are usually viewed as pioneers of leadership training (Kets de Vries, 2005).

Bushido and Leadership

"Samurai" refers to the military aristocracy of pre-industrial and agricultural Japan. Bushido emphasizes the art of self-discipline in the process of growing or perfecting oneself, advocating that one should be more thoughtful, intelligent, and ever-victorious than their enemies or opponents. Low (2010) argued that Bushido is deeply influenced by Confucianism, emphasizing concepts such as loyalty to the master, self-discipline, respect, and ethical behavior. The ethic and values of samurai are derived from Confucianism, Zen Buddhism, and Shinto, which include rectitude, courage, benevolence, respect, honesty, honor, and loyalty.

In terms of its influence on leadership thinking, first of all, leaders are supposed to study diligently and strive to acquire profound knowledge. Second, Bushido emphasizes the role of introspection in avoiding mistakes (Low, 2018). A leader should adopt the samurai way, constantly asking themselves whether their policies and judgments are correct. Finally, the leaders who follow Bushido should also be a good listener and be able to put forward specific solutions.

Confucianism and Leadership

Compared with Chinese Confucianism, Japanese Confucianism is more external and concrete (Ames & Hershock, 2018). In China, Confucianism emphasizes "Ren" and "Shu" (putting oneself in the other's place), while the dominant value in Japanese Confucianism is "Zhong" (loyalty), which was regarded as the primary virtue in the Edo period. In fact, this value orientation was closely related to the social structure of Japan at that time. Unlike the Chinese political structure with the "Shi" (literati), the samurai class was the ruling class, so it was very important for samurai to be loyal to their monarch and lord.

In Japan, Confucianism demands that employees should respect and obey leaders who take a paternalistic attitude to their subordinates (Dorfman et al., 1997). Although Japanese organizations are hierarchical and highly organized (Haghirian, 2010), Japanese managers are expected to help and take care of their employees and involve themselves in employees' personal lives (Dorfman et al., 1997). When an organization is regarded as a big family, the primary role of a leader is to be a father and to preserve harmony, respect, and cohesion within the organization (Rarick, 1994).

Contemporary Leadership Research

Among the existing research on Japanese leadership, some have verified the application of Western leadership theories in Japan. For example, some scholars have explored the application of transformational leadership (Kimura, 2012), participative leadership (Hwang et al., 2015), charismatic leadership (Brocklehurst et al., 2013), directive leadership (Fukushige & Spicer, 2011), supportive leadership (Ishikawa, 2012), and ethical leadership (Kimura & Nishikawa, 2018) in Japanese organizations.

Empirical studies have shown the specificity of Japanese leadership by applying Western leadership theories and concepts. Yokochi-Bryce (1990) proposed that Japanese leaders tend to show more transformational leadership than transactional leadership. Studies have shown that although Japan shares common cultural characteristics with other Confucian-oriented Asian countries, the Japanese appreciate participative leadership more than other countries (Graen, 2006; Hwang et al., 2015). Kimura and Nishikawa (2018) suggested that Japanese ethical leadership has specific components under the influence of the cultural and institutional context of business ethics.

Enlightened from business practices in Japanese organizations, some scholars have summarized the characteristics of Japanese leaders. Japanese leadership mainly focuses on team harmony and interpersonal relationships, which is closely related to Confucian philosophy in Japan. For example, Low (2018) summarized Matsushita's and Akio Morita's thoughts (Sony) and their leadership ways. Matsushita believed that leaders should lead in a paternal way and treat their employees as part of a family. Similarly, Morita emphasized the value of teamwork and of creating a familial feeling within the corporation. Based on the traditional myth and religious background of Japan, Shibata and Kodama (2009) examined the leadership style of elite Japanese organizations. Innovative leadership was proposed to describe the leadership style that these elite Japanese organizations use to create and transform their organizational values and myths. These styles fit well with the characteristics of Japanese culture and business practices.

Leadership in Indonesia

Historical and Cultural Background

Indonesia is the world's largest archipelago with more than 17,000 islands, and has been an important maritime hub in Asia since the 2nd century AD. Indonesia is a nation with various cultures, races, and languages. In 700 BC, under the influence of the Dong Son culture, early Indonesians mastered the techniques of rice cultivation and bronze casting. They were animists who believed that all objects had a life force or soul. Around the 2nd century, Indian culture was introduced to Indonesia, and some small kingdoms emerged in West Java. At the end of the 10th century, Hinduism and Buddhism gradually syncretized, and Javanese culture began to emerge (Brown, 2003). The spread of Islam among the Indonesian inhabitants can be traced back to the 13th century in North Sumatra, and by the end of the 16th century, Islam had become the dominant religion in Java and Sumatra. In the 16th century, the Dutch colonized Indonesia. It was not until 1942 that the Japanese invasion and subsequent occupation ended Dutch rule. Indonesia eventually achieved its independence from Japan in 1945 (Ricklefs, 2008). After Indonesia's independence, Dutch reoccupation and various separatist movements against the new republic all hindered the economic and social development of Indonesia. In 1968, Suharto seized power from Sukarno and ruled as a dictator. Suharto's administration was named the New Order era. After Suharto's 32-year autocratic rule, he resigned in May 1998 (Ricklefs, 2008). In 1999, Indonesia held its first democratic elections, marking a new period of a democracy with openness and liberty. At the beginning of the 21st century, the Indonesian economy began to recover and grow steadily. Indonesia is now the largest economy in Southeast Asia and is classified as a newly industrialized country.

Traditional Culture and Leadership

Javanese Culture and Leadership

The Javanese people make up the largest ethnic group in Indonesia. Javanese culture has a dominant influence on modern Indonesia (Irawanto, Ramsey, & Ryan, 2011). The Javanese share three core values: nature, harmony, and hierarchy. The Javanese worship god and their ways of life are full of devotion to god. It is crucial for Javanese people to sustain harmonious relationships among individuals, nature, and society (Ali, 1986). They respect other people and avoid conflicts for maintaining harmony. Javanese people are classified by their social group, and each person behaves based on the hierarchical social rank (Irawanto, Ramsey, & Tweed, 2012).

In terms of leadership, first of all, the Javanese leadership style is based on "bapakism" (father-ism), which reflects a strong respect for the father. "Babakism" emphasizes power, authority, and legitimacy (Irawanto et al., 2011). Leaders are expected to act as protectors, mentors, and father-like figures for their followers, displaying wise and honest behavior. Secondly, Javanese leaders also are "andhap-ashor," which indicates that leaders should perform moral deeds and be moral models. Finally, "tepo seliro" (sympathy) indicates that leaders are expected to act with gracious sympathy (Irawanto et al., 2012).

Ethnicity and Leadership

Indonesia is a country that has many languages and religions and is a composite culture. Such cultural diversity provides a broad background for understanding the influence of culture on the management system and leadership style in Indonesia (Sahertian & Graha, 2016). For historical reasons, indigenous values and cultures of Indonesia have been gradually integrated with other religions such as Islam, Confucianism, Hinduism and Taoism.

Ethnicity is one of the important characteristics of the organizational environment – leadership styles vary according to race and ethnicity (Haney-Brown, 2017).

The organizational structure in Indonesia consists of leaders from different ethnic backgrounds, so East Asian, South Asian, and Southeast Asian styles of leadership may all exist within organizations. Sahertian and Graha (2016) pointed out that it may be inappropriate to classify Indonesia as the country with a unique leadership style because of its ethnic diversity shaped by local conditions. Recent research has shown the diversity of indigenous leadership styles. Hamzah, Saufi and Wafa (2002) found that Malaysian and Indian Indonesian managers prefer performing participative leadership, and Chinese Indonesian managers tend to prefer a delegation style. However, Indonesian leaders in Indonesian organizations lead in a father-like way, which is identical to the characteristic of paternalistic leadership style (Irawanto, 2009). Karim, Mardhotillah, and Samadi (2019) proposed a new Indonesian leadership style: ethnic leadership, which is "the ability to spread the belief, value, culture, and norm of ancestry." Besides, multicultural backgrounds also influence Indonesian leadership styles. Sahertian and Graha (2016) pointed out that there is a significant difference between Chinese ethnic leaders and indigenous leaders on the perception of leadership excellence in Indonesian organizations. Indigenous leaders pay more attention to organizational demand, while Chinese ethnic leaders think managerial behavior is more important. Indonesian leadership should be understood based on the multicultural context of Indonesia.

Contemporary Leadership Research

Among the existing research on Indonesian leadership, some scholars have verified the application of Western leadership theories in Indonesia. For example, some scholars have explored the application of transformational leadership (Rawung, Wuryaningrat and Elvinita, 2015), paternalistic leadership (Irawanto & Ramsey, 2011), servant leadership (Harwiki, 2013), ethical leadership (Cintya & Yustina, 2019), and spiritual leadership (Supriyanto, Soetjipto & Maharani, 2016) in Indonesian organizations.

Some research has tailored Western leadership theories to an Indonesian context. Irawanto and Ramsey (2011) summarize the relationship between paternalistic leadership based on Chinese Confucian values and Indonesian leadership in a Javanese context, and discuss effective leadership in Indonesia from a cross-cultural perspective. Siregar (2013) has found that charismatic leadership theory can be used to explain the leadership role of "Kyai" in the context of Javanese culture. Kyai refered to the intelligent and respected Islamic religious leaders who are the most influential figures in shaping the social, cultural and religious life for Muslim society in Indonesia.

Recently researchers have discussed the influence of indigenous Indonesian values on leadership styles. Selvarajah et al. (2017) examined the association between the eight principles of "Asta Brata" (Javanese statesmanship) and Indonesian leadership traits. These principles represent various personal abilities: (1) "Chandra" (the moon): decisiveness; (2) "Surya" (the sun): authority; (3) "Kartika" (the star): external realities;

(4) "Bumi" (the earth): patience; (5) "Agni" (fire): governance; (6) "Tirta" (water): trustworthiness; (7) "Maruto" (the wind): discerning; (8) "Samudra" (the ocean): progressive. Their study has proved that these abilities are conducive to the perceptions of leadership excellence in Javanese organizations.

Leadership in Thailand

Historical and Cultural Background

Before the 13th century, Hinduism was prevalent in Thailand (Anurit, Selvarajah and Meyer, 2011). Then the country began to embrace Buddhism. In the 19th century, under the influence of European colonial powers, Thailand's monarchs Monkhuat (Rama IV, 1851–1868) and Chulalongkorn (Rama V, 1868–1910) promoted reforms that modernized the country to protect Thailand's sovereign status and to avoid colonization. In 1932, the Siamese Revolution ended the absolute monarchy and established a constitutional monarchy supervised by military personnel (Mishra, 2010). Since the drastic changes in 1932, Thailand's political system has evolved unsteadily. After 1973, Thailand underwent a difficult transition from military rule to civilian rule, with several drastic reversals of its political system. From 2001, Thailand has experienced a series of political crises bringing about large-scale violence, regular protests, marches, and unstable governance. Tensions and polarized politics have negatively affected Thailand's economy and Thai people's lives in the past decade.

Traditional Culture and Leadership

Religion and Leadership

Religions in Thailand include Buddhism, Islam, Hinduism, Confucianism, Taoism, and Christianity. The main religion in Thailand is the Theravada school of Buddhism. The main idea of Theravada Buddhism is based on the teachings of Gautama Buddha, which holds that desire, craving and the human ego are sources of suffering. One can achieve *nirvana* (a state of freedom) through self-awakening and the Noble Eightfold Path, getting rid of desire and suffering.

Buddhism plays an important role in management practices and constructions of leadership in Thailand. Kemavuthanon and Duberley (2009) focused on the influence of Buddhism leadership in Thai community organizations. The study found that characteristics of effective leadership in Thailand are consistent with three principles of Buddhist teachings concerning the interests or life goals: (1) *Attatha* (oneself or one's own benefit); (2) *Parattha* (the benefits to others); (3) *Ubhayattha* (the mutual benefit, happiness, and virtue of the community or society) (Kemavuthanon & Duberley, 2009). These three-level models of effective leadership are derived from the Buddhist context of Thailand.

Cultural Values and Leadership

In terms of Thai values, Komin (1990) analysed the cultural context of the social and cultural system of Thailand from the perspective of work-related values. They pointed out nine work-related values of Thailand: (1) ego orientation or *Kreng Chai* (to be considerate); (2) *Bunkhun* (grateful relationship orientation); (3) smooth interpersonal relationship orientation; (4) flexibility and adjustment orientation; (5) religion-psychical orientation (e.g. Buddhism belief orientation); (6) education and competence orientation; (7) interdependence orientation; (8) fun-pleasure orientation; (9) achievement-task orientation. These values show a Thai emphasis on building harmonious relationships, showing respect and concern for others. Maintaining harmonious relationships with others is an important characteristic of the Thai people, which directly relates to Thai leadership styles (Anurit et al., 2011). An effective leader in a Thai context should build a good relationship with their subordinates to make sure tasks and projects are successfully completed. Moreover, given the emphasis on "relationships" in Thai culture, Thai people prefer benevolent paternalistic leadership instead of impersonal and system-based leadership (Komin, 1990). Further, Selvarajah, Meyer and Donovan (2013) discussed the cultural factors that influence the perception of what constitutes an excellent leader in Thai organizations, which reflect the cultural values and characteristics of Thailand, including a deference for authority, a non-confrontational style, environmental harmony, respect (face), current work focus, decision-making style, and organizational climate.

Contemporary Leadership Research

Among the existing research on Thai leadership, some studies have verified the application of Western leadership theories in Thailand. For example, some scholars have explored the application of transformational leadership (Ariyabuddhiphongs & Kahn, 2017), sustainable leadership (Suriyankietkaew, 2014), responsible leadership (Hansen, 2008), paternalistic leadership (Duangekanong et al., 2017), authentic leadership (Kulophas et al., 2018), affirmative leadership (Mandhachitara & Allapach, 2017), and other leadership theories in Thai organizations.

Some scholars have proposed Thai characteristic leadership theories from a Western perspective. For example, based on Thai culture and ethical leadership theory, Kanokorn, Wallapha and Ngang (2013) discuss the ethical leadership indicators of school principals in Thailand. Amornpipat, and McLean (2016) have found that there are cultural differences between Thai authentic leadership and existing Western theories. In addition to the four dimensions of self-awareness, relationship transparency, balanced processes, and internal ethics, there is an additional dimension of authentic leadership in Thailand: relational harmony, which means that leaders are expected to respect others and build harmonious relationships among their group members.

Empirical studies have shown the specificity of Thai leadership. In Thai organizations, members pay attention to interpersonal relationships and tend to save their face and avoid any criticism. In addition, the concept of "Chai Yen Yen" in Thai (Buddhism belief orientation) also requires Thai people to learn to keep their temper under control and respect others. According to the cultural context of Thailand, Thai leaders tend to adopt democratic and transformational leadership styles rather than authoritarian leadership styles (Piansoongnern, 2016). Yukongdi (2010) found that Thai employees' preferred leadership style is consultative leadership, followed by participative, paternalistic, and autocratic leadership. Piansoongnern (2013) also reported that successful leaders in Thai organizations are trustworthy and open-minded individuals who are considerate of their employees and are willing to encourage employees to voice their concerns and suggestions.

Comparing Leadership among Asian Countries

The previous sections demonstrated the unique cultures and traditions that are related to leadership for different countries. The next question is whether we can compare leadership across these five countries. In this section we present such empirical evidences that are primarily emic or culture-universal in nature. Using the Hofstede framework, a meta-analysis of different countries across 40 years provides comparable information of four cultural dimensions, including power distance, individualism, masculinity and uncertainty avoidance (Taras et al., 2010). The standardized country means for power distance are: China (0.71), India (0.83), Japan (0.32), Indonesia (0.69), and Thailand (0.50). All of these five countries have positive means, suggesting that they tend to have above-average power distances from the rest of the world. The mean differences among five countries are rather small. For individualism, scores are China (-0.13), India (-0.55), Japan (-0.23), Indonesia (-0.58), and Thailand (-0.88). All scores are negative, suggesting that these countries tend to be more collectivistic rather than individualistic. For masculinity, the means are as follows: China (-0.44), India (-0.18), Japan (1.31), Indonesia (0.13), and Thailand (-0.58). We can see that Japan has a high level of masculinity, while China and Thailand are rather high on levels of femininity. Masculinity at the national level is negatively correlated with gender equality of the country (Steel and Taras, 2010). The last dimension scores of uncertainty avoidance means are: China (0.42), India (-0.63), Japan (1.33), Indonesia (-0.58), and Thailand (0.16). We can see that Japan is very high on uncertainty avoidance, while India and

Indonesia are rather low. While Japanese does not like unstructured, unpredictable and unclear situations, Indian and Indonesian have a preference of such.

The GLOBE Project also provides scores of culture practices and values for different countries, including the five countries mentioned in this chapter (Hanges & Dickson, 2004). The GLOBE Project culture dimensions are much more complex than those from Hofstede and are difficult to be summarized here. We just want to highlight a couple of salient scores for culturally endorsed leadership theory (CLT) leadership dimensions: Indonesia is very high on the charismatic/value-based leadership dimension, while Thailand is relatively high on autonomous leadership. For other dimensions and countries, the differences or patterns are not so obvious. In the GLOBE report, culture and leadership dimensions are grouped to the region level. China and Japan were both in *Confucian Asia*, while India, Indonesia, and Thailand are all lumped together into *Southern Asia*. Given those countries' distinctively different cultural and historical backgrounds, this aggregation does not provide much help in facilitating the interpretation and comparison of country-specific results.

Looking at the culture and leadership aspects across these five countries, we can see some commonalities. Harmony is a cherished culture value for China, Japan, Indonesia and Thailand, which is embedded in their traditional religions or moral systems of Buddhism, Confucianism, Taoism, Shinto and Javanese worship. In the workplace, harmony means that leaders should maintain a good relationship with their subordinates with a high level of mutual trust. Paternalistic leadership, although not unique to Asian countries, is emphasized across all these five countries. This leadership style is in line with the relatively high-power distance among these five countries. Another commonality among these five countries is the moral and ethical aspect of leadership. Leaders are expected to hold high moral standards and serve as role models for their subordinates.

Challenges and Opportunities to Develop Asia-Centric Leadership Research

The fast economic development in the past decades has created an urgent need for Asian countries to identify and promote leadership frameworks that not only reflect their own traditions, but also have wider implications outside their national borders. Existing mainly Western-originated leadership frameworks may not be able to serve such a need. An Asian-centric approach of leadership is in demand. This is a great time for Asian leadership scholars to reflect their own cultural heritages, and at the same time look forward to building new leadership frameworks that have a global significance. The seemingly contradictory forces of globalization and localization call for genuine and scientific ways to study leadership in Asia. Here we want to highlight some challenges and opportunities to establish the new Asian-centric leadership research.

Indigenous or Universal Theories?

When culture is considered, leadership can be approached from the indigenous or universal angles. The indigenous approach's primary concern is the validity of the research within the boundary of a culture or society, while the universal approach assumes that a leadership concept or assessment is generalizable or compatible across the boundaries of different cultures or societies. As we reviewed some leadership literature from these five Asian countries, each country has plenty of studies using either approach. The universal approach studies often test the generalizability of theories or measures mostly originating in Western cultures. They are more likely to use explanations and terminologies that are familiar to scholars in other countries, and thus tend to receive more global attention than indigenous research. However, the indigenous research is more powerful than the universal research in revealing culturally bounded ideas, values, and traditions. To build the Asian-centric leadership, we need to rely on both universal and indigenous approaches. The universal frameworks can serve as stepping stones for approaching more nuanced indigenous thinking. If we want to understand Asian leadership in its totality, we need to look both from inside and outside. The integration of both universal and indigenous approaches is needed. In his work to compare different psychological approaches in relationship with culture, Yang (2000) suggested that the indigenous and universal approaches are not necessarily contradictory to each other. They can just mean different levels of maturity of the research. It is possible that a monocultural indigenous framework can find its validity in other cultures, and thus become universal. He calls for an indigenous-derived global psychology. The same logic can be applied to leadership research. We should strive to find indigenous-derived Asian leadership that has global implications.

Context-Specific or Context-Free?

When we make a claim that the leadership in one country has a certain unique feature, the underlying assumption is that across the board, most leadership positions in that country share that feature. However, there are different requirements in business domains, non-profit domain, and political domain for leaders. It is hard to generalize knowledge from one domain into another. Furthermore, even within the business domain, different industries may have different demands for their leaders. The GLOBE Project (House et al., 2004) showed consistencies within a society in terms of leadership styles, in comparison with other countries. This was an evidence of context-free leadership practices or values in one country. The study also found different association patterns of leadership with some outcome variables in different industries. This was evidence of a context-specific leadership style. Even for the same leadership position, different tasks (e.g., more innovative vs. more traditional tasks) or different situations (e.g., business as usual vs. under crisis) require different leader responses, which may also interact with the culture. More studies are needed to map the commonalities and specificities of leadership styles across different social, organizational or industry domains and situations.

Parsimony or Comprehensiveness?

How many dimensions are sufficient to cover leadership within a culture or across cultures? There is no good answer for this question. For the culture dimensions, Hofstede proposed four dimensions, but later added two extras. Meta-analyses show good validity of the original four dimensions (Steel & Taras, 2010; Taras et al., 2010). The premise of the GLOBE Project is that Hofstede's framework is insufficient in covering leadership-related culture factors. The project examined seven cultural dimensions across four different cultural manifestations, thus leading to 28 different culture specifications. The much more refined culture specifications may help reveal more subtle differences across countries, but the complexity of such a framework may become an obstacle for further implications. For the leadership measure, the GLOBE Project had 6 so-called second-order factors mainly based on existing leadership frameworks. There were 21 subscales or leadership dimensions (Hanges & Dickson, 2004). This leadership assessment may be useful for practice, but it is hard for academic research to use the full leadership survey to conduct cross-cultural comparisons. We can see it is hard to strike a balance between parsimony and comprehensiveness in terms of leadership dimensions. For indigenous leadership research, as shown in our country review, every country has a set of unique leadership concepts and frameworks based on its own traditions, but it is hard to figure out how many dimensions are needed for each country to capture its special leadership expectations or behaviors. Additional empirical studies are still needed for us to reach a parsimonious understanding of Asian-centric leadership.

New Methods?

Considering the rich contextual factors, it requires new research methods to examine indigenous leadership in each country with the balance of parsimony and comprehensiveness. One of the major issues we need to address is creating fairly large sets of data that contain comprehensive leadership information (e.g., behaviors, demographics, evaluations and expectations) in different contexts. We then need to extract insightful knowledge from such data. In terms of possible sources of data, publicly available online texts, pictures and videos that contain information about leaders' demographics, behaviors, opinions and evaluations are abundant. The current challenge is to find feasible approaches and algorithms to extract the relevant insights. Another source of data is the collection of existing empirical studies on leadership.

Meta-analysis has proven useful in obtaining new knowledge that is different from the original studies that it is built on (Steel & Taras, 2010). There is hope of converting findings from possibly millions of existing empirical studies into a large set of data, then using some online analytical tools (i.e. hubmeta) to do large-scale meta-analysis (Bosco, Uggerslev, & Steel, 2017). It is possible to use such a new method to identify new leadership patterns with the consideration of many contextual factors.

If the 21st century is truly "the Asian century," Asia has to assume the leadership to lead the rest of the world. A precondition for that to happen is the emergence and wide acceptance of new Asian-centric leadership frameworks, which should be deeply rooted in Asian cultures but have wide implications for other parts of the world.

References

Adler, N. J. (1983). Cross-cultural management: Issues to be faced. *International Studies of Management & Organization, 13* (1–2), 7–45.

Ali, F. (1986). *Refleksi paham "kekuasaan Jawa" dalam Indonesia modern*. Jakarta: Gramedia.

Alok, K. (2014). Authentic leadership and psychological ownership: Investigation of interrelations. *Leadership and Organization Development Journal*, *35*(4), 266–285.

Alok, K. (2017). Sāttvika leadership: An Indian model of positive leadership. *Journal of Business Ethics*, *142*(1), 117–138.

Ames, R. T. & Hershock, P. D. (2018). *Confucianisms for a changing world cultural order*. Honolulu: University of Hawaii Press.

Amornpipat, I. & McLean, G. N. (2016). *Cultural influence on authentic leadership in Thailand*. Paper presented at the Proceedings of the 17th International Conference on Human Resource Development Research and Practice across Europe, Manchester.

Anurit, P., Selvarajah, C. & Meyer, D. (2011). Exploring relevant dimensions to leadership excellence in Thailand. *International Journal of Academic Research in Business and Social Sciences, 37*, 3993–4006.

Ariyabuddhiphongs, V. & Kahn, S. I. (2017). Transformational leadership and turnover intention: The mediating effects of trust and job performance on café employees in Thailand. *Journal of Human Resources in Hospitality & Tourism*, *16*(2), 215–233.

Bai, X. & Roberts, W. (2011). Taoism and its model of traits of successful leaders. *Journal of Management Development*, *30*(7/8), 724–739.

Banerjee, R. (1998). *Mother leadership*. Allahabad: Wheeler Publishing.

Bass, B. M. & Avolio, B. J. (1993). Transformational leadership and organizational culture. *Public administration quarterly*, *17*(1), 112–121.

Bass, B. M. & Riggio, R. E. (2006). *Transformational leadership*. New York, NY: Psychology Press.

Bass, B. M., Stogdill, R. M. & Bass, R. R. (2008). *Stogdill's handbook of leadership: A survey of theory and research*. New York, NY: Free Press.

Bhatta, C. P. (2000). Leadership values: insights from Ashoka's inscriptions. *Journal of Human Values*, *6*(2), 103–113.

Bird, A. & Mendenhall, M. E. (2016). From cross-cultural management to global leadership: Evolution and adaptation. *Journal of World Business*, *51*(1), 115–126.

Bosco, F. A., Uggerslev, K. L. & Steel, P. (2017). MetaBUS as a vehicle for facilitating meta-analysis. *Human Resource Management Review*, *27*(1), 237–254.

Brocklehurst, P., Nomura, M., Ozaki, T., Ferguson, J. & Matsuda, R. (2013). Cultural differences in clinical leadership: a qualitative study comparing the attitudes of general dental practitioners from Greater Manchester and Tokyo. *British Dental Journal*, *215*(10), 1–6.

Brown, C. (2003). *A short history of Indonesia: The unlikely nation?* Crows Nest: Allen & Unwin.

Brown, M. E. & Treviño, L. K. (2006). Ethical leadership: A review and future directions. *The Leadership Quarterly*, *17*(6), 595–616.

Bruning, N. S. & Tung, R. L. (2013). Leadership development and global talent management in the Asian context: An introduction. *Asian Business & Management*, *12*(4), 381–386.

Chakrabarti, S. K. (1999). *Wisdom leadership: Dialogues and reflections*. New Delhi: Wheeler Publishing.

Chandra, B., Mukherjee, M., Mukherjee, A., Panikkar, K. N. & Mahajan, S. (2016). *India's struggle for independence*. London: Penguin UK.

Chatterjee, D. (1998). *Leading consciously: A pilgrimage to self-mastery*. New Delhi: Viva Books.

Cheng, B. S., Chou, L. F., Wu, T. Y., Huang, M. P. & Farh, J. L. (2004). Paternalistic leadership and subordinate responses: Establishing a leadership model in Chinese organizations. *Asian Journal of Social Psychology*, *7*(1), 89–117.

Cheung, C. K. & Chan, A. C. F. (2005). Philosophical foundations of eminent Hong Kong Chinese CEOs' leadership. *Journal of Business Ethics*, *60*(1), 47–62.

Cintya, L. & Yustina, A. I. (2019). From intention to action in whistleblowing: Examining ethical leadership and effective commitment of accountants in Indonesia. *International Journal of Business*, *24*(4), 412–433.

Dai, L., Chin, T. & Rafiq, M. (2019). Understanding the role of psychological capital in humorous leadership-employee creativity relations. *Frontiers in Psychology, 10*, 1–11.

Dhulla, T. V. (2014). Transformational leadership & triguna theory: A short literature Review. *2*(5), 341–356.

Dorfman, P. W., Howell, J. P., Hibino, S., Lee, J. K., Tate, U. & Bautista, A. (1997). Leadership in Western and Asian countries: Commonalities and differences in effective leadership processes. *Leadership Quarterly*, *8*(3), 233–274.

Duangekanong, D. D., Duangekanong, S., John, V. K., Wichayachakorn, A. & Vikitset, N. (2017). Dimensions of paternalistic leadership and employee outcomes in small thai firms. *AU-eJournal of Interdisciplinary Research 2*(2), 56–64.

Farh, J. L. & Cheng, B. S. (2000). A cultural analysis of paternalistic leadership in Chinese organizations. In J. T. Li, A. S. Tsui, & E. Weldon (Eds.), *Management and organizations in the Chinese context* (pp. 84–127). New York, NY: Springer.

Fukushige, A. & Spicer, D. P. (2011). Leadership and followers' work goals: A comparison between Japan and the UK. *The International Journal of Human Resource Management*, *22*(10), 2110–2134.

Graen, G. B. (2006). In the eye of the beholder: Cross-cultural lesson in leadership from project GLOBE: A response viewed from the third culture bonding (TCB) model of cross-cultural leadership. *Academy of Management Perspectives*, *20*(4), 95–101.

Greenleaf, R. K. (2002). *Servant leadership: A journey into the nature of legitimate power and greatness*. New York, NY: Paulist Press.

Haghirian, P. (2010). *Understanding Japanese management practices*. New York, NY: Business Expert Press.

Hamzah, M., Saufi, R. A. & Wafa, S. (2002). Leadership style preferences of Malaysian managers. *Malaysian Management Review*, *37*(1), 1–10.

Haney-Brown, K. R. (2017). *The Relationship between Ethnic Identity and Leadership Style*. Walden University, Minneapolis.

Hanges, P. J. & Dickson, M. W. (2004). The development and validation of the GLOBE culture and leadership scales. In R. J. House, P. J. Hanges, M. Javidan, P. W. Dorfman, & V. Gupta (Eds.), *Leadership, Culture, and Organizations: The GLOBE Study of 62 Societies, 62*, 122–151. Thousand Oaks, CA: SAGE.

Hansen, E. G. (2008). *Responsible leadership requires responsible leadership systems: The case of Merck Ltd., Thailand*. Paper presented at the the 8th EURAM conference 2008: Managing Diversity: European Destiny and Hope, Ljubljana and Bled.

Harwiki, W. (2013). The influence of servant leadership on organization culture, organizational commitment, organizational citizenship behavior and employees performance (Study of Outstanding Cooperatives in East Java Province, Indonesia). *Journal of Economics and Behavioral Studies, 5*(12), 876–885.

Hofstede, G. (1984). *Culture's consequences: International differences in work-related values*. Thousand Oaks, CA: SAGE.

Hofstede, G. (2001). *Culture's consequences: Comparing values, behaviors, institutions and organizations across nations*. Thousand Oaks, CA: SAGE.

Hofstede, G. (2002). Dimensions do not exist: A reply to Brendan McSweeney. *Human Relations, 55*(11), 1355–1360.

Hofstede, G. (2010). The GLOBE debate: Back to relevance. *Journal of international business studies, 41*(8), 1339–1346.

Hofstede, G. & Milosevic, D. (2011). Dimensionalizing cultures: The Hofstede model in context. *Online Readings in Psychology and Culture, 2*(1), 1–16. Retrieved from https://doi.org/10.9707/2307-0919.1014

House, R. J., Hanges, P. J., Javidan, M., Dorfman, P. W. & Gupta, V. (2004). *Culture, leadership, and organizations: The GLOBE study of 62 societies*. Thousand Oaks, CA: SAGE.

Hwang, K. K. (2008). Leadership theory of legalism and its function in Confucian Society. *Advances in Dental Research, 2*(2), 364–367.

Hwang, S. J., Quast, L. N., Center, B. A., Chung, C.-T. N., Hahn, H.-J. & Wohkittel, J. (2015). The impact of leadership behaviours on leaders' perceived job performance across cultures: Comparing the role of charismatic, directive, participative, and supportive leadership behaviours in the US and four Confucian Asian countries. *Human Resource Development International, 18*(3), 259–277.

Irawanto, D. W. (2009). An analysis of national culture and leadership practices in Indonesia. *Journal of Diversity Management (JDM), 4*(2), 41–48.

Irawanto, D. W. & Ramsey, P. (2011). Paternalistic leadership and employee responses in Javanese culture. *Gadjah Mada International Journal of Business, 13*(2), 185–203.

Irawanto, D. W., Ramsey, P. L. & Ryan, J. C. (2011). Tailoring leadership theory to Indonesian culture. *Global Business Review, 12*(3), 355–366.

Irawanto, D. W., Ramsey, P. L. & Tweed, D. C. (2012). *Exploring paternalistic leadership and its application to the Indonesian public sector*. Massey University, Palmerston North.

Ishida, T. & Park, S. J. (1985). *The 21st Century, the Asian Century?* Berlin: EXpress Edition.

Ishikawa, J. (2012). Leadership and performance in Japanese R&D teams. *Asia Pacific Business Review, 18*(2), 241–258.

Javidan, M., House, R. J., Dorfman, P. W., Hanges, P. J. & De Luque, M. S. (2006). Conceptualizing and measuring cultures and their consequences: a comparative review of GLOBE's and Hofstede's approaches. *Journal of International Business Studies, 37*(6), 897–914.

Kanokorn, S., Wallapha, A. & Ngang, T. K. (2013). Indicators of ethical leadership for school principals in Thailand. *Procedia-Social and Behavioral Sciences, 93*, 2085–2089.

Karim, A., Mardhotillah, N. F. & Samadi, M. I. (2019). Ethical leadership transforms into ethnic: exploring new leader's style of Indonesia. *Journal of Leadership in Organizations, 1*(2), 146–157.

Keller, G. F. & Kronstedt, C. R. (2005). Connecting Confucianism, communism, and the Chinese culture of commerce. *The Journal of Language for international business*, *16*(1), 60–75.

Kemavuthanon, S. & Duberley, J. (2009). A Buddhist view of leadership: The case of the OTOP project. *Leadership & Organization Development Journal*, *30*(8), 737–758.

Kets de Vries, M. F. (2005). Leadership group coaching in action: The Zen of creating high performance teams. *Academy of Management Perspectives*, *19*(1), 61–76.

Khanna, P. (2019). *The Future is Asian: Commerce, Conflict and Culture of 21st Century*. New York, NY: Simon and Schuster.

Khuntia, R. & Suar, D. (2004). A scale to assess ethical leadership of Indian private and public sector managers. *Journal of Business Ethics*, *49*(1), 13–26.

Kimura. (2012). Transformational leadership and job satisfaction: The mediating effects of perceptions of politics and market orientation in the Japanese context. *7*(1), 29–42.

Kimura, T. & Nishikawa, M. (2018). Ethical leadership and its cultural and institutional context: An empirical study in Japan. *Journal of Business Ethics*, *151*(3), 707–724.

Kirkman, B. L., Lowe, K. B. & Gibson, C. B. (2006). A quarter century of culture's consequences: A review of empirical research incorporating Hofstede's cultural values framework. *Journal of International Business Studies*, *37*(3), 285–320.

Kishore, M. (2008). *The New Asian Hemisphere: The Irresistible Shift of Global Power to the East*. New York, NY: Public Affairs.

Komin, S. (1990). Culture and work-related values in Thai organizations. *International Journal of Psychology*, *25* (3–6), 681–704.

Kulophas, D., Hallinger, P., Ruengtrakul, A. & Wongwanich, S. (2018). Exploring the effects of authentic leadership on academic optimism and teacher engagement in Thailand. *International Journal of Educational Management*, *32*(1), 27–45.

Leung, K. (2007). Asian social psychology: Achievements, threats, and opportunities. *Asian Journal of Social Psychology*, *10*(1), 8–15.

Li, C. & Shi, K. (2008). The Structure and Measurement of Transformational Leadership in China. *Acta Psychological Sinica*, *37*(4), 803–811.

Li, C., Zhao, H. & Begley, T. M. (2015). Transformational leadership dimensions and employee creativity in China: A cross-level analysis. *Journal of Business Research*, *68*(6), 1149–1156.

Li, S. L., He, W., Yam, K. C. & Long, L. R. (2015). When and why empowering leadership increases followers' taking charge: A multilevel examination in China. *Asia Pacific Journal of Management*, *32*(3), 645–670.

Lin, C. (2010). Studying Chinese culture and conflict: A research agenda. *International Journal of Conflict Management*, *21*(1), 70–93.

Ling, W., Chen, L. & Wang, D. (1987). Construction of CPM Scale for Leadership Behavior Assessment. *Acta Psychologica Sinica*, *19*(2), 199–207.

Ling, W., Chia, R. C. & Fang, L. (2000). Chinese implicit leadership theory. *The Journal of Social Psychology*, *140*(6), 729–739.

Liu, P. (2017). A framework for understanding Chinese leadership: a cultural approach. *International Journal of Leadership in Education*, *20*(6), 749–761.

Low, K. C. P. (2018). *Leadership in Japan*. New York, NY: Springer.

Low, P. K. C. (2010). *Successfully negotiating in Asia*. Berlin: Springer Science & Business Media.

Low, P. K. C. & Muniapan, B. (2011). Organisational development and the Hindu trinity: Brahma, Vishnu and Shiva on leadership, culture and change. *International Journal of Indian Culture and Business Management*, *4*(5), 491–505.

Lyu, Y., Wang, M., Le, J. & Kwan, H. K. (2019). Effects of authentic leadership on work–family balance in China. *Journal of Managerial Psychology*, *34*(2), 110–123.

Ma, L. & Tsui, A. S. (2015). Traditional Chinese philosophies and contemporary leadership. *The Leadership Quarterly*, *26*(1), 13–24.

Mandhachitara, R. & Allapach, S. N. (2017). Small business performance in Thailand: key success factors. *Journal of Research in Marketing and Entrepreneurship*, *19*(2), 161–181.

McElhatton, E. & Jackson, B. (2012). Paradox in harmony: Formulating a Chinese model of leadership. *Leadership*, *8*(4), 441–461.

McSweeney, B. (2002a). The essentials of scholarship: A reply to Geert Hofstede. *Human Relations*, *55*(11), 1363–1372.

McSweeney, B. (2002b). Hofstede's model of national cultural differences and their consequences: A triumph of faith-a failure of analysis. *Human Relations*, *55*(1), 89–118.

Mishra, P. P. (2010). *The history of Thailand*. Santa Barbara: ABC-CLIO.

Muniapan, B. (2006). *Can the Bhagavad-Gita be used as a manual for management development of Indian managers worldwide*. Paper presented at the 5th Asia Academy of Management Conference, Tokyo.

Muniapan, B. (2009). *The Bhagavad-Gita on leadership for good governance and sustainable development*. Paper presented at the 15th Annual International Sustainable Development Research Conference,'Taking up the Global Challenge: Analyzing the Implementation of Innovations and Governance for Sustainable Development', Utrecht.

Muniapan, B. & Satpathy, B. (2010). Ancient Indian wisdom for managers: the relevance of Valmiki Ramayana in developing managerial effectiveness. *International Journal of Indian culture and business management*, *3*(6), 645–668.

Muthia, A. & Krishnan, V. R. (2015). Servant leadership and commitment: Role of transformational leadership. *International Journal on Leadership*, *3*(1), 9–20.

Natesan, N. C., Keeffe, M. J. & Darling, J. R. (2009). Enhancement of global business practices: lessons from the Hindu Bhagavad Gita. *European Business Review*, *21*(2), 128–143.

Pareek, U. (1981). *Beyond Management: Essays on the process of institution building*. New Delhi: Prakash.

Piansoongnern, O. (2013). Flexible leadership for managing talented employees in the securities industry: a case study of Thailand. *Global Journal of Flexible Systems Management*, *14*(2), 107–113.

Piansoongnern, O. (2016). Chinese leadership and its impacts on innovative work behavior of the Thai employees. *Global Journal of Flexible Systems Management*, *17*(1), 15–27.

Pradhan, R. K., Panda, M. & Jena, L. K. (2017). Transformational leadership and psychological empowerment. *Journal of Enterprise Information Management*, *30*(1), 82–95.

Rarick, C. A. (1994). The philosophical impact of Shintoism, Buddhism, and Confucianism on Japanese management practices. *International Journal of Value-Based Management*, *7*(3), 219–226.

Rawat, P. S. & Lyndon, S. (2016). Effect of paternalistic leadership style on subordinate's trust: an Indian study. *Journal of Indian Business Research*, *8*(4), 264–277.

Rawung, F. H., Wuryaningrat, N. F. & Elvinita, L. E. (2015). The influence of transformational and transactional leadership on knowledge sharing: An empirical study on small and medium businesses in Indonesia. *20*(1), 123–145.

Ren, S. & Chadee, D. (2017). Ethical leadership, self-efficacy and job satisfaction in China: the moderating role of guanxi. *Personnel review*, *46*(2), 371–388.

Ricklefs, M. C. (2008). *A History of Modern Indonesia since c. 1200*. New York, NY: Macmillan International Higher Education.

Sahertian, P. & Graha, A. N. (2016). Exploring leadership dimension among organizations (the analysis against leadership excellence based on cultural and ethnical backgrounds in Indonesia). *Indian Journal of Commerce and Management Studies*, *7*(1), 1–7.

Satpathy, B. & Muniapan, B. (2008). The knowledge of "Self" from the Bhagavad-Gita and its significance for human capital development. *Asian Social Science*, *4*(10), 143–150.

Sawada, J. A. (1998). Mind and morality in nineteenth-century Japanese religions: Misogi-Kyō and Maruyama-Kyō. *Philosophy East and West*, *48*(1), 108–141.

Schneid, M., Isidor, R., Li, C. & Kabst, R. (2015). The influence of cultural context on the relationship between gender diversity and team performance: A meta-analysis. *The International Journal of Human Resource Management*, *26*(6), 733–756.

Selvarajah, C., Meyer, D. & Donovan, J. (2013). Cultural context and its influence on managerial leadership in Thailand. *Asia Pacific business review*, *19*(3), 356–380.

Selvarajah, C., Meyer, D., Roostika, R. & Sukunesan, S. (2017). Exploring managerial leadership in Javanese (Indonesia) organisations: engaging Asta Brata, the eight principles of Javanese statesmanship. *Asia Pacific Business Review*, *23*(3), 373–395.

Shah, S. J. (2010). Re-thinking educational leadership: exploring the impact of cultural and belief systems. *International Journal of Leadership in Education*, *13*(1), 27–44.

Sharma, S. (1995). Towards enlightened leadership: A framework of leadership & management. In K. B. Akhilesh, L. Prasad, & P. Singh (Eds.), *Evolving performing organisations through people: A global agenda* (pp. 209–214). New Delhi: New Age International Publishers.

Sharma, S. (2001). Routes to reality: Scientific and Rishi approaches. *Journal of Human Values*, *7*(1), 75–83.

Sharma, S. (2007). *Management in new age Western windows Eastern doors*. New Delhi: New Age International.

Shenkar, O., Ronen, S., Shefy, E. & Chow, I. H. S. (1998). The role structure of Chinese managers. *Human Relations*, *51*(1), 51–72.

Shibata, T. & Kodama, M. (2009). Cultural mythology and global leadership in Japan. In E. Kessler & D. Wong-Mingji (Eds.), *Cultural Mythology and Global Leadership* (pp. 343–358). Cheltenham: Cheltenham.

Singh, A. (2000). Learning to lead: The leadership journey of middle managers. *Finance India*, *14*(3), 983–983.

Singh, N. & Krishnan, V. R. (2005). Towards understanding transformational leadership in India: A grounded theory approach. *Vision*, *9*(2), 5–17.

Singh, P. & Bhandarker, A. (1990). *Corporate success and transformational leadership*. New Delhi: New Age International.

Sinha, J. (1980). *The Nurturant Task Leader*. New Delhi: Concept.

Siregar, F. M. (2013). Religious leader and charismatic leadership in Indonesia: the role of Kyai in Pesantren in Java. *Jurnal Kawistara*, *3*(2), 117–226.

Smith, P. B. (2006). When elephants fight, the grass gets trampled: The GLOBE and Hofstede projects. *Journal of International Business Studies*, *37*(6), 915–921.

Smith, V. A. (1999). *The early history of India*. New Delhi: Atlantic Publishers & Dist.

Song, X. R. & Beckett, D. (2013). Conceptualizing Leadership for a Globalizing China. In J. Rajasekar & L. S. Beh (Eds.), *Culture and Gender in Leadership* (pp. 64–81). New York, NY: Springer.

Steel, P. & Taras, V. (2010). Culture as a consequence: A multi-level multivariate meta-analysis of the effects of individual and country characteristics on work-related cultural values. *Journal of International Management*, *16*(3), 211–233.

Sun, H. F., Chen, C. C. & Zhang, S. H. (2008). Strategic leadership of Sunzi in the Art of war. In C. C. Chen & Y. T. Lee (Eds.), *Leadership and management in China: Philosophies, theories, and practices* (pp. 143–168). Cambridge: Cambridge University Press.

Supriyanto, A. S., Soetjipto, B. E. & Maharani, V. (2016). The effect of spiritual leadership on workplace spirituality, job satisfaction and ihsan behaviour: A study on nurses of Aisyiah

Islamic hospital in Malang, Indonesia. *International Journal of Applied Business and Economic Research*, *14*(11), 7675–7688.

Suriyankietkaew, S. (2014). Effects of sustainable leadership on customer satisfaction: Evidence from Thailand. *Asia-Pacific Journal of Business Administration*, *8*(3), 245–259.

Suzuki, D. T. (2019). *Zen and Japanese culture*. Princeton, NJ: Princeton University Press.

Taras, V., Kirkman, B. L. & Steel, P. (2010). Examining the impact of culture's consequences: A three-decade, multilevel, meta-analytic review of Hofstede's cultural value dimensions. *Journal of Applied Psychology*, *95*(3), 405–439.

Venaik, S. & Brewer, P. (2010). Avoiding uncertainty in Hofstede and GLOBE. *Journal of International Business Studies*, *41*(8), 1294–1315.

Walker, B. L. (2015). *A concise history of Japan*. Cambridge: Cambridge University Press.

Walumbwa, F. O., Avolio, B. J., Gardner, W. L., Wernsing, T. S. & Peterson, S. J. (2008). Authentic leadership: Development and validation of a theory-based measure. *Journal of management*, *34*(1), 89–126.

Wang, M., Guo, T., Ni, Y., Shang, S. & Tang, Z. (2019). The effect of spiritual leadership on employee effectiveness: An intrinsic motivation perspective. *Frontiers in psychology*, *9*(1), 1–11.

Wang, M., Kwan, H. K. & Zhou, A. (2017). Effects of servant leadership on work–family balance in China. *Asia Pacific Journal of Human Resources*, *55*(4), 387–407.

Williamson, D. (2002). Forward from a critique of Hofstede's model of national culture. *Human Relations*, *55*(11), 1373–1395.

Wong, K. C. (2001). Chinese culture and leadership. *International Journal of Leadership in Education*, *4*(4), 309–319.

Wu, M. & Wang, J. (2012). Developing a charismatic leadership model for Chinese organizations: The mediating role of loyalty to supervisors. *The International Journal of Human Resource Management*, *23*(19), 4069–4084.

Xiao, X., Liu, F., Zhou, F. & Chen, S. (2018). Narcissistic Leadership and Employees' Knowledge Sharing: Influence of Organizational Identification and Collectivism. *Social Behavior and Personality: An International Journal*, *46*(8), 1317–1329.

Yang, K. S. (2000). Monocultural and cross-cultural indigenous approaches: The royal road to the development of a balanced global psychology. *Asian Journal of Social Psychology*, *3*(3), 241–263.

Yokochi-Bryce, N. (1990). *Leadership styles of Japanese business executives and managers: Transformational and transactional*. United States International University, Nairobi.

Yukongdi, V. (2010). A study of Thai employees' preferred leadership style. *Asia Pacific business review*, *16* (1–2), 161–181.

Zhang, H., Cone, M. H., Everett, A. M. & Elkin, G. (2011). Aesthetic leadership in Chinese business: A philosophical perspective. *Journal of Business Ethics*, *101*(3), 475–491.

Zhang, Y. & Foo, S. F. (2012). Balanced leadership: Perspectives, principles and practices. *Chinese Management Studies*, *6*(2), 245–256.

Zheng, B. (2006). The Pattern of Difference Sequence and Chinese Organizational Behaviors. *Indigenous Psychological Research in Chinese Societies*, *3*(2), 142–219.

Zhou, F. & Wu, Y. J. (2018). How humble leadership fosters employee innovation behavior. *Leadership & Organization Development Journal*, *39*(3), 375–387.

Melody Pui Man Chong and Malika Richards

Chapter 2
Asian Global Leaders: The Eight Leadership Essentials

West Meets East: Leadership Theory Problems Continue

Asia remains the world's most economically dynamic region. According to a recent International Monetary Fund (IMF) report, this region has had a GDP growth rate of 5.6 percent in recent years. The report also shows that despite recent impressive performance in Asian markets, long-term growth prospects are impacted by factors such as demographic shifts, slowing productivity growth and the rise of the digital economy (International Monetary Fund, 2018). These factors present challenges for global leaders. We argue that, through their unique leadership behaviors, Asian leaders have been successful in the global economy. Given the growth in the Asian economies, it is essential to explore the driving forces behind its momentum, especially that of the essentials of effective Asian leaders who lead in the global context (McDonald, 2012).

Although recent global leadership studies provide new definitions and have important managerial implications based on alternative approaches in understanding global leadership, these models are not without limitations. For instance, the Western construct may not be easily expanded to global dimensions, and some approaches also fail to include the cultural underpinnings arising from local circumstances, subordinates and the leaders themselves (Steers, Sanchez-Runde & Nardon, 2012). Therefore, the old problem remains: The majority of leadership research and theories have been conducted and developed in the Western context, which may not fully explain organizational behaviors in other cultural contexts because the key variables may have very different meanings and implications (Leung & White, 2004).

Ancient Philosophies and Values

To date, extensive leadership research has studied the relationships between Asian/ Chinese traditional philosophies and contemporary leadership (e.g., Alves, Manz & Btterfield, 2005; Chong, 2018; Ma & Tsui, 2015; McDonald, 2012; Rowley & Ulrich, 2012; Tsui, et al., 2004). Nevertheless, most studies only link leadership to the widely discussed values of Confucianism and Daoism. Recently, some scholars also discuss the role of Legalism and relate it to the development of leadership

https://doi.org/10.1515/9783110671988-002

theory and practices. For instance, Ma and Tsui (2015) discuss Legalism together with Daoism and Confucianism, and the authors believe that they relate to Western-originated leadership theories. Rowley and Ulrich (2012), based on Confucianism, Daoism and Legalism, raise the importance of moving beyond the overly dominant and ethnocentric Western leadership theories by exploring Asian leadership on a different cultural foundation. Hwang (2008) suggests that among the various Chinese indigenous leadership theories, Legalism is only second to Confucianism. Further, Hwang suggests that Chinese society is characterized by the reality that Confucianism is mostly discussed and praised in public while Legalism is in use in private.

Han Fei (ca. 280–233 BC), as a representative of the Legalism school of thought, is considered one of the most influential political philosophers in Chinese history. His leading philosophies echo the ideas of contemporary scholars because he is also a pioneer of "change and innovation" (Chong, 2018). Witzel (2012) points out that Han Fei's ideas on leadership have resonance with other ideas, not just in contemporary Asian leadership, but also in the Western philosophies. Han Fei's work, the *Hanfeizi*, is a synthesis of the agendas of his predecessors, including Shang Yang's emphasis on "law," the preoccupation with "tactics" from Shen Buhai, and the concept of "position" from Shen Dao (Denecke, 2010). Scholars have generally linked and emphasized the Legalism school to the dark side of leadership in terms of authoritarianism (e.g., control, authority and centralization) but have often ignored other positive and productive behaviors (e.g., innovativeness, flexibility, discipline and strategy) that are exemplified by successful Asian global leaders.

Similarly, Sun Tzu's *The Art of War* has had a significant impact on many Asian countries and has been applied to the discussion of modern management and business by many scholars from the East and the West (e.g., Chen, 1994; Chow, 1994; Dimovskid et al., 2012; McCann, 2012; Pars, 2013; Rarick, 1996, 2007). Sun Tzu's military strategies were heavily influenced by Daoism, which stresses the interrelatedness and relativity of everything in the world. Many Asian business leaders have attached great importance to this treatise on classic military strategy (Chen, 1994). The first chapter of *The Art of War*, "Laying Plans," discusses five important factors a commander should possess: "The commander stands for the virtues of Wisdom, Sincerity, Benevolence, Courage, and Strictness" (Giles, 2014). Tsui and colleagues (2004) investigate the variation of leadership styles among Chinese CEOs and show that the most effective leadership dimensions do not always only include strong interpersonal relationship skills and benevolence, but also other behaviors such as creativity and risk-taking behaviors, monitoring operations and being authoritative (Tsui et al., 2004). These behaviors resemble both the teachings of Legalism and the School of Military Strategy.

However, most leadership studies do not discuss the importance of how these ancient philosophies and values might have an impact on global leadership development. In a recent special issue, Chong and Fu (2020) highlight the Asian perspective in global leadership and discuss four essential qualities of global leaders based on Daoism and Confucianism. This book chapter continues to discuss and highlight the importance of the value system in Asian leadership. Specifically, the ancient Chinese pearls of wisdom from Legalism (or the School of Law, *Hanfeizi* by Han Fei) and the School of Military Strategy (*The Art of War* by Sun Tzu) will be the major sources for this article.

Figure 2.1 presents a summary of the core ideas of these two Chinese classics. These concepts will be introduced in the next section in greater detail. Approximately 2,400 years have passed since these classics were written, but ancient wisdom still holds and can be applied to contemporary leadership. These four ancient philosophies, like universal phenomena, are shaped by the integration of two opposite cosmic energies, namely *yin* and *yang*. The left represents the *yin* or female energy – softness – while the right is the *yang* or male energy – hardness (Fang, 2012). The discovery of indigenous management theory continues to be challenging, but we believe that these ancient Chinese philosophies contribute to the formation and understanding of Asian leaders in the global context.

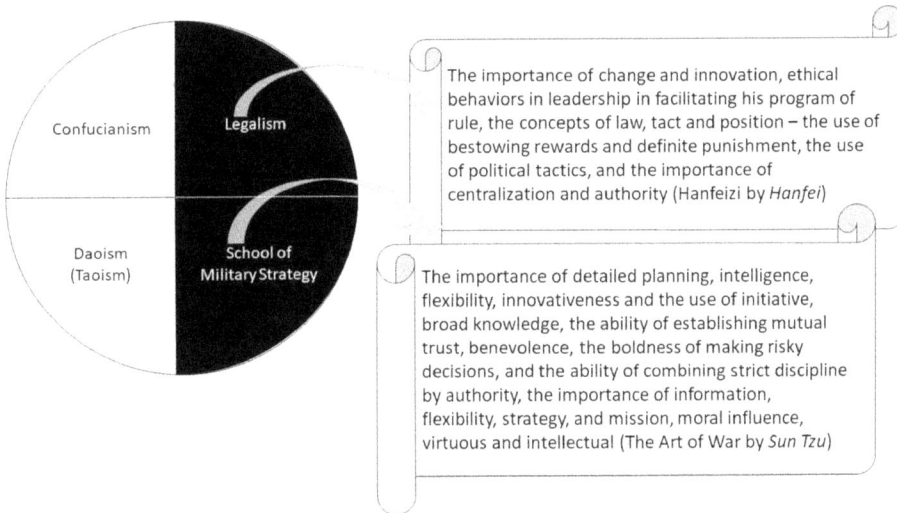

The importance of change and innovation, ethical behaviors in leadership in facilitating his program of rule, the concepts of law, tact and position – the use of bestowing rewards and definite punishment, the use of political tactics, and the importance of centralization and authority (Hanfeizi by *Hanfei*)

The importance of detailed planning, intelligence, flexibility, innovativeness and the use of initiative, broad knowledge, the ability of establishing mutual trust, benevolence, the boldness of making risky decisions, and the ability of combining strict discipline by authority, the importance of information, flexibility, strategy, and mission, moral influence, virtuous and intellectual (The Art of War by *Sun Tzu*)

Confucianism / Legalism / Daoism (Taoism) / School of Military Strategy

Figure 2.1: *Hanfeizi* (Legalism) and *The Art of War* (The School of Military Strategy) (For details, see Giles, 2014; Liao, 1939).

Culture affects an individual's values, attitudes and leadership behavior (Chong & Fu, 2020). Jack Ma always openly talks about Daoism, Buddhism, Confucianism and even the Tai Chi philosophy. These ancient thoughts have a significant impact on his management styles. As he once said, "Tai Chi's view on accommodation and transformation, yin and yang, ebb and flow, all thread through our company's management philosophy" (Tsui, Zhang & Chen, 2017). The founder of Huawei, Ren

Zhengfei's military background, has been a legendary example of how company vision and leadership behaviors are reflected from his philosophies and values. Ren says, "We shall drink in our heart's content to celebrate our success, but if we should fail, let us fight to our utmost until we all die" (De Cremer & Tao, 2015a). This quote resembles the Moral Law (shared vision and harmony among all people), which is a critical success factor in *The Art of War*.

Leadership Qualities in Asian Leaders

Chong and Fu (2020) discuss the importance of value systems in Asian leaders, based on Confucianism and Daoism (Taoism). The four leadership qualities are:
- *Humanistic leadership*
- *Moral leadership*
- *Invisible leadership*
- *Paradoxical leadership*

In addition to these four leadership qualities, we introduce four additional essential qualities of successful Asian leaders (Figure 2.2) as follows:

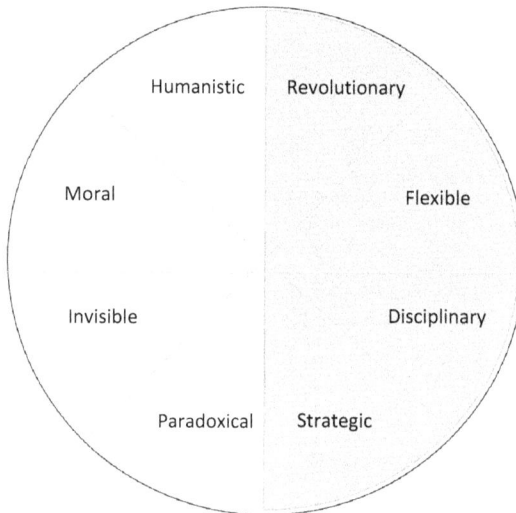

Figure 2.2: The Eight Essential Leadership Qualities of Asian Leaders (Own source).

Revolutionary Leadership

With accelerating change facing business organizations, leaders need to alter their response to these changing environments (Norton, 2010). Successful leaders of the 21st century are those who can lead their people to think innovatively (Basadur, 2004).

Han Fei argues that whether to choose change depends upon the question of whether or not existing traditions or institutions are still valid and useful for the present political purposes (Liao, 1939, see also Chong, 2018). Similarly, in *The Art of War*, Sun Tzu offers insights on how to manage change. He lists several essential components, such as innovation and the use of initiative (Chow, 1994). From the Western perspective, both transformational and change leadership styles suggest the capability of a leader to communicate a vision in meeting the changing and competitive marketplace (Yukl, 2002). These behaviors are consistent with Sun Tzu's suggestions regarding the importance of the Moral Law (see Giles, 2014).

There are similarities shared by Western and Eastern leaders, but also significant differences regarding how they achieve change and innovation. Based on *The Art of War*, Chow (1994) offers insights on how to manage change by detailed planning, intelligence, flexibility and innovativeness, and suggests that the positive qualities an active CEO should have are: broad knowledge, the ability to establish mutual trust, benevolence, boldness in making risky decisions, and strict discipline.

By referring to Han Fei's suggestions, Rowley and Ulrich (2012) point out that leadership includes numerous duties, responsibilities and the necessity of interactive relationships with followers. Legalism also carries strong authoritarian elements, but these are also important and offer compelling leadership implications. As Han Fei suggests, authority and position should not be lent to anybody else. If the sovereign loses them, the minister can borrow the power and position from the ruler. The ruler loses the control of his state, while the power of his ministers is multiplied (Liao, 1939). However, Han Fei also points out that natural law should be established with the consensus of all members. A wise leader should understand the principles of nature operating in the state and use them as the foundation for constituting rules (Hwang, 2012).

As we can see, although decision making for strategic direction is centralized and set by the founder, it is widely accepted by the subordinates. Asian leaders are more willing to take higher risks and are bold with innovation. The founders of many Asian companies started their business from nothing and successfully made a revolutionary transformation from small family businesses to diversified industries.

– **Toyota**'s leaders set "impossible" goals to create breakthrough innovations and stick to their long-term focus. There are no deadlines for innovation projects. The ideas of a "never-give-up" culture has led to revolutionary innovation (Rosing, Rosenbuschm & Frese, 2010).

- **Uniqlo**'s reasonable prices, excellent quality, and a value-adding brand image of "made for all" has transformed the company into a unique global fashion company. As founder Tadashi Yanai notes, "We are not a fashion company . . . We are a technology company" (Chu, 2012).
- **Alibaba**'s competitiveness is deeply rooted in its strong commitment to helping small and medium enterprises (SMEs) grow and expand in both the domestic and global markets. Jack Ma believes "small is beautiful." This principle focuses on SME projects, which has allowed small Chinese businesses to reach out to the global market (Lai, 2010).
- **Haidiloa**'s success is attributed to the founder's unique entrepreneurial values. These shared corporate values motivate employees to deliver extraordinary and creative customer service (McFarlan, Xiaoming & Zhao, 2011).

There is a Chinese saying: "Crises create opportunities." Risk-taking behaviors are commonly found in Asian leaders. In particular, Korean leaders deliberately create crises inside their companies in order to push their organizations into extraordinary performance. With the centralization of authority, the Korean business group chairperson sets the strategic direction (Hemmert, 2012).

- **Samsung**'s advancement into a top-tier innovative company was driven by the top management's anticipation of the market potential of the semiconductor industry and the ensuring aggressive commitment to this seemingly high-risk investment (Lee & Slater, 2007).
- **Hyundai** continued its practice of internally-generated crises, such as aggressive construction deadlines, demanding production targets and quality benchmarks, as a catalyst to the intensity of its learning efforts (Wright, Suh & Leggett, 2009).

Flexible Leadership

Due to increased globalization, rapid technological change, virtual interaction, a diversified workforce and concerns about sustainability and ethical outcomes, we need more flexible leaders (Burke & Cooper, 2004; Yukl & Mahsud, 2010).

In Western literature, flexible leadership is about the ability to deal with ambiguity and uncertainty. Those who can keep the experience of uncertainty to a tolerable level can keep more options open (White & Shullman, 2010). It also means adjusting one's leadership style, method or approach in response to different or changing contextual demands to facilitate employee performance. Flexible leaders require a full behavioral repertoire corresponding to the many different roles they need to perform (Kaiser & Overfield, 2010). Han Fei indicates that this is the reason why the sage neither seeks to follow the ways of the ancients nor establishes any fixed standard for all times, but examines the things of his age and then prepares to deal with them (Liao, 1939).

In line with Sun Tzu's sayings, in order to cope with ever-changing situations, one should maintain a high degree of flexibility (Chen, 1994). Sun Tzu suggests many methods to deal with ambiguity and uncertainty, including the effective use of both direct and indirect methods to secure victory. The direct method is used for joining battle, while indirect methods are needed in order to secure victory. Indirect tactics, if efficiently applied, are powerful and inexhaustible (Giles, 2014). For strategies to be effective, they must be flexible. Strategic plans must be monitored to be appropriate for different situations, but no one single strategy can be applied in all situations. Therefore, the strategy depends upon a number of contingency variables because "In the business of war, there is no invariable strategic advantage which can be relied upon at all times" (Rarick, 1996, based on *The Art of War*).

– **Hyundai** competes in the global markets by accepting environmental uncertainty and risk as a part of its flexible daily operations. The top management encourages employees to take calculated risks to resolve pressing operational problems as rapidly as possible (Shim & Steers, 2012).
– **Huawei**'s flexible, customer-first attitude, and innovative problem-solving approaches have helped the company to gain several large business accounts in the Middle East. When Huawei expanded its 3G market to Europe, it won this market by creating innovative base stations that enable radio access. This enabled lower costs and became popular with European carriers (De Cremer & Tao, 2015a).
– **Toyota** handles mistakes and identifies problems publicly. Their flexible business strategy, a long-term perspective, together with short-term profitable customization and organic growth, all contribute to its growth and success (Hogan & Benson, 2009).

Disciplinary Leadership

Disciplined leaders are those who concentrate on task-oriented functions, such as planning, scheduling work, coordinating subordinates' activities, providing necessary supplies and technical assistance, and guiding subordinates in setting performance goals (Yukl, 2002).

Like the Western task-oriented leadership, Sun Tzu also stresses proactive measures and detailed planning because with "careful and detailed planning, one can win; with careless and less detailed planning, one cannot win. From the way planning is accomplished beforehand, leaders can predict victory or defeat" (Chow, 1994). As Sun Tzu writes in the chapter "Laying Plans," "By method and discipline are to be understood the marshalling of the army in its proper subdivisions, the graduations of rank among the officers, the maintenance of roads by which supplies may reach the army, and the control of military expenditure" (Giles, 2014).

An effective Asian leader understands the importance of information, flexibility, strategy and mission, according to Sun Tzu. This is primarily based on an authority who also enforces discipline and imposes order and purpose (Chen, 1994; Rarick, 1996, 2007). The founder of the Hangzhou Wahaha Group, Qinghou Zong, points out that leaders who lack authority will find it difficult to manage Chinese companies (Tsui, Zhang & Chen, 2017). While task orientation is common among Western leaders, being authoritative is not typical behavior. However, this behavior is viewed as legitimate in Asian culture (Chen, 2004; Hemmert, 2012; Tsui et al., 2004). Drawing from Sun Tzu's work, Rarick (1996) discusses the importance of authority and the essential task-oriented characteristics of a military leader. Based on paternalism, leaders are expected to act as a disciplinarian. As Sun Tzu said, "For the masses, nothing is more exalted than authority. If the commander acts with authority over his men and enforces discipline among his officers, the entire army will have faith in his authority and will conquer the enemy" (Rarick, 1996).

The meaning of strictness in *The Art of War* can also be interpreted as the ability to enforce strict discipline, including how to use rewards and punishment timely, decisively and fairly (Chen, 1994). Similarly, Han Fei also indicates that it is essential for a leader to consistently enforce specific rewards and punishment because these two "handles" will make his followers exert their best efforts to reach their full potential. According to Han Fei, "punishment for fault never skips ministers; reward for good never misses commoners." The law applies to everyone fairly in society (Liao, 1939).

In transactional leadership, a contingent reward refers to how a leader rewards his or her subordinates' efforts (Bass, 1998). Kipnis, Schmidt and Wilkinson (1980) also propose the sanction influence tactics, which include assertive behaviors such as threatening the subordinate's job security, an unsatisfactory performance evaluation, the loss of promotion, and no salary increase. However, there are also differences because Han Fei points out that in order to make the tactics effective, the punishment must be "definite," and the reward should be "attractive." These two strategies are used in many Asian enterprises.

- In **Samsung**, while there is not much differentiation in basic salary for a given job, employees can receive high rewards based on their work achievements. The mechanism through which Samsung propagates its management philosophy is by employing "message-driven management," such as the use of an achievement-based performance system: the principles of competition, and reward and punishment (Iwai, 2020).
- In **Haier**, bonuses and promotions are given to those who consistently exceed their daily targets while those who fall short have their pay docked or are demoted to probationary status (Hawes & Chew, 2011).
- "The stranger principle" in **Vantone** demonstrates the strict discipline of using both rewards and punishment. As indicated by one of the founders, Lun Feng, if the person introduced exhibits outstanding performance and makes a significant contribution to the company, the friend who introduced him or her would be rewarded. In contrast, if the person did something wrong and caused a loss

for the company, this friend's performance appraisal would be negatively affected (Chen, 2012).
- She Chen, CEO of **Chengdu Bus Group**, linked wages to safe mileage accumulation. The company reduced drivers' wages each time they had accidents and rewarded those drivers with fewer accidents by increasing their wages. The safety records were also linked to promotions and demotions. As a result, accidents were significantly reduced. Insurance rate expenses per bus also dropped 75 percent within two years (Jing & Van de Ven, 2014).

The successes of Huawei and Lenovo are credited to the alignment of corporate values with their incentive systems (rewards and recognition) and monitoring processes.
- The performance incentive and employee shareholder systems implemented by **Huawei** have encouraged employees to act like owners and have enhanced corporate performance (De Cremer & Tao, 2015a). The idea of this employee profit-sharing system is effective in serving both the individual and collective interests because it enhances employee motivation to behave as an entrepreneur/owner and helps the company achieve its vision (De Cremer & Tao, 2015b).
- When Chuanzhi Liu, founder of **Lenovo**, left the position of chairman, he reminded the top management that their salaries would not be raised before those salaries of the frontline employees. This salary incentive system was also successfully implemented in Europe and the United States. The strategy not only enhanced the morale of the overseas employees, but also helped build a positive image that Lenovo sincerely cares about all its employees (Tsui, Zhang & Chen, 2017).

Strategic Leadership

Hambrick, Cannella and Pettigrew (2001) suggest two distinctive differences between leadership and strategic leadership. "Leadership" refers to leaders at any level, whereas "strategic leadership" refers to the top management of an organization. According to these authors, "the most effective strategic leadership practices in the 21st century will be ones through which strategic leaders find ways for knowledge to breed still more knowledge" (Ireland & Hitt, 1999). Global companies that are able to adapt in a rapidly changing technological world are those able to invest in knowledge development (Lusch, Vargo & Malter, 2006).

By developing strategic products, such as Heattech in 2006, **Uniqlo** refined its business model by integrating technology and innerwear into the fashion industry. By its accumulated knowledge in the fashion industry, Uniqlo has established a method of creating innovation by imitation and learning, which has generated new values (Huang, Kobayashi & Isomura, 2014).

Sun Tzu stated: "The general who wins a battle makes many calculations." Sun Tzu is also famous for the aphorism, "If you know the enemy and know yourself, you need not fear the result of a hundred battles. If you know yourself but not the enemy, for every victory gained, you will also suffer a defeat" (Giles, 2014). These strategies are exercised by a number of Asian leaders:

- **Tencent**'s WeChat took only a year to draw one hundred million users. Like Facebook and Twitter, it has evolved into a full-fledged social network platform, outperforming China Mobile's home-grown app – Fetion – with more functional features, such as drifting bottles, friend shake and music sharing (Wu & Wan, 2014).
- In 2003, **Alibaba** entered the C2C and B2C arenas with the introduction of Taobao. The timing was partly prompted by the arrival of eBay in China. In 2004, Alipay facilitated payments without credit cards and has now become the leader in global mobile payment. The launches of Alibaba Cloud Computing in 2009 and Ant Finance in 2014 are also crucial milestones that turned Alibaba into a global giant (Leavy, 2019).

Similar to Sun Tzu's strategies regarding the calculation and observation of self and others, Crossan, Vera and Nanjad (2008) propose that transcendent leadership involves a strategic leader who leads within and among the levels of self, others and the organization. It includes the responsibility of self-awareness and proactivity in developing personal strengths, the mechanisms of interpersonal influence a leader has upon followers, and the alignments of three interrelated areas: environment, strategy and organization. Similarly, Han Fei also stresses the importance of using strategies and single tactics, because smart leaders that are well-versed in the principles of tactics have foresight and keen observational skills. If not for these, the leaders cannot discern selfishness and problems (Liao, 1939).

Strategic leaders should use their time and energy to predict future competitive conditions and challenges and seek information that will allow them to accurately predict changes in various global markets (Ireland & Hitt, 1999). They should also facilitate organizational learning by studying failures openly and constructively to find hidden lessons (Schoemaker, Krupp & Howland, 2013). Jack Ma of **Alibaba** said he would never use a general who always wins; instead, he would choose the one who has failed often but has sometimes succeeded, because his failures would give him the wisdom to avoid these errors in future (Tsui, Zhang & Chen, 2017).

Apart from knowledge, strategic leadership should have leadership wisdom and absorptive capacity. Quoting Robert Sternberg's words, "wisdom" is about successful intelligence, balancing of interests and timeframes, mindful infusion of values, responsiveness to the environment and the application of knowledge for the common good. Absorptive capacity means to absorb new information, assimilate it, learn from it, and, importantly, to apply it to new ends (Cohen & Levinthat, 1990). Boal and Hooijberg (2000) also propose that absorptive capacity, the capacity to change and managerial wisdom are the essence of strategic leadership, while the social intelligence and behavioral complexity of strategic leaders positively affect the essence of strategic leadership.

Sun Tzu expounded on the importance of human intelligence: "The reason why the enlightened ruler and the wise general are able to conquer the enemy is . . . because of foreknowledge" (Chow, 1994). Like Western leaders, Asian leaders generally make strategic decisions based on knowledge and wisdom. They learn from mistakes and adjust their strategies from time to time. But one significant difference is that Asian leaders also tend to make bold decisions by intuition, foreknowledge and hands-on experience (Chen, 2004).

– The case of **Hyundai** Motor shows that they were not ready for their initial move into offshore production. However, they rebounded from these early failures remarkably quickly and learned from their mistakes. One of the critical ways Hyundai Motor was able to learn was through the codification of experience, resulting in explicit knowledge that could guide future success (Wright, Suh & Leggett, 2009).

– **Samsung** wisely and flexibly managed to overcome the crisis of the Samsung Galaxy Note 7 battery explosions by holding themselves accountable again. They did well in getting to the root of the cause and then communicating to their employees and consumers effectively. Samsung used the opportunity to develop a bigger brand and create a corporate culture of change that encourages and prides itself on taking risks (Dua, 2017).

– The failures of **Uniqlo** in London and Beijing provided its founder, Tadashi Yanai, with valuable experiences to expand Uniqlo as a global brand again. Now the group is back in New York and London and has been expanding at breakneck speed in Asia, including a plan of opening 1,000 stores in the greater China area. Uniqlo is no longer just a maker of affordable casual wear, but a global brand capable of sharing prime real estate with luxury retailers in New York City or Paris (Nakamoto, 2012).

What is Asian Global Leadership?

Confucius said, "By nature, men are nearly alike; by practice, they get to be wide apart" (The Analects, see Muller, 2018).

Various streams of leadership research have examined effective Asian leadership or global leadership, but not much work has discussed the relationship between the two, such as Asian leadership in the global context, or global leadership in the Asian context. As suggested by Confucius, we believe that the effective leadership qualities we present in this book chapter are universally applicable. However, there are also differences in terms of how leaders exercise these behaviors.

In this article, we review this body of knowledge in Asian philosophies and synthesize it under a global construct of Asian leadership, which we define as follows: "Asian Global Leadership refers to Asian leaders, who lead others in a global context, use a combination of leadership behaviors which originated from the Eastern (Chinese) philosophies and values. These leadership behaviors are comprised of both soft and hard elements, like the yin and yang energies. They resemble very closely, but also show significant differences from Western leadership practices." Under this unifying construct, we summarize the characteristics and conceptualizations that we observe among Asian global leaders. These ideas are shown in Table 2.1.

Table 2.1: Comparison of the eight leadership qualities between the West and the East (Own source).

Global Leadership Qualities	The West	The East Similar to the West but:
Humanistic	**Benevolence and care:** but work-life only	also touching the personal lives of employees and a more long-term relationship
Moral	**High ethical standards:** but more explicit, image building	more on implicit and self-cultivation
Invisible	**Non-intervention:** based on a common purpose	also by following "Dao" and the flow quietly; doing nothing but achieving everything
Paradoxical	**Embrace inconsistencies:** that provoke conflict and defensive reactions	the opposite elements mutually transform one another in a balancing process and achieve harmony or equilibrium
Revolutionary	**Innovation and deal with change:** by a communicated vision	also by bold decisions, internally-generated crises and centralization of authority
Flexible	**Deal with ambiguity and uncertainty:** by adjusting one's leadership style, method or approach	no one best method; using both direct and indirect methods
Disciplinary	**Task-oriented functions:** by careful planning and operations	also by strict disciplines; using both bestowing reward and definite punishment
Strategic	**Knowledge and wisdom:** by responsiveness to the environment and application of knowledge for the common good	also by intuition, foreknowledge and hands-on experience

Conclusion

Many Asian leaders have successfully transformed their companies over the years, adapting to changes in the global markets. For instance, the Hong Kong tycoon and **CK Hutchison Holdings** founder Li Ka-shing said that his management philosophies reflect the Confucian values while also adopting a Western management style (Bloomberg, 2016). Our model in global leadership is consistent with the universal approach (see Steers, Sanchez-Runde & Nardon, 2012), which considers leadership to be generalizable. These leadership behaviors (see Table 2.1) are widely used by Asian leaders both domestically and in their overseas affiliates, though the leadership qualities are derived from the ancient Eastern/Chinese philosophies. We believe these leadership essentials, which combine *yin* and *yang* energies, are useful in the global context, and can be learned and exercised by Western leaders.

Although this article offers insights, distinctive aspects and real-life examples of Asian leadership in the global context, there are also limitations. The ancient philosophies and values are profound, and cover wisdom, knowledge and implications that we might not be able to capture in this short article. We conclude this article by quoting Jack Ma's words when describing a powerful feature of effective Asian leaders: "Everyone has a different personality. I hope my company can be like a zoo of different animals with different characteristics . . . . With different animals, a company can have a good ecosystem . . . . I died thousands of times, and have no fear of another death. Young people can easily catch up with your skills, but courage is what makes a leader" (Tsui, Zhang & Chen, 2017).

References

Alves, J. C., Manz, C. C. & Butterfield, D. A. (2005). Developing leadership theory in Asia: The role of Chinese philosophy. *International Journal of Leadership Studies*, *1*(1): 3–27.

Basadur, M. (2004). Leading others to think innovatively together: Creative leadership. *The Leadership Quarterly*, *15*(1): 103–121.

Bass, B. (1998). Transformational leadership: Industry, military, and educational impact. Mahwah, NJ: Erlbaum Associates.

Bloomberg (2016). *Hong Kong Billionaire Li Ka-Shing: An In-Depth Interview* [Video file]. Retrieved from https://www.bloomberg.com/news/videos/2016-06-29/hong-kong-billionaire-li-ka-shing-an-in-depth-interview.

Boal, K. B. & Hooijberg, R. (2000). Strategic leadership research: moving on. *The Leadership Quarterly*, *11*(4): 515–549.

Burke, R. J. & Cooper, C. L. (2004). *Leading in Turbulent Times*. Blackwell (Oxford, UK).

Chen, M. (1994). Sun Tzu's strategic thinking and contemporary business. *Business Horizons*, *37*(2): 42–48.

Chen, M. (2004). *Asian Management Systems: Chinese, Japanese and Korean Styles of Business*. Thomson (London, UK).

Chen, X. P. (2012). Morality and integrity keep a company away from trouble: An interview with Mr. Feng Lun, Chairman of Vantone Holdings Co. Ltd. *Chinese Management Insights*, *1*(3): 88–96.

Chong, M. P. M. & Fu, P. P. (2020). Global leadership: An Asian perspective. *Journal of Leadership Studies*, *14*(2): 58–62.

Chong, M. P. M. (2018). *Organizational political tactics: Hanfei's Legalist doctrines of leadership*. Paper presented at the 78th Annual Meeting of the Academy of Management, Chicago, Illinois, USA.

Chow, H. W. (1994). Managing change: Perspectives from Sun Tzu's *Art of War*. *Journal of Strategic Change*, *3*(4): 189–199.

Chu, J. (2012). Cheap, chic and made for all: How Uniqlo plans to take over casual fashion. *Fast Company*. Retrieved from https://www.fastcompany.com/1839302/cheap-chic-and-made-all-how-uniqlo-plans-take-over-casual-fashion.

Cohen, W. M. & Levinthal, D. (1990). Absorptive capacity: A new perspective on learning and innovation. *Administrative Science Quarterly*, *35*(1): 128–152.

Crossan, M., Vera, D. & Nanjad, L. (2008). Transcendent leadership: Strategic leadership in dynamic environments. *The Leadership Quarterly*, *19*(5): 569–581.

De Cremer, D. & Tao, T. (2015a). Huawei's culture is the key to its success. *Harvard Business Review*. Retrieved from https://hbr.org/2015/06/huaweis-culture-is-the-key-to-its-success.

De Cremer, D. & Tao, T. (2015b). Huawei: A case study of when profit sharing works. *Harvard Business Review*. Retrieved from https://hbr.org/2015/09/huawei-a-case-study-of-when-profit-sharing-works.

Denecke, W. (2010). *The Dynamics of Masters Literature: Early Chinese Thought from Confucius to Han Feizi*. Harvard University Asia Center for the Harvard-Yenching Institute and Harvard University Press (Cambridge, MA).

Dimovskid, V., Marič, M., Miha, U., Durica, N. & Ferjan, M. (2012). Sun Tzu's "The Art of War" and implications for leadership: Theoretical discussion. *Organizacija*, *45*(4): 151–158.

Dua, T. (2017). From a 'cultural meme' to a comeback kid: How Samsung overcame its Galaxy Note 7 fiasco. *Business Insider*. Retrieved from https://www.businessinsider.com/how-samsung-overcame-its-galaxy-note-7-fiasco-2017-10.

Fang, T. (2012). Yin Yang: A new perspective on culture. *Management and Organization Review*, *8*(1): 25–50.

Giles, L. trans. (n.d.). *The Art of War by Sun Tzu*, Retrieved from https://suntzusaid.com/artofwar.php.

Hambrick, D. Cannella, A. A. & Pettigrew, A. (2001). Upper echelons: Donald Hambrick on executives and strategy. *Academy of Management Executive*, *15*(3): 36–44.

Hawes, C. & Chew, E. (2011). The cultural transformation of large Chinese enterprises into internationally competitive corporations: Case studies of Haier and Huawei. *Journal of Chinese Economic and Business Studies*, *9*(1): 67–83.

Hemmert, M. (2012). *Tiger Management: Korean Companies on World Markets*. Routledge (London, UK).

Hogan, R. & Benson, M. J. (2009). Personality, leadership, and globalization: Linking personality to global organizational effectiveness. *Advances in Global Leadership*, *5*: 11–34.

Huang, P.-Y., Kobayashi, S. & Isomura, K. (2014). How UNIQLO evolves its value proposition and brand image: Imitation, trial and error and innovation. *Strategic Direction*, *30*(7): 42–45.

Hwang, K. K. (2008). Leadership theory of Legalism and its function in Confucian society. In C. C. Chen & Y. T. Lee (Eds.), *Leadership and Management in China: Philosophies, Theories and Practices* (pp. 108–142). Cambridge University Press (Cambridge, UK).

Hwang, K. K. (2012). Confucian and legalist basis of leadership and business ethics. In C. Luetege (Ed.), *Handbook of the Philosophical Foundations of Business Ethics* (pp. 1005–1026). Springer (Berlin, Heidelberg).

International Monetary Fund. (2018). *Regional Economic Outlook, Asia Pacific: Good Times, Uncertain Times: A Time to Prepare.* International Monetary Fund (Washington, DC).

Ireland, R. D. & Hitt, M. A. (1999). Achieving and maintaining strategic competitiveness in the 21st century: The role of strategic leadership. *Academy of Management Perspectives, 13*(1): 43–57.

Iwai, H. (2020). Practicing the company philosophy to survive: The competitive world of Samsung Group. In I. Mitsui (Ed.), *Cultural Translation of Management Philosophy in Asian Companies: Its Emergence, Transmission, and Diffusion in the Global Era* (pp. 121–135). Springer (Singapore).

Jing, R. & Van de Ven, A. H. (2014). A Yin-Yang model of organizational change: The case of Chengdu Bus Group. *Management and Organization Review, 10*(1): 29–54.

Kaiser, R. B. & Overfield, D. V. (2010). Assessing flexible leadership as a mastery of opposites. *Consulting Psychology Journal: Practice and Research, 62*(2), 105–118.

Kipnis, D., Schmidt, S. M., & Wilkinson, I. (1980). Intraorganizational influence tactics: Explorations in getting one's way. Journal of Applied Psychology, 65(4):440–452.

Lai, L. S. (2010). Chinese entrepreneurship in the internet age: Lessons from Alibaba.com. *International Journal of Economics and Management Engineering, 4*(12): 2252–2258.

Leavy, B. (2019). Alibaba strategist Ming Zeng: "Smart business" in the era of business ecosystems. *Strategy & Leadership, 47*(2): 11–18.

Lee, J. & Slater, J. (2007). Dynamic capabilities, entrepreneurial rent-seeking and the investment development path: The case of Samsung. *Journal of International Management, 13*(3): 241–257.

Leung, K. & White, S. (2004). Taking stock and charting a path for Asian management research. In K. Leung & S. White (Eds.), *Handbook of Asian Management* (pp. 3–18). Springer (Boston, MA).

Liao, W. K. trans. (1939). *The Complete Works of Han Fei Tzu.* Retrieved from http://www2.iath. virginia.edu:8080/exist/cocoon/xwomen/texts/hanfei/tpage/tocc/bilingual.

Lusch, R. F., Vargo, S. L. & Malter, A. J. (2006). Marketing as service-exchange: Taking a leadership role in global marketing management. *Organizational Dynamics, 35*(3): 264–278.

Ma, L. & Tsui, A. S. (2015). Traditional Chinese philosophies and contemporary leadership. *The Leadership Quarterly, 26*(1): 13–24.

McCann, D. P. (2012). On reading Sun-Tzu: The promise and perils of appropriating a Chinese classic in international business ethics. *Journal of International Business Ethics, 5*(2): 27–37.

McDonald, P. (2012). Confucian foundations to leadership: A study of Chinese business leaders across Greater China and South-East Asia. *Asia Pacific Business Review, 18*(4): 465–487.

McFarlan, F. W., Xiaoming, Z. & Zhao, Z. (2011). *The Haidilao Company.* Harvard Business Review Case Serial. Harvard Business School Press (New York, NY).

Muller, A. C. trans. (n.d.). *The Analects of Confucius.* Retrieved from http://www.acmuller.net/con-dao/analects.html.

Nakamoto, M. (2012). Japan's king of casual smartens up. *Financial Times.* Retrieved from https:// www.ft.com/content/afae506a-cb51-11e1-b896-00144feabdc0.

Norton, L. W. (2010). Flexible leadership: An integrative perspective. *Consulting Psychology Journal: Practice and Research, 62*(2): 143–150.

Pars, M. (2013). Six strategy lessons from Clausewitz and Sun Tzu. *Journal of Public Affairs, 13*(3): 329–334.

Rarick, C. (1996). Ancient Chinese advice for modern business strategies. *SAM Advanced Management Journal, 61*(1): 38–43.

Rarick, C. (2007). The "other" art of war: Strategic implication of Sun Pin's bing fa. *SAM Advanced Management Journal, 72*(4): 4–8.

Rosing K., Rosenbusch N. & Frese M. (2010). Ambidextrous leadership in the innovation process. In Gerybadze, A., Hommel, U., Reiners, H. W. & Thomaschewski, D. (Eds.), *Innovation and International Corporate Growth* (pp. 191–204). Springer (Berlin, Heidelberg).

Rowley, C. & Ulrich, D. (2012). Introduction: setting the scene for leadership in Asia. *Asia Pacific Business Review, 18*(4): 451–463.

Schoemaker, P. J. H., Krupp, S. & Howland, S. (2013). Strategic leadership: The essential skills. *Harvard Business Review, 91*(1), 131–134.

Shim, W. S. & Steers, R. M. (2012). Symmetric and asymmetric leadership cultures: A comparative study of leadership and organizational culture at Hyundai and Toyota. *Journal of World Business, 47*(4): 581–591.

Steers, R. M., Sanchez-Runde, C. & Nardon, L. (2012). Leadership in a global context: New directions in research and theory development. *Journal of World Business, 47*(4): 479–482.

Tsui A. S., Zhang, Y. & Chen X. P. (2017). *Leadership of Chinese Private Enterprises: Insights and Interviews*. Palgrave Macmillan (London, UK).

Tsui, A. S., Wang, H., Xin, K., Zhang, L. & Fu, P. P. (2004). "Let a thousand flowers bloom": Variation of leadership styles among Chinese CEOs. *Organizational Dynamics, 33*(1): 5–20.

White, R. P. & Shullman, S. L. (2010). Acceptance of uncertainty as an indicator of effective leadership. *Consulting Psychology Journal: Practice and Research, 62*(2): 94–104.

Witzel, M. (2012). The leadership philosophy of Han Fei. *Asia Pacific Business Review, 18*(4): 489–503.

Wright, C., Suh, C. S. & Leggett, C. (2009). If at first you don't succeed: Globalized production and organizational learning at the Hyundai Motor Company. *Asia Pacific Business Review, 15*(2): 163–180.

Wu, J. & Wan, Q. (2014). From WeChat to we fight: Tencent and China mobile's dilemma. *PACIS 2014 Proceedings*. Retrieved from http://aisel.aisnet.org/pacis2014/265.

Yukl, G. A. (2002). *Leadership in Organizations*. Prentice-Hall (New York, NY).

Yukl, G. & Mahsud, R. (2010). Why flexible and adaptive leadership is essential. *Consulting Psychology Journal: Practice and Research, 62*(2): 81–93.

David De Cremer, Hannah De Cremer and Jess Zhang

Chapter 3
Asian Global Leadership: Looking at the World in Patient, Collective and Humble Ways

For the last year, my daughter Hannah has developed a strong interest in drawing and constructing her own stories about reality. It's been a fascinating journey so far to witness how she manages to get her own ideas down on paper about how people live. The style of her drawings has quickly developed into shapes that have gradually become more and more recognizable. In itself, this is already a testimony to how creatively and beautifully the human brain develops and allows us to take perspective. But the most interesting thing has been how she truly has become an artist able to look at both the bigger picture (such as a castle, playground or city) and the individual characters that are supposed to live in that context (such as dinosaurs, princesses and parents) at the same time. She seems to have transformed herself into someone who looks both at the overall scene and the details within that scene to shape the stories that she tells her parents. Why do I consider this an interesting development?

The reason for telling this story is that Hannah has a Chinese mother and a Belgian father. In a way, she brings together Asian and Western perspectives, and in my view, this has surfaced in how she approaches her drawings. When she starts drawing, she has a story in mind that gradually builds when she starts adding more and more details. This approach ultimately delivers a drawing in which a lot of action is happening within the context of a bigger setting. In more psychological terms, Hannah is clearly looking at the world in what can be called a "holistic" way – she focuses on the context at hand, but, in her case, this tendency goes hand in hand with an eye for details that she considers fixed, such as the personality of a dinosaur or a princess. Interestingly, within the psychology literature, this focus on the context at hand is suggested to be more present in collectivistic societies (a proxy for most Asian countries), whereas the focus on analytic details and salient (fixed) characteristics is more present in individualistic societies (a proxy for most Western countries). So it seems she is truly embracing her dual culture by integrating it in how she looks at the world. This integrative way of looking at the world may, in my view, be what we will need to define the kind of leadership required in a global world that is becoming increasingly influenced by Asia.

The idea that culture has an influence on how people look at the world has received much empirical support. One of the first studies of its kind indeed revealed that when people were asked to look at an image, significant differences were found between individuals from East Asia and those from the US (Chua, Boland & Nisbett, 2005). Specifically, participants from East Asia spent more time focusing on

https://doi.org/10.1515/9783110671988-003

and working with the context of the image, whereas participants from the US were focusing most of the time on what was clearly the core and details of the image. So, depending on where you are from, or, more specifically, depending on which culture you were raised in, you tend to focus initially at different aspects (context or more analytical details) of an image. Interestingly, this different way of looking at reality was also observed in children's drawings. In this study, researchers compared children from Japan and Canada who were asked to draw a landscape (Senzaki, Masuda & Nand, 2014). Their findings revealed that participants from Japan were more context-oriented and those from Canada focused more on the specific objects within the context, as such supporting that Asian societies seem to differ from Western societies in how they process information that they see (Masuda et al., 2008).

Of course, as any cultural phenomenon, this difference between different cultures in what they look at is psychologically motivated. This means that independent of the specific cultural influences that have been observed, humans have been shown to process incoming information such as an image in two different ways (Smith & Trope, 2006). And, these two ways nicely correspond with the way Eastern versus Western societies look at reality (i.e. context-oriented versus detail- and object-oriented). Specifically, in focusing on elements from incoming information, people either engage in more abstract information processing or in more concrete information processing. Abstract processing involves looking more at the central aspects that make up the context. It also includes detecting relationships between the different objects within the image. This tendency to zoom in on the possible relationships between the parts of a whole corresponds with being a holistic thinker, which would be more pronounced in Asian societies. For example, in exercises where one is asked to name two related items in a list of words like "train, bus and track," participants from the East would say "train" and "track" because they are functionally related, whereas participants from the West would be more likely to say "train" and "bus" because they are both different objects (vehicles). Concrete processing, on the other hand, involves looking more at the exact details within an image and identifying the differences between objects. From this, it thus follows that people from Eastern societies are more likely to engage in abstract processing, whereas those from Western societies would be more inclined to engage in concrete processing. We do note that, of course, within Western and Eastern societies, variability exists and both modes of processing do occur.

How we look at the world can have a significant influence on how we make decisions and treat people. As such, understanding information processing capacities becomes important to those who are in leadership positions. Moreover, as the world has become smaller due to the increased engagement to "globalization," it becomes more important than ever to be able to take different perspectives and understand how people perceive reality to make legitimate decisions. We can look at leadership as "a process of social influence in which one person is able to enlist the aid and support of others in the accomplishment of a common task" (Chemers, 2000). Leaders thus drive and motivate others to accomplish a shared goal. How influential one can be will be determined by how complex and large-scale the context one operates in as a leader will be. At the global level, being a leader is then also defined as "an individual who inspires a group of people to willingly pursue a positive vision in an effectively organized fashion while fostering individual and collective growth in a context characterized by significant levels of complexity, flow, and presence" (Mendenhall et al., 2012). Given these definitions, it stands to reason that our processing modes are likely to significantly influence the kind of leadership we will need in a more global context. As our processing modes are influenced by culture, in this chapter, we focus on how Asian ways of looking at the world will influence global leadership.

The Rise of the East and Global Leadership

The region of Asia is developing quickly and its global impact has never been bigger. Looking at the size of its population, this should not be a surprise. More people live in Asia than in any other continent (Brown, 2020). This simple numerical observation also helps forecast that Asian economies will increasingly have more impact on the global economy (De Cremer, 2020a). In fact, Asian economies are expected to be larger than the rest of the world combined in 2021, for the first time since the 19th century. Together with this rise in population and economic power, Asian households will be on track to become the major consumer segment at a global scale. Indeed, in 2016, there were about 3.2 billion people in the middle class and at this moment in time a majority of the world's population is now considered middle-class or rich households (Kharas, 2017). Kharas (2017) estimated that the next billion of new entrants to the middle class (since 2016) will live in Asia. As a result, it is expected that by 2030, about 66 percent of the world's middle classes will live in Asia.

The rise of the East in modern times has initially been motivated by the rise of China and India, with China accounting for 19 percent of the world output in 2019, making it the second economy in the world (for now!) and India being the world's third-largest economy (Romei & Reed, 2019). But it's not only China and India – other smaller and midsize countries in Asia are making the difference with, for example, Indonesia and Vietnam being on the fast track to entering the top 10 and top 20 of economic power holders, respectively. This economic rise of Asia has recently been demonstrated by one of the biggest free trade deals in history, with a deal that was signed on 15 November 2020 between the leaders of China and another 14 countries in the Asia-Pacific region. This deal covers 2.2 billion people and 30 percent of the world's economic output.

It is thus clear that Asian economies have become increasingly important global players (Cappelli et al., 2010), and this will have an impact on how businesses worldwide have to think about how to run their organizations to successfully reach this important economic region. As running an organization requires effective leadership (Hogan & Kaiser, 2005), it is then also necessary that leadership at the global level becomes savvy enough to understand how business works in Asia. Even more so, because of Asia's emerging worldwide influence, the notion of what we understand as global leadership will also be challenged. Until today, organizations operating globally are looking for talented people to run projects and guide transformational processes across cultures.

One common observation in how talented employees are being nurtured to become global leaders is the adoption of Western leadership models (Hanges et al., 2016). In fact, because of global competition and the major influence of Western education, Western textbooks have been used in Asian management and business schools for a long time and have subsequently even instilled an academic research culture in Asia that relies on leadership approaches grounded in Western values and practices (Tsui et al., 2004; Zhang et al., 2014).

Today, the 21st century, however, is believed to be Asian. As well as a growing Asian dominance, we also see the emergence of more Asian talents at the global leadership level (McDonald, 2012). As such, it is time to examine more carefully how patterns of contemporary Asian cognitions and behaviors, which are important parts of the Asian cultural fabric, are displayed in leadership practices, and hence are likely to influence what global leadership will constitute in the 21st century. Specifically, in this chapter we argue that the mode of processing information that we discussed earlier in our introduction (and which is subject to cultural influences) will have a major influence on the shape that global leadership will have to take.

Mode of Processing and Asian Global Leadership

Focusing and thinking more in terms of concrete objects, which is the more prevalent view in Western societies, can be linked to the tendency of Western management traditions focusing on leadership as the activity of an individual. In contrast, the tendency to look more at the bigger picture and consider the relationships between the different objects, which is the more prevalent view in Eastern societies, aligns more with the Asian way of looking at leadership as a collective and group-focused kind of behavior. As such, the way people process information is a function of culture, and this mode of processing shows a natural relationship with expectations and behaviors that come along with the concept of leadership. Specifically, in Asia, the "holistic" perspective is therefore more closely related to understanding leadership in a collective (rather than an individual) context. This collective-oriented way of processing information has several consequences that we expect to influence the shape of Asian Global Leadership. In the following sections, we describe three of such consequences.

Being Patient to Change

Because a holistic approach means that leaders in the East will initially look at the problem in more of an abstract manner and therefore will evaluate the general idea first. After having engaged in a more abstract way of looking at the situation as a whole (e.g. considering the idea more generally), they will start looking at the details and determining how to move on with the idea. Or, in other words, after having looked at the idea in an abstract way, after some time they will start looking at the more concrete features of the situation and idea proposed. Leaders in Western societies will more quickly focus on the concrete features and thus be more inclined to start working on its execution. This is not to say that in the East, leaders do not move fast. On the contrary – they can move very fast, but only when the general idea is accepted and well understood (De Cremer, 2015; 2020b). Once they buy into the idea, things move fast – often much faster than in the West. What this kind of reasoning implies is that in Eastern societies, patience is a key element in getting things to change, as they look at the change event initially at an abstract level, moving in their own pace towards the concrete level, subsequently moving fast.

The Group Comes First

A consequence of holistic thinking is that initially the whole is looked at, and objects (or individuals) are seen as interrelated. This more abstract way of looking at the situation as a whole then translates to Eastern leaders' tendency to consider the group as more important than one individual. Indeed, in the West, people process information about individuals more in terms of their personality and abilities, rather than in terms of their relationship to the broader context (and thus others). As such, they will see their identity as more of an autonomous sense of self to pursue whereas in the East, people will see their identity as more embedded in interpersonal relationships within the given context of a collective. In short, differences in modes of processing thus also drive the level of focus, which in the West will be more on the individual and in the East will be more on the group. As a result, leaders in Asian societies will be less inclined to sell themselves too much, as they cannot be seen as putting their personal interest above the group interest (Markus & Kitayama, 1991). Indeed, if people in Asian societies are emphasizing too many of their own achievements and abilities, they are liked less (Bond, Leung & Wan, 1982). This brings up the point that leaders in the East are concerned more about the value of humility.

Being Humble Means Prestige

A holistic mindset motivates people to primarily focus on the interrelationships between themselves and others. As a result, their primary concern lies in fostering and taking care of those relationships, which is usually achieved by showing empathy, building trust and relying on cooperation. Is this the idea of a leader? It is definitely the case for New Zealand Prime Minister Jacinda Ardern, who noted, "One of the criticisms I've faced over the years is that I'm not aggressive enough or assertive enough, or maybe somehow, because I'm empathetic, it means I'm weak. I totally rebel against that. I refuse to believe that you cannot be both compassionate and strong." Because leaders like Ardern do not put themselves above everyone else, they are often called humble leaders. The management literature has clearly demonstrated that being humble is one of the key determinants of leadership effectiveness (Owens & Hekman, 2012) and is considered as central to Asian conceptualizations of leadership (e.g. ethocracy, or "ruling by ethical values" (Cheung & Chan, 2005). This means that in cultures where the relationships between the individual parts of the whole are paid more attention to, these cultures will also have a strong natural inclination toward being humble. Indeed, research finds that in Asian societies, "humility is the desired response, or the culturally appropriate response, and that it is wise not to gloat over performance or to express confidence in ability" (Markus & Kitayama, 1991).

Being humble also aligns well with what has been called a "prestige" strategy. That is, rather than being assertive and controlling (i.e., a dominance strategy), humble leaders do care about how they treat others, as they want to display cooperative behavior and share knowledge that is valuable to other group members (Cheng & Tracy, 2014). This kind of behavior is more likely to increase leaders' adaptability as more prestige (which is necessary to obtain a sustainable social standing within a group) is attributed to the leader (Henrich & Gil-White, 2001). So as the group interest is considered the starting point when a holistic mindset is influencing how information is processed, leaders naturally pursue a long-term positive social standing, which is displayed by means of being a humble person to others.

Asian Global Leadership: Looking at the Whole Picture

With the growing economic and social power of the Asian continent, how global leadership is portrayed will change as well. Gradually, Asian-specific ways of acting and thinking will become part of the behavioral repertoire of any global leader, and in this process it is important to bring together the strengths of both Western and Eastern approaches to processes relevant to promoting effective leadership. Indeed, the necessity of looking at what Asian leadership at the global level means requires Western and Eastern leadership perspectives and ideas to converge (King & Zhang,

2014). In both the East and the West, there is a common understanding that effective leadership mobilizes groups of people in the direction of a goal that the collective wants to achieve. How the process of mobilizing is activated and executed still may reveal important differences between Asian and Western leaders. We argue that this is primarily the case because their ways of looking at the world differ.

The Asian way of looking at the world is more holistic and, as such, shapes decisions and actions in specific ways. That is, by looking more at the context and how the objects within that context are connected, Asian leadership is more characterized by integrating elements that focus on the whole (the collective) rather than the parts (the individual). This kind of leadership focuses on the relationships that exist between the parts and respecting each of them in their contribution to the whole (i.e., being humble and respectful). Finally, this way of leading also allows for taking more time to secure that the collective interest is served rather than moving on quickly by means of individual actions (i.e. patience). Given Asia's prominence in the world economy, these ways of looking at reality will greatly influence how global leaders will have to change how they approach their different stakeholders, hence rendering a new notion of Asian global leadership. It is by integrating both the Eastern and Western ways of looking at the world that international businesses will be successful in adapting to the current economic power shift, as they will be able to look at the world in new and more inclusive ways.

References

Bond, M., Leung, K. & Wan, K. C. (1982). The social impact of self-effacing attributions: The Chinese case. *Journal of Social Psychology, 118*, 157–166.

Brown, G. D. (2020). *XL: Asia: Exponential leadership in the Asian Century*. Pikkal & Co.

Capelli, P., Singh, H., Singh, J. & Useem, M. (2010). The India way: Lessons for the U.S. *Academy of Management Perspectives, 24*(2), 6–24.

Chemers, M. M. (2000). Leadership research and theory: A functional integration. *Group Dynamics, 4*, 27–43.

Cheng J. T. & Tracy J. L. (2014). Toward a unified science of hierarchy: Dominance and prestige are two fundamental pathways to human social rank. In Cheng J. T., Tracy J. L., Anderson C. (Eds.), *The Psychology of Social Status* (pp. 3–27). Springer (New York, NY).

Cheung, C. & Chan, A. C. (2005). Philosophical foundations of eminent Hong Kong Chinese CEOs' leadership. *Journal of Business Ethics, 60*(1), 47–62.

Chua, H. F., Boland, J. E. & Nisbett, R. E. (2005). Cultural variation in eye movements during scene perception. *Proceedings of National Academy of Science, 102*(35), 12629–12633.

De Cremer, D. (2015). Understanding trust, in China and the West. *Harvard Business Review*.

De Cremer, D. (2020a). Asian Global Leadership: An introduction to the special issue. *Journal of Leadership Studies, 14*(2), 52–54.

De Cremer, D. (2020b). On the trust management challenge of Asian global leadership. *Journal of Leadership Studies, 14*(2), 67–70.

Hanges, P. J., Aiken, J. R., Park, J. & Su, J. (2016). Cross-cultural leadership: Leading around the world. *Current Opinion in Psychology*, *8*, 64–69.

Henrich, J. & Gil-White, F. J. (2001). The evolution of prestige: Freely conferred deference as a mechanism for enhancing the benefits of cultural transmission. *Evolution and Human Behavior*, *22*, 165–196.

Hogan, R. & Kiaser, R. B. (2005). What we know about leadership. *Review of General Psychology*, *9*(2), 169–180.

King, P. & Zhang, W. (2014). Chinese and Western leadership models: A literature review. *Macrothink Institute Journal of Management Research, 6*(2). Retrieved on 21 January 2021 from: http://dx.doi.org/10.5296/jmr.v6i2.4927.

Kharas, H. (2017). The unprecedented expansion of the global middle class: An update. Global Economy & Development Working Paper 100. Retrieved on 21 January 2021 from: https://www.brookings.edu/wp-content/uploads/2017/02/global_20170228_global-middle-class.pdf.

Markus, H. R. & Kitayama, S. (1991). Culture and the self: Implications for cognition, emotion, and motivation. *Psychological Review*, *98*, 224–253.

Masuda, T., Gonzalez, R., Kwan, L. & Nisbett, R. E. (2008). Culture and aesthetic preference: Comparing the attention to context of East Asians and Americans. *Personality and Social Psychology Bulletin*, *34*(9), 1260–1275.

McDonald, P. (2012). Confucian foundations to leadership: A study of Chinese business leaders across greater China and south-east Asia. *Asia Pacific Business Review*, *18*(4), 465–487.

Mendenhall, M. E., Reiche, B. S., Bird, A. & Osland, J. S. (2012). Defining the "global" in global leadership. *Journal of World Business*, *47*(4), 493–503.

Owens, B. P. & Hekman, D. (2012). Modeling how to grow: An inductive examination of humble leader behaviors, outcomes, and contingencies. *Academy of Management Journal*, *55*(4), 787–818.

Romei, V. & Reed, J. (2019, March 26). The Asian Century is set to begin. *The Financial Times*. Retrieved on 21 January 2021 from: https://www.ft.com/content/520cb6f6-2958-11e9-a5ab-ff8ef2b976c7.

Senzaki, S. Masuda, K. & Nand, K. (2014). Holistic versus analytic expressions in artworks: cross-cultural differences and similarities in drawings and collages by Canadian and Japanese School-Age Children. *Journal of Cross-Cultural Psychology*, *45*(8), 1297–1316.

Smith, P. K. & Trope, Y. (2006). You focus on the forest when you're in charge of the trees: Power priming and abstract information processing. *Journal of Personality and Social Psychology*, *90*(4), 578–596

Tsui, A. S., Wang, H., Xin, K., Zhang, L. & Fu, P. P. (2004). Let a thousand flowers bloom: Variation of leadership styles among Chinese CEOs. *Organizational Dynamics*, *33*(1), 5–20.

Zhang, Z.-X., Chen, G. Z. X., Chen, Y.-R. & Ang, S. (2014). Business leadership in the Chinese context: Trends, findings, and implications. *Management and Organization Review*, *10*(2), 199–221.

Part II: **On the Challenges of Asian Leadership in a Global Setting**

Audrey Chia and Lim Yee Wei

Chapter 4
Social Innovators Leading Change in Health

Health and Social Challenges in Asia

Asia is home to 60 percent of the world's population (United Nations, 2020) and is socially and economically diverse. While it is home to some of the world's wealthiest individuals, Asia is also home the world's poorest individuals, with 1.2 billion people in Asia living beneath the international poverty line of US$3.20 a day. Of these, the poorest 400 million live on less than US$1.90 a day (Shuvojit & Ng, 2019). When it comes to health, education and other basic services, low-income and vulnerable communities lack the three "A's": access, affordability and availability. Many people live in rural and remote areas that are underserved or in urban areas where these services are unaffordable to them.

In this chapter, we examine the leadership of successful social innovators who have addressed the challenges of the three A's and have received international recognition for their work. These innovators are people whose work we have studied as part of our program of empirical research on social innovation for health in Asia. While the social innovators introduced here are based in countries in Asia – the Philippines, India, Singapore and Indonesia – their work has extended beyond their country of residence to benefit others in Asia and across the world.

In Indonesia, villagers in some rural communities without access to electricity or water systems light their homes with low-cost solar lanterns, cook with clean-burning stoves, and drink filtered water. Unlike other rural communities, they have escaped the health risks from kerosene fumes, burns and diarrhea and are safer because their homes and surroundings are lit. Distribution networks and financing have made the technologies affordable and available to rural dwellers.

In Cambodia, India and Mozambique, people with low incomes have learnt about the dangers of open defecation. Those who can afford to do so buy affordable toilets from local entrepreneurs who have been trained to make and supply them. Around the globe, World Toilet Day (November 19, as declared by the United Nations) and the Urgent Run draw attention to the plight of 2.4 billion people who do not have access to proper sanitation.

In several hundred remote and rural areas of the Philippines – an archipelago of over 7,000 islands – maternal mortality rates have significantly decreased in the last ten years. The intervention that led to this decrease was mostly non-medical. Mayors, health officials and others were trained in leadership and governance and change management.

https://doi.org/10.1515/9783110671988-004

Who has been leading all this? They are the social innovators who have founded or led organizations such as Kopernik, World Toilet Organization (WTO) and the Zuellig Family Foundation (ZFF): Ewa Wojkowska & Toshi Nakamura, Jack Sim, and Ernesto Garilao, respectively. Social innovators have gained prominence in the last few decades. A well-known and successful example is Aravind Eye Care System, which was founded by ophthalmologist Dr. Govindappa Venkataswamy. Aravind Eye Care System offers high-quality eye surgery at a low cost, restoring sight to people with cataracts.

All over Asia, social innovators have emerged, stepping up to lead where governments and markets have failed to meet basic needs, whether for water, sanitation, primary healthcare or specialist care. In our earlier research (Lim & Chia, 2016), we noted that social innovators search for frugal yet effective solutions to deliver healthcare and social services to low-income and underserved communities. They do not act alone, but they act together with the communities that they aim to serve. In Asia and beyond, social innovators have addressed multiple health and social problems – from individual healthcare to population health; from capacity building of community health workers to responding to environmental health threats such as air and water pollution.

Often, a single social innovator can tackle more than one health or social problem. E-Health Point in India was co-founded by Amit Jain to provide clean water at an affordable cost of USD$2 per month, addressing public health threats of water pollution, dysentery, diarrhea and other water-borne diseases. Jain and his co-founders subsequently used the water collection points (prefabricated structures installed in underserved areas) to provide basic primary care, generic medicines and on-point diagnostics to villagers in Punjab. This network of points was then scaled up to other areas of India.

Similarly, although the main aim of Aravind Eye Care System was to prevent and cure blindness, it also trained health professionals, uplifting the skills and livelihood of the community. Faced with the high cost of imported intraocular lenses, Aravind developed its own research arm, Aurolab, and produced its own lenses, now providing a new stream of revenue. The Aravind model of care delivery has since been adopted by the Tilganga Institute of Ophthalmology in Nepal and adapted by the John Fawcett Foundation in Indonesia.

How were these leading social innovators able to deliver sustainable and scalable solutions to seemingly intractable health problems? The leadership of these social innovators displayed three major strengths. First, they were highly entrepreneurial and open to taking risks. This is what led them to address problems that governments and markets had failed to address. Second, when developing their solutions, they elicited ideas and feedback from the communities that they sought to serve. For instance, Kopernik employed local Indonesians and conducted experiments with the farmers whom they sought to help. They were open to methods and solutions from multiple sources. Third, they practiced inclusive and bridging leadership, and nurtured networks of supportive relationships. These three practices enabled them to develop frugal products, deliver health services at an affordable cost and scale and spread their impact.

Innovation and Entrepreneurship

Operating in resource-poor environments, social innovators had to make the most of what was available to develop cost-effective solutions to difficult and complex problems. Their assumptions and approaches differed markedly from those of traditional philanthropists and aid donors. Social innovators did not assume that the underserved communities were helpless or dependent. Rather, they viewed the people whom they served as having valuable local knowledge, experience and non-financial resources. In some cases, the underserved communities became partners and co-designers of solutions. They fostered mutual dependence rather than a one-way relationship between themselves and these communities (Lim & Chia, 2016).

Social innovation was also fueled by their freedom from sectoral boundaries. Not fitting neatly into the public or private sectors, social innovators were freed from sectoral and disciplinary conventions and could create solutions that were different and innovative. In doing so, social innovators served as bridges – bridging ideas across sectors and disciplines; bridging underserved communities to services and products they needed; and bridging stakeholders who could work together to improve health, including funders, volunteers and other resource providers.

Such unbounded thinking allowed social innovators to question and break prior assumptions about healthcare delivery. Social innovators adopted, transplanted and blended technologies and solutions from one realm to another. Dr. Venkataswamy, founder of Aravind Eye Care System, wondered why eye surgery could not be like fast food chains – delivering a product in the same way, quickly and of consistent quality, regardless of where it operated. He then adopted the McDonald's production line approach to cataract surgery (*Infinite Vision*).

The founder of the World Toilet Organization, Jack Sim, promoted toilets in the same way that luxury brands market their goods, promoting toilets as an aspirational product for lower-income consumers. In his words, he strove to make toilets an "object of desire that if you don't have, you are not keeping up with the Joneses . . . We want to make toilets a status symbol, just like a Louis Vuitton handbag" (*Meet Mr. Toilet*). Inspiration from other industries or businesses has spurred social innovators' creativity and has led to the development of unusual approaches and solutions.

Connecting Key Stakeholders: Building Bridges

In attempting to meet the needs of the vulnerable and poor, social innovators have faced geographical, cultural and economic divides. In response, they have adopted leadership practices characterized by connection and bridging. This is illustrated by ZFF's interventions to reduce maternal mortality rates in remote and rural areas. Instead of supplying more medicines or building more health centers, Garilao and his team chose as their first intervention a health leadership and governance program. Through their analyses, Garilao and his team determined that one of the major causes of maternal mortality was mayors of municipalities giving insufficient attention to health. The program brought together the different officers in charge of rural health: elected mayors, government-appointed health leaders and local health providers. The program introduced "bridging leadership," the process of engaging and collaborating with stakeholders to foster a sense of personal and shared ownership of a complex problem, and co-creating solutions. ZFF also provided a framework (Health Change Model) that clearly indicated the steps that mayors and local health officials could take to systematically improve community health. Goals were set and indicators of progress were identified. After their training, the mayors and local health officials applied their lessons in bridging leadership to rally the local health boards, village chiefs, religious leaders, tribal leaders, families and traditional healers behind the cause of reducing maternal mortality rates (Chia & McAllister, 2016).

ZFF's bridging style extended even to those unexpected stakeholders. Their analysis had identified home births, attended to by traditional healers instead of skilled birth attendants, as a major cause of maternal mortality. Together, ZFF and the local leaders and communities found a solution. The traditional healers were not alienated but were rather paid for a new role of accompanying mothers to birth facilities with skilled birth attendants. By training the leaders, activating the community and enabling them to develop their own solutions, ZFF encouraged them to take ownership of maternal health and other community health problems (Chia & Lim, 2016).

Social innovators often find themselves leading groups of people over whom they have no formal authority or power. Innovators such as ZFF realize the importance of building social capital to gain information, advice, knowledge, help and assistance to inspire volunteers, and to learn from and share experiences.

The social innovators we studied actively built networks of exchange and reciprocity. There is an element of risk because not everyone will reciprocate. Jack Sim of WTO operated on a leverage model (described in the next section). Kopernik built a network of rural women entrepreneurs who would educate their peers on the advantages of the low-cost technologies, sell them and provide after-sales service, enabling beneficiaries to strengthen and grow their own networks.

Emotional appeal was helpful to social innovators who worked on taboo or unappealing topics, such as sanitation. Sim of WTO used various forms of emotional appeal, associating access to sanitation with a better future for children and with safety for women and the elderly. Giving one's family a toilet was framed as an expression of love, and toilets were depicted as aspirational goods. Similarly, maternal mortality, ZFF's focal point, was something tangible and visible, having a poignancy that aroused emotions.

Keeping it Going

Social innovators not only sought innovative solutions, but also strove to make their solutions sustainable. They created multiple resource and income streams. For ZFF, these included initial grants and donations but later included funding from the United States Agency for International Development, Merck, the United Nations, and others. Other social innovators like WTO, Kopernik, Aravind and E-Health Point focused not on donating to lower-income individuals but on providing affordable solutions.

E-Health Point collected revenue from water subscriptions and from fees for on-point diagnostics and telemedicine consultations. The revenue was then used to cover the costs of service delivery while enabling the venture to continue serving its social purpose: to scale up operations and to spread to other areas.

Besides crowdfunding to cover the cost of deploying affordable technologies and emergency equipment such as masks, Kopernik also received financial and in-kind support from corporate partnerships with companies such as Japan Airlines and Cisco Systems. It also received grants and donations from the Rockefeller Foundation, the governments of Australia, Sweden and Finland, and pro-bono services from Deloitte. It earned revenue from consulting services on last-mile delivery.

WTO developed a leverage model to obtain services for free. These included the design of its logo and short films featuring the problem of sanitation (such as "Meet Mr. Toilet"). As Sim explained, these designers and filmmakers wanted publicity for their work, and Sim gave them an interesting topic with a high potential for publicity in exchange for the use of their work. Revenue was raised from hosting fees for the World Toilet Summit and Expo, and other income was derived from donations and grants (including from the Gates Foundation). The resources were used for capacity building and education, pilot programs and the development of new models of low-cost toilets.

The approach described here illustrates one of the strengths of social innovators, which is their ability to obtain financial and non-financial resources (time, expertise and social capital) from a wide range of organizations and people. These range from grants, loans, seed funding, competitions, venture philanthropy, crowdfunding, corporate social investing and others.

Extending the Bridge: More Stakeholders and Supporters

To attain their goals, social innovators forge collaborations among unlikely partners united by a shared purpose. WTO's cause has attracted support from Hollywood actors (including Matt Damon) and Bollywood actors (such as Salman Khan, Vidya

Balan), religious leaders, and businesses such as Reckitt-Benckiser and Unilever. Social innovators have connected groups that did not collaborate in the past. They often assumed the role of network broker, creating beneficial links among many stakeholders.

Social media and technology platforms (adopted by WTO, Kopernik and E-Health Point) were effectively used to support collaborations, mobilize resources, and create awareness. Technology and connections sometimes created impressive multiplier effects, increasing advocacy and awareness. To create global awareness about the plight of people without access to sanitation, Jack Sim also encouraged people all over the world to participate in "the Big Squat," a demonstration in which participants took one minute to squat in a public place to draw attention to the plight of those who do not have access to toilets. The Big Squat, which started in 2009, was easy to accomplish and share on social media, and made an interesting news story, leading to even greater publicity. Later, Sim and the government of Singapore lobbied the United Nations to declare the inaugural World Toilet Day on November 19, 2012. The first World Toilet Day went viral, with tweets about it being only second to those about Harry Potter and surpassing those about Justin Bieber. In 2014, the Urgent Run, inspired by the Olympic Torch relay, took place in different countries, starting on November 1 and culminating in the Urgent Run to the office of the United Nations on November 19.

Growth and Further Development

Like other entrepreneurs, social innovators work toward growth. This means spreading the successful model to other localities and scaling their work to include other services or products. While not all social innovators can achieve spread and scale, there are successful examples – for example, E-Health Point India, which not only spread and increased the number of health points, but also scaled to provide telehealth and diagnostics.

Social entrepreneurs have captured the imagination of the public with their inspiring and moving stories. The social innovators whom we studied effectively complemented the work done by the government, non-governmental organizations and international agencies to meet health needs, especially of lower-income and underserved populations. Sometimes, social innovators succeed perhaps too well. ZFF has become inextricably linked with healthcare in the Philippines. As one now-retired official from the Philippines Department of Health put it, "You cannot talk about health in the Philippines without mentioning the Zuellig Family Foundation."

The social innovators whom we studied displayed agility and adaptability. Because of its success, E-Health Point became an attractive buy for private sector companies. After it was sold, Amit Jain continued to help underserved populations in other ways, such as mentoring social start-ups in agricultural technology and leading an organization that built capacity for women entrepreneurs. Inspired by the idea of providing innovative toilets to lower-income populations, Sim broadened his focus to the training of local entrepreneurs who would develop affordable solutions. He built a Sustainable Development Goals Hub to attract frugal innovators, encouraging them to collaborate and develop solutions for sustainable development. ZFF's model attracted international attention. Garilao and his team were invited to share their experiences and Bridging Leadership model with Indonesia's National Population and Family Planning Board.

Kopernik reduced its focus on platform sourcing and technology distribution in favor of a Living Lab conducted in collaboration with the farmers and communities it served. As Wojkowska explained, the initial platform model enabled them to "work with partners in 26 countries, distributing more than 160,000 units of technology to 570,000 people . . . . A few years into our work, companies began to approach Kopernik to partner with us . . . to enter emerging markets. Fast forward four years, we have gained additional insights (into) the urgent need for more evidence and more experimentation in the development sector in order to achieve the Sustainable Development Goals." (Wojkowska, 2020). Despite its new focus, Kopernik's platform was active during the Southeast Asian pollution caused by forest fires, the eruption of Mount Agung in 2019, and the COVID-19 pandemic beginning at the end of 2019 and continuing through 2021.

The social innovators profiled here are among thousands who work in Asia. Like other social innovators, these leaders challenged assumptions and conventional boundaries of sectors, geography or business registration. In doing so, they created change and transformation. Their leadership extended beyond their own organizations. These leaders did not work alone, but worked with other leaders in the community such as religious leaders, village heads and informal leaders of women's groups. Showing a high level of consideration, these leaders recognized the needs of disadvantaged communities; they then harnessed the strengths and potential of those communities as they developed solutions, improving skills and livelihoods in the process. Their leadership was characterized by values (often associated with Asia) of compassion and collectivism. Their impact has extended beyond their geographic origin to other regions, amplifying social good.

References

Aravind Eye System. https://aravind.org/. Retrieved on 8 May 2020.

BL for Indonesian Family Planning. https://zuelligfoundation.org/bl-for-indonesian-family-planning/. Retrieved on 8 May 2020.

Chia, A. & McAllister, M. (2016). The Zuellig family foundation: A bridge to a better future. *Ivey Business Publishing*.

Chia, A. & Lim, Y. W. (2016). The Zuellig family foundation: A strategic philanthropic approach to integrated care. *International Journal of Integrated Care*, *16*(6): A193. http://doi.org/10.5334/ijic.2741.

Infinite Vision. https://youtu.be/hHLzsuAueEM. Retrieved on 8 May 2020.

"Delivering Quality Healthcare at <$2 a month" Innovation & Entrepreneurship Seminar by Amit Jain, CEO, HealthPoint. https://www.youtube.com/watch?v=R-QlNKrjESE. Retrieved on 8 May 2020.

Kopernik. https://kopernik.info/. Retrieved on 8 May 2020.

Lim, Y. W. & Chia, A. (2016). Social entrepreneurship: Improving global health. *Journal of the American Medical Association (JAMA)*, *315*(22): 2393–2394. http://doi:10.1001/jama.2016.4400.

Meet Mr. Toilet. https://vimeo.com/34792993. Retrieved on 8 May 2020.

Population. United Nations. https://www.un.org/en/sections/issues-depth/population/index.html. Retrieved on 8 May 2020.

Shuvojit, B. & Ng, P. L. (2019). Why can't dynamic Asia-Pacific beat poverty? UNESCAP blog. https://www.unescap.org/blog/why-cant-dynamic-asia-pacific-beat-poverty. Retrieved on 8 May 2020.

Wojkowska, E. (2020). Looking back and moving forward: The evolution of Kopernik. https://kopernik.info/en/news-events/news/looking-back-and-moving-forward-the-evolution-of-kopernik. Retrieved on 8 May 2020.

World Toilet Organization. https://worldtoilet.org/. Retrieved on 8 May 2020.

Zuellig Family Foundation. https://zuelligfoundation.org/. Retrieved on 8 May 2020.

Dean Tjosvold and Alfred Shiu-Ho Wong

Chapter 5
Asian Managers Learn from Experience in Collectivist Cultures

Organizations may be the most useful social innovation ever created. Of course, organizations are not always successful and may go bad when they fail to respond effectively to changes in their environment (Sull, 2005). Organizations do not operate by magic; they must be made effective. Members of an organization have to contribute to its functioning, and with the right leadership and management in place, members are able to fully embrace their potential and work efficiently by choosing the right priorities.

Our theory and research suggest that effective leadership relies on open-minded discussions to facilitate collaboration. These discussions can resolve many issues and manage various conflicts. On the basis of 109 primary studies, a meta-analytic investigation was conducted, and the outcome shows that members with cooperative rather than competitive goals discuss issues open-mindedly that in turn promote work outcomes such as performance, creativity, interpersonal relationships, leader-member exchange and commitment (Tjosvold et al., 2020). Specifically, organizational members with cooperative goals discuss problems and issues open-mindedly that in turn stimulate work outcomes, whereas those with competitive or independent goals do not. Results of the meta-analyses support the theory that cooperative goals develop mutual-benefit motivation and integrative conflict management, which in turn induce organizational members to be more open-minded and to combine their best ideas that result in high-quality contributions to organizations.

This article argues that Asian managers have the advantage of considerable experiences working in collectivist organizational cultures that emphasize the value of mutual, cooperative relationships. They have daily experience and ongoing learning on how to develop and maintain cooperative relationships. We have reviewed research that suggests that experience with collectivist, cooperative relationships can contribute to the leadership competence and development of Asian managers. Results of the meta-analyses suggest that these effects are reliable; they occur in a wide range of collaborations and work on a range of issues. Asian managers can benefit by developing their leadership capabilities in many ways.

The first section focusses on the idea that managers are effective leaders by developing cooperative relationships. The second part argues that these cooperative relationships are useful in large part because they help organizational managers and employees engage in open-minded discussions. The third section clarifies the nature of open-minded discussions and how managers and employees can demonstrate open-mindedness. The fourth and final part proposes that Asian organizations are

https://doi.org/10.1515/9783110671988-005

generally collectivistic whereas Western organizations are individualistic. Asian managers have more experience working with cooperative relationships. Therefore, they have a higher competence and inclination for developing cooperative, open-minded and effective relationships and productive organizational work.

Quality Relationships for Effective Leadership

Cultures generally recognize that they must invest resources into learning and developing leadership. Societies and organizations reward people for their leadership with money and other tangible resources as well as status and additional intangible benefits. The need and value of promoting coordination are well recognized. However, developing the capability to coordinate the work of others is a major undertaking.

Effective leaders help individuals and groups to collaborate so that they can combine their resources and energy and integrate their abilities and insights. With this coordination, organizations can fulfill their potential to accomplish large, complex goals as well as to complete more mundane tasks and functions.

Recognizing that effective leaders can help individuals and groups to coordinate their effort and ideas does not mean that we know how to develop those effective leaders. Developing leaders is often very challenging – managers, trainers and coaches very much debate the methods that leaders should use to facilitate coordination and how those methods should be implemented.

Cooperative Relationships for Productive Leadership

Our research suggests that cooperative relationships are the foundation for effective leadership. Quality relationships among team members and between leaders and team members are the basis of successful organizations.

Kurt Lewin (1935) and Morton Deutsch (1949a, 1949b) developed the modern theory of cooperation and competition. Deutsch (1973) theorized that goal interdependence influences the way individuals, teams and organizations relate with each other, and that the way of relating in turn affects cooperation and competition outcomes. The nature of interdependence, which considers how goals are related to each other, can vary depending on the goals; these can be either aiding, hindering or independent with regard to other goals. Deutsch identified three types of interdependence: cooperation, competition and independence.

Cooperation exists when individuals' goals are positively related to each other; as one individual moves toward reaching his or her own goals, others move toward reaching their goals as well. With cooperative goals, individuals motivate each other to succeed; the success of one person has a spill-over effect among other individuals.

Thus, people work together to reach goals and settle disputes for mutual benefits (Tjosvold, Wong & Chen, 2014a, 2014b).

Individuals' goals in competition oppose each other's goals, making others reaching their goals less likely. Individuals realize that they have a higher chance to achieve their own goals when others do not achieve their goals. Therefore, individuals tend to seek their own interests at the cost of others. They want others to "lose" as they succeed and "win."

Independence occurs when an individual's goal achievement or failure is not related to other individuals' goals. They are oriented toward their own goals and are disinterested in whether others reach their goals or not.

Effects of Cooperation and Competition in Organizations

Organizational partners integrate their actions when they understand that their goals are cooperative rather than competitive. Studies confirm the theory that cooperative and competitive goals lead to quite different social interaction patterns in organizations (e.g., Tjosvold et al., 2014b; Wong, Tjosvold & Yu, 2005). This section discusses the constructive impact of cooperative goals by showing that they develop mutual-benefit motivation and integrative conflict management. Mutual-benefit motivation involves the desire to combine work and to cooperate. Integrative conflict management provides the intellectual flexibility to combine diverse ideas. This results in team members with cooperative goals having the energy and understanding to develop integrated, high-quality resolutions to issues and problems.

Cooperative Goals for Mutual-Benefit Motivation

Individuals with cooperative goals aid one another using their energy and capabilities; they recognize that if they help their partners achieve their goals, they help themselves reach their own goals. Their ongoing mutual help consolidates their team cohesion and reinforces the belief that in the future they will continue to provide mutual help (Deutsch, 1973, 1980; Johnson & Johnson, 2005; Lee, Farh & Chen, 2011). Believing that goals will be achieved with mutual help provides the foundation to a strong mutual-benefit motivation (Deutsch, 1973; Hempel, Zhang & Tjosvold, 2009). Individuals come to expect that partners will assist, share knowledge and support one another (Lewicki, McAllister & Bies, 1998).

Competitive goals, though, result in mutual frustration, as individuals suspect that others are trying to prevent them from achieving their goals so that the others can achieve their own. They are likely to interfere with each other by constructing barriers. In other words, they think that they can only achieve their own goals if others cannot achieve theirs. Individuals in competition tend to impede others' goals to develop more opportunities to achieve their own goals. They form a pattern of preventing each other from achieving their own goals.

Independent goals occur when the progress of one person has no relevance to the progress of others. Consequently, independent goals tend to not have powerful, stable mutual benefit or mutual frustration.

Empirical research lends support to these predictions. For example, in a study of joint venture partnerships, competitive goals led to concerns about free-riding where one party tried to hide their attempts to gain an advantage over another party and frustrate joint performance (Wong et al., 2018). Cooperative goals on the other hand reduced free-riding concerns and promoted joint performance.

Integrative Conflict Management

Cooperation and competition theories have contributed to the understanding of collaboration by identifying constructive ways to define and manage conflict (Deutsch, 1973). Conflict has traditionally been confounded with competition and was defined as opposing goals and scarce resources (e.g., Pondy, 1967). People are thought to be in conflict because their goals are incompatible and cannot be achieved simultaneously (Korsgaard et al., 2008).

However, regarding conflict as conflicting interests strengthens the popular view that conflict is win-lose; each side tries to win the conflict to achieve their own goals. The assumption that conflict is win-lose reinforces the idea that conflict is negative. Barki and Hartwick (2004) explicitly argue that negative emotion is a core aspect of conflict. The idea that conflict develops from opposing interests reinforces common misconceptions and attitudes that conflict pits people against each other in a battle to dominate.

Competitive goals have been found to induce closed-minded discussion (Etherington & Tjosvold, 1998). Believing that they are in a battle to win, discussants want their ideas and plans to prevail and win. They emphasize the strengths of their positions while not much attention is drawn to the weaknesses of their own arguments. They fail to integrate their thinking as they attempt to have their own ideas "win."

Deutsch (1973) argued that conflict could be usefully defined as incompatible activities. This definition is unconfounded with competition and cooperation; conflict develops in both cooperative and competitive goal situations. But whether disputants understand their goals as cooperative or competitive significantly influences how they deal with their conflicts.

Considerable research indicates that cooperative goals are key to constructive conflict management (Tjosvold et al., 2014a). With cooperative goals, discussants have been found to express their opinions while simultaneously listening and understanding their partners' ideas to incorporate the best ideas from each side and develop alternative solutions that both sides are committed to (Tjosvold et al., 2014b).

Cooperative goals help discussants to be effective problem solvers by developing integrative solutions that incorporate the best ideas from all participants.

In summary, cooperative goals develop mutual-benefit motivation and integrative conflict. Mutual-benefit motivation promotes an integrative effort, as collaborators realize that they want each other to succeed. Integrative conflict management combines diverse ideas so that discussants can put together the best ideas to develop innovative solutions. The next section illustrates how cooperative mutual-benefit motivation and integrative conflict management form the basis for open-minded discussions. These discussions in turn help organizational members contribute to effective problem resolutions that strengthen their organizations.

Open-Minded Discussions

Open-mindedness is the willingness to actively search for evidence against one's favored beliefs and ideas and to weigh such evidence impartially and fully (Baker & Sinkula, 1999; Cegarra-Navarro & Sánchez-Polo, 2011; Mitchell, Nicholas & Boyle, 2009; Sinkula, Baker & Noordewier, 1997). Open-minded discussion occurs when people mutually seek to understand each other's ideas and positions, consider each other's reasoning for these positions impartially, and work to integrate their ideas into mutually acceptable solutions.

In open-minded discussions, protagonists express their own views directly to each other. They are open with their own views, open to those of others, and are open to new solutions to resolve the conflict. Evidence indicates that these aspects of openness are reinforcing, and they constitute open-minded discussion (Johnson & Johnson, 2005; Tjosvold, 1990; Tjosvold, Dann & Wong, 1992; Tjosvold & Halco, 1992).

Studies have used survey items to measure and offer a more specific understanding of open-mindedness (Chen, Liu & Tjosvold, 2005; Wong et al., 2005). These items include expressing our own views directly to each other, listening carefully to each other's opinions, trying to understand each other's concerns, and working to use each other's ideas. These items are not trying to measure the same specific action but the same approach; they are typically strongly correlated with each other, and the scale has high reliability.

It takes two to have a conflict and it takes two to manage a conflict. One protagonist can make bold, persistent and skilled actions that encourage an otherwise closed-minded protagonist to discuss conflict open-mindedly. Generally, open-mindedness is needed by all protagonists to make conflict constructive. Evidence also suggests that protagonists develop similar levels of open-mindedness; one protagonist's open-mindedness encourages others to be open-minded and their closed-mindedness fosters others to be closed-minded (Tjosvold, 1990; Tjosvold et al., 1992; Tjosvold &

Halco, 1992). Conflicts are more likely to be constructively managed when protagonists discuss their views openly and integrate them into solutions.

Cooperative Relationships for Open-Mindedness

Of course, managers and employees do not always discuss their differences open-mindedly and, according to the contingency perspective, under certain conditions it would be inappropriate and dysfunctional to do so. Commitments to competitive and independent goals are apt to lead to closed-minded discussions with an emphasis on promoting individual interests without concern for others' ideas and aspirations. Indeed, with competitive goals they are apt to actively prevent the achievement of each other's goals as they understand that it is a way of promoting their own.

This review argues that a cooperative relationship underlies open-minded discussion. Previous research with both experimental and survey data has directly tested and found that cooperative relationships promote open-mindedness (Deutsch, 1973; Deutsch et al., 2014). Research has demonstrated both the causal relationship that cooperative goals promote open-mindedness and survey results that support that cooperative relationships support open-minded discussion in a wide variety of organizational situations (Tjosvold et al., 2014a). In addition, we can identify social psychologists such as Morton Deutsch, David W. Johnson and Karl Smith, whose research supports our understanding of cooperation.

Collectivist Asian Organizations Develop Cooperative Skills

According to Hofstede (1980), Western countries have similar cultures and Eastern countries have similar cultures (Kirkman, Lowe & Gibson, 2017). On one hand, Eastern cultures are characterized by maintaining harmonious social relationships (Triandis, McCusker & Hui, 1990). As such, employees in Eastern cultures may be more likely to express their feelings of support and caring for each other. Research suggests that relationships will be more supportive and cooperative in the East than in the West; managers in Western cultures may confront different views directly with each other and are more likely to show a higher level of antagonism (Bond & and Smith, 1996).

Because of their frequent experiences of developing and maintaining supportive relationships, Asian managers can become effective, cooperative leaders. Cooperative relationships require considerable maintenance (Chen, Kang & Tjosvold, 2017). To remain effective, managers and employees have to be convinced that their goals continue to be positively related and that they find effective and fair ways to share information (Chen, Tjosvold & Liu, 2006). They are under pressure to develop and enhance their ways of working together. They want to resolve tensions and settle disputes so that they can continue to collaborate efficiently. They iron out differences so that their collaboration remains vibrant and mutually advantageous (Mohr & Spekman, 1994). Making cooperative goals productive requires an ongoing and continuing application of diverse, mutually supportive relationship skills.

Asian managers then potentially have an important advantage, in that they have considerable experience in developing cooperative goals and practices, while Western managers are oriented toward developing individualistic and sometimes even antagonistic ways of working (Bond & Smith, 1996). Asian managers have the values upon which to develop cooperative relationships, open-mindedness and collectivist action. Research reviewed in this article suggests that Asian managers have values and skills that help them appreciate and develop cooperative relationships. Furthermore, there is potential for global leaders to learn values and skills from Asian managers in terms of working collaboratively and helping others work collaboratively with other people.

Research reviewed also indicates that these cooperative relationships are the basis for open-minded discussions that result in productive organizational work. This superior performance can take such forms as creativity, efficiency, high quality relationships and strong commitment. Asian managers have an important potential advantage of developing cooperative relationships that in turn stimulate ongoing, productive and open-minded discussions that integrate ideas, solve problems and drive organizational productivity. Nowadays, a global leader not only needs to integrate the work of individuals or teams dispersed across multiple countries, but also has to face the more important challenge of managing the interdependence between the people they lead and connecting them to one another across boundaries (IMD, 2014). The emphasis on cooperative relationships and open-minded discussions of Asian managers can help them develop into effective global leaders by better equipping them with the experience, values and skills to connect with employees in multiple countries.

References

Baker, W. E. & Sinkula, J. M. (1999). The synergistic effect of market orientation and learning orientation on organizational performance. *Journal of the Academy of Marketing Science*, *27*, 411–427.

Barki, H. & Hartwick, J. (2004). Conceptualizing the construct of interpersonal conflict. *International Journal of Conflict Management*, *15*(3), 216–244.

Bond, R. & Smith, P. B. (1996). Culture and conformity: A meta-analysis of studies using Asch's (1952b, 1956) line judgment task. *Psychological Bulletin*, *119*(1), 111–137.

Cegarra-Navarro, J.-G. & Sánchez-Polo, M. T. (2011). Influence of the open-mindedness culture on organizational memory: An empirical investigation of Spanish SMEs. *The International Journal of Human Resource Management*, *22*(1), 1–18.

Chen, G., Liu, C. & Tjosvold, D. (2005). Conflict management for effective top management teams and innovation in China. *Journal of Management Studies*, *42*(2), 277–300.

Chen, G., Tjosvold, D. & Liu, C. (2006). Cooperative goals, leader people and productivity values: Their contribution to top management teams in China. *Journal of Management Studies*, *43*(5), 1177–1200.

Chen, N. Y.-F., Kang, Y. & Tjosvold, D. (2017). Constructive controversy and guanxi relationships for disaster recovery. *International Journal of Conflict Management*, *28*(4), 410–436.

Deutsch, M. (1949a). An experimental study of the effects of co-operation and competition upon group process. *Human Relations*, *2*, 199–231.

Deutsch, M. (1949b). A theory of co-operation and competition. *Human Relations*, *2*, 129–152.

Deutsch, M. (1973). *The Resolution of Conflict*. Yale University Press (New Haven, CT).

Deutsch, M. (1980). *Fifty years of conflict*. In L. Festinger (Ed.), *Retrospections on Social Psychology* (pp. 46–77). Oxford University Press (New York, NY).

Deutsch, M., Coleman, P. T. & Marcus, E. C. (2014). *The Handbook of Conflict Resolution: Theory and Practice* (3rd ed.). Jossey-Bass Publishers (San Francisco, CA).

Etherington, L. & Tjosvold, D. (1998). Managing budget conflicts: Contribution of goal interdependence and interaction. *Canadian Journal of Administrative Sciences/Revue Canadienne des Sciences de l'Administration*, *15*, 142–151.

Hempel, P. S., Zhang, Z. X. & Tjosvold, D. (2009). Conflict management between and within teams for trusting relationships and performance in China. *Journal of Organizational Behavior*, *30*(1), 41–65.

Hofstede, G. (1980). Motivation, leadership, and organization: do American theories apply abroad? *Organizational Dynamics*, *9*, 42–63.

IMD (2014). Global leadership and global teams. Retrieved from http://www.imd.org/research-knowledge/articles/global-leadership-and-global-teams/.

Johnson, D. W. & Johnson, R. T. (2005). *Teaching Students to Be Peacemakers* (4th ed.). Interaction Book Company (Edina, MN).

Kirkman, B. L., Lowe, K. B. & Gibson, C. B. (2017). A retrospective on Culture's Consequences: The 35-year journey. *Journal of International Business Studies*, *48*(1), 12–29.

Korsgaard, M. A., Jeong, S. S., Mahony, D. M. & Pitariu, A. H. (2008). A multilevel view of intragroup conflict. *Journal of Management*, *34*(6), 1222–1252.

Lee, C., Farh, J.-L. & Chen, Z.-J. (2011). Promoting group potency in project teams: The importance of group identification. *Journal of Organizational Behavior*, *32*(8), 1147–1162.

Lewicki, R. J., McAllister, D. J. & Bies, R. J. (1998). Trust and distrust: New relationships and realities. *Academy of Management Review*, *23*(3), 438–458.

Lewin, K. (1935). Psycho-sociological problems of a minority group. *Character & Personality: A Quarterly for Psychodiagnostic & Allied Studies*, *3*, 175–187.

Mitchell, R., Nicholas, S. & Boyle, B. (2009). The role of openness to cognitive diversity and group processes in knowledge creation. *Small Group Research*, *40*(5), 535–554.

Mohr, J. & Spekman, R. (1994). Characteristics of partnership success: Partnership attributes, communication behavior, and conflict resolution techniques. *Strategic Management Journal*, *15*(2), 135–152. doi:10.1002/smj.4250150205.

Pondy, L. R. (1967). Organizational conflict: Concepts and models. *Administrative Science Quarterly*, *12*(2), 296–320.

Sinkula, J. M., Baker, W. E. & Noordewier, T. (1997). A framework for market-based organizational learning: Linking values, knowledge, and behavior. *Journal of the Academy of Marketing Science*, *25*, 305–318.

Sull, D. (2005). Why Good Companies Go Bad. *Harvard Business Review, 77*(4):42–8, 50–2, 183.

Tjosvold, D. (1990). The goal interdependence approach to communication in conflict: An organizational study. In M. A. Rahim (Ed.), *Theory and Research in Conflict Management* (pp. 15–27). Praeger Publishers (New York, NY).

Tjosvold, D., Dann, V. & Wong, C. (1992). Managing conflict between departments to serve customers. *Human Relations, 45*(10), 1035–1054.

Tjosvold, D. & Halco, J. A. (1992). Performance appraisal of managers: Goal interdependence, ratings, and outcomes. *The Journal of Social Psychology, 132*(5), 629–639.

Tjosvold, D., Li, W. D., Wong, A. & Zhang, X. (2020). Open-minded discussion: A meta-analytic evaluation of cooperation and competition theory. Paper presented at 79th Annual Meeting of the Academy of Management, Boston, MA.

Tjosvold, D., Wong, A. S. H. & Chen, N. Y. F. (2014a). Constructively managing conflicts in organizations. *Annual Review of Organizational Psychology and Organizational Behavior, 1*, 545–568.

Tjosvold, D., Wong, A. S. H. & Chen, N. Y. F. (2014b). Cooperative and competitive conflict management in organizations. In N. Ashkanasy, K. Jehn, & R. Ayoko (Eds.), *Handbook of Conflict Management Research* (pp. 33–50). Edgar Elgard Publishers (Cheltenham, UK).

Triandis, H. C., McCusker, C. & Hui, C. H. (1990). Multimethod probes of individualism and collectivism. *Journal of Personality and Social Psychology, 59*, 1006–1020.

Wong, A., Tjosvold, D. & Yu, Z.-Y. (2005). Organizational partnerships in China: Self-interest, goal interdependence, and opportunism. *Journal of Applied Psychology, 90*(4), 782–791.

Wong, A., Wei, L., Wang, X. & Tjosvold, D. (2018). Collectivist values for constructive conflict management in international joint venture effectiveness. *International Journal of Conflict Management, 29*(1), 126–143.

Prem Shamdasani

Chapter 6
Leadership of the Brand: Time for Asian Leaders to Leverage Branding to Build Passionate and High-Performing Organizations

> More than any other communications medium, employees can breathe life, vitality and personality into the brand.   – Leonard L. Berry and A. Parasuraman (1991)

In the last decade, Asian brands have only accounted for 10 percent of the top 100 most valuable global brands (Interbrand, 2010–2019). Out of these top Asian brands, Japan accounted for a higher proportion and was represented by a few established global brands such as Toyota, Nissan, Sony, Canon, Nintendo and Panasonic. The other Asian brands were South Korean brands such as Samsung and Kia, and more recently, Chinese brands such as Huawei and Lenovo.

Interbrand's ranking methodology quantifies the brand value of global companies in dollar terms based on a financial analysis of profits; the unique influence of the brand on customer choices other than price, convenience and features, for example; and the ability of the brand to create loyalty, which is based on internal and external factors. Internal factors are organizational and include brand clarity, commitment, governance and responsiveness. External factors include brand authenticity, differentiation, relevance, consistency, presence and engagement. It is evident from the Interbrand's ranking of the most valuable global brands over the past decade that Asian brands are lagging behind their Western counterparts in prioritizing and harnessing the value of branding to both external stakeholders (customers and corporate partners) and internal stakeholders (employees and shareholders).

According to Brand Finance (2020), the brand value of 205 brands in the US account for about 45.4 percent of the total enterprise value, amounting to US$3.2 trillion. The brand value as a percentage of total enterprise value of the top three Asian economies is as follows: China at 18.9 percent or US$1.33 trillion (70 brands); Japan at 6.8 percent or US$4.83 billion (36 brands) and South Korea at 2.4 percent or US$1.71 billion (7 brands). With brand values growing and with Asia now accounting for more than 40 percent of the global GDP and about 50 percent of the world's population, it is imperative that Asian business leaders start taking the *leadership of their brands* seriously.

While Asian companies have increasingly demonstrated global leadership and organizational capabilities, leveraging on technologies, business models, manufacturing, supply chains and markets to drive business growth, they have largely ignored the

https://doi.org/10.1515/9783110671988-006

strategic role and value of branding in achieving customer loyalty and in building passionate and high-performing organizations. Alibaba, Toyota and Samsung are good examples of Asian brands that are making global business impact through their strong visions and leadership while building strong, purposeful brands that resonate with internal and external stakeholders. Howard Schultz, executive chairman of Starbucks, underscores this point from both the customer and employee branding perspective: "If people believe they share values with a company, they will stay loyal to the brand."

Davis (2018) highlights that since branding is seen through the eyes of internal and external stakeholders, leaders should demonstrate a deliberate and resilient commitment to creating value for all stakeholders. He cautions against "short-termism" where organizations focus on KPIs and protecting revenues/profits while avoiding risks and innovation that would provide growth and meaningful brand value for all stakeholders. He identifies four brand value dimensions:

1. Reputational – building trust in the brand by embracing best practices and consistently delivering value to customers
2. Organizational – building pride in the brand among employees by aligning values with the organizational purpose
3. Societal – building trust by doing business in an ethical and environmentally sustainable manner that contributes to the well-being of society
4. Financial – deriving higher financial value from the brand by realizing the reputational, organizational and societal values

Leading the Brand from Within

Sir Richard Branson – founder and head of the Virgin Group, and who has built one of the most iconic and valued brands in the world – emphasizes the role of leadership and organization-wide commitment to building a brand that both employees and customers value: "Branding demands commitment; commitment to continual re-invention; striking chords with people to stir their emotions; and commitment to imagination. It is easy to be cynical about such things, much harder to be successful." (McKoy, 2014)

Leading the brand from within or using internal branding represents the commitment an organization has in living the brand values and delivering on its brand promise (Mitchell, 2002). It is manifested in the communications, activities and processes of the brand that inform and inspire employees.

Internal branding activities help to communicate, educate and reinforce employees about the brand values and the desired behaviors to deliver on the brand promise (De Chernatony & Segal-Horn, 2001; Mosley, 2007). Several research studies in social identity, organizational identity and organizational commitment suggest that internal branding motivates employees to embrace organizational values, to strongly and uniquely identify with the organization, and be more committed to achieve the organization's strategic objectives (Foster et al., 2010).

Davis & Dunn (2002) emphasizes that although internal branding requires significant leadership and organizational resources and commitment, it provides many benefits, including creating a positive and more productive work environment, fostering a strong organizational identity and providing a platform for change. Companies such as Starbucks, IBM and Walmart have launched brands internally with great success (Marshall, 2013), and this has enabled them to achieve profitable growth and brand loyalty.

In this VUCAH (volatile, uncertain, complex, ambiguous and hyper-connected) world, internal branding may be key to helping organizations anticipate and manage change brought about by technological, regulatory, environmental, biological and geopolitical disruption. Higher internal engagement with the brand enables organizations to better fulfill their brand promise to external stakeholders, notably customers.

The success of global technology companies such as Google and Microsoft in driving business disruption and growth can be attributed to their ability to align the corporate culture with the brand vision, values and promise. Google's internal brand broadly defined as "Googliness" provides the basic code of conduct for its employees who are encouraged to strike a balance between short-term and long-term objectives, to be proactive and passionate, and to collaboratively solve problems for the company, partners and customers.

Microsoft's successful transformation from a siloed, product-centric organization to a collaborative, customer-obsessed organization can be largely attributed to the business vision and strong internal branding efforts under the leadership of Satya Nadella and his management team. This has enabled Microsoft to be one of the most valuable companies in the world and to be recognized for its innovation and thought leadership.

Lessons from the technology giants Google and Microsoft and the sustainability of food and beverage and hospitality brands such as Starbucks and Ritz Carlton reveal that the key in driving internal branding has been the commitment of the leadership to creating a brand-centric culture and recognizing and rewarding employees who live out those values and deliver on the brand promise.

Corporate leadership in Asia needs to recognize that they play a pivotal role in driving internal branding and building a brand-based culture supported by resources, governance and rewards tied to the brand's purpose and values (Davis, 2009).

Internal Branding Inertia: Why Are Asian Leaders Holding Back?

Some of reasons for the internal brand inertia among Asian leaders and organizations can be attributed to strategic, economic, structural and cultural factors.

The leadership of many Asian companies tend to be more product-centric and preoccupied with competing on price, specifications and the speed to market, leading to a more commoditized approach to their markets. As a result, they tend to dehumanize the corporate culture and interactions with employees and customers which in turn impacts both the employee and customer experiences.

Another reason for the inertia is that building a strong brand takes time – sometime decades. This requires a deep and long-term organizational commitment to researching and understanding customers' tangible and intangible needs, then using these insights to engage customers at the emotional level and develop appropriate brand communications that resonate with them.

Many Asian conglomerates are still family-owned or founder-led and hierarchical, in which decision-making is concentrated at the top and is supported by a face-driven culture where there is strong adherence to the management structure. Additionally, leadership is more focused on aggressively pursuing growth and profitability, often at the expense of fostering a values-based culture which reinforces the company's vision, brand values and promise.

Therefore, employees do not have a good understanding of the brand and how to consistently and passionately deliver on the brand promise. In short, Asian companies have historically not prioritized building brand leadership, nor have they recognized the role of branding in creating both internal and external value.

Overcoming the Internal Branding Inertia: What Can Asian leaders Do?

Two interesting perspectives exist to better enable Asian leaders to build a brand-centric organization and to align their values with the brand promise.

Roll (2015) argues that several changes are needed in the Asian boardroom to foster a more brand-centric culture and bring about a paradigm shift. First and foremost, there needs to be a shift in mindsets from a tactical to a long-term, strategic view of branding and aligning the entire organization toward delivering the brand promise rather than limiting it to the marketing function. Second, it is necessary to abandon parochial mindsets and imagery rooted in Asia's colonial past that hamper the growth of modern, progressive global brands. Third, a better understanding of customer behavior is necessary – one that goes beyond local borders and embraces global cultures, mindsets and behaviors. Finally, it is essential to create iconic brands that capture the spirit of the regions of Asia.

Jack Ma, founder of Alibaba, has created one of the largest business-to-business and business-to-consumer e-commerce companies in the world. He has also made Alibaba arguably one of the most iconic brands not only in Asia but in the world. For a start, he chose a recognizable and easily pronounced brand name, Alibaba, a character from *One Thousand and One Nights* who used the phrase "open sesame" to a enter a cave full of treasures. According to Alibaba's website, the brand name is aligned with the company's purpose of opening doors and providing opportunities for small businesses. Second, weaving an inspiring brand story about Jack Ma's humble beginnings as a technopreneur – where he started Alibaba in his living room in Hangzhou with no government connections or *quanxi* – has resonated not only with Chinese audiences but with global audiences as well (Doland, 2014). Finally, leading by example and actively cascading the values throughout the organization has resulted in stronger brand buy-ins and advocacy among employees and corporate partners.

Davis (2002) highlights important principles that should guide Asian leaders in the brand assimilation process within their companies. The first step involves making the brand relevant so that every employee understands and embraces the brand's meaning. Second, make the brand accessible so that employees know where and from whom to get brand-related information and answers. Third, reinforce the brand continuously through ongoing activities and make brand education a regular program that continues after the initial employee onboarding and orientation. The fourth step involves recognizing and rewarding employees for on-brand behaviors. Finally, align hiring practices with the brand culture and encourage the ability to live out the brand values.

Singapore Airlines (SIA) has built one of the most iconic and respected service brands in the hyper-competitive aviation space in Asia and globally. Singapore Airlines has created the SIA Way, where every flight attendant is trained and evaluated on consistently delivering their service attributes – being caring, warm, professional, enterprising and dedicated – to passengers in every class of travel. The SIA Way is a concerted and ongoing attempt by the leadership to ensure that every flight attendant understands and lives the values of the SIA brand. This strong commitment to internal branding through training, engagement and recognition has enabled SIA flight attendants to internalize the values and behaviors that enhance the passenger experience. As a result, SIA has been able to sustainably differentiate itself from other premium airlines and has been a regular recipient of the best airline in the world award.

Toyota is another good example of a strong global Asian brand that has successfully aligned its brand promise with its business philosophy, values and operations. It is encapsulated in the Toyota Way, which is based on two fundamental pillars – Continuous Improvement and Respect for People (Liker, 2004). The Toyota Way has provided strong internal and external brand alignment and is evident in Toyota's sustainable performance and consistent brand leadership in the automotive space. Despite the highly competitive and fragmented automobile industry, Toyota is the one of the two automotive brands that has made it to Interbrand's top 10 most valuable brands in the world.

Haidilao Hot Pot, a chain of hot pot restaurants founded in China in 1994, is a brand that that is seeing great success within and outside China and now operates internationally in many markets including the United States, Singapore, Taiwan, South Korea, Japan, Canada, Australia, Malaysia and Indonesia. In addition to its tasty and spicy cuisine, Haidilao's more than 60,000 employees are highly engaged and are passionate about delivering its brand promise through great customer service and experiences that go beyond food and beverages. For example, free nail art and hand care, free leather shoe cleaning, free photo taking and massage chairs are examples of services that are offered to customers.

In the next decade, Asia is expected to account for over 50 percent of the world's population and about 60 percent of the global GDP. A significant proportion of the economic growth will be driven by the technology and services sectors. This presents a good opportunity for Asian companies to learn, benchmark and adapt the best practices in branding of Western companies such as Google, Microsoft and Starbucks, and build sustainable global leadership by leveraging their unique Asian values and competitive advantages that are rooted in Asia.

The SIA, Alibaba, Toyota and Haidilao examples should inspire Asian leaders to recognize the long-term benefits of effectively aligning internal branding with the delivery of the brand promise to customers. Doing so will enable Asian leadership to build passionate, high-performing global organizations that consistently live the brand values, and earn the trust and loyalty of both employees and customers.

It is All About the Experience!

There is growing evidence that internal branding efforts enhance employee experience and the subsequent organizational commitment – management and employee behaviors and attitudes – to deliver satisfying, meaningful and memorable customer experiences. This in turn translates to strong brand loyalty both internally and externally, which enables organizations to be purpose-led and to achieve sustainable and profitable growth. Creating the inspired mindset and better aligning to the values of the organization through internal branding helps to create a virtuous circle that benefits all stakeholders.

Lee Yohn (2018), a writer on brand leadership, strongly advocates that organizations should start to prioritize employee experience as the next frontier of competitive advantage. Employee experience is the sum of all interactions an employee has during his or her employment with the company, from recruitment to termination. Companies leading in employee experience performed better in terms of having four times the average profitability and twice the average revenue of companies that lagged.

According to Mercer's (2019a) Global Talent Trends Study, 97 percent of the executives acknowledge that the competition for talent is getting harder, and about a third of satisfied employees are still contemplating leaving their jobs. As such, companies are starting to focus on employee experience and treating employees like customers who have the same needs, wants and aspirations. This requires a shift in organizational mindset and a commitment to human-centric design of the end-to-end employee journey, which enhances the employee experience and strengthens the sense of belongingness and pride.

Mercer (2019b) advocates that for organizations to pivot successfully, they must adopt their customer experience playbook for their own employees. This is done by treating employees like customers and understanding the experience from the employee's perspective; differentiating employee engagement and interactions – human or digital – based on the desired experience; and co-creating solutions where leaders and employees collaborate to improve employee experiences. This results in a stronger emotional buy-in and better and faster execution, thereby improving organizational agility, which is critical to succeeding in a fast-paced and competitive business environment.

Mercer's research has identified that employees desire experiences that are: *enriching* – meaningful, fulfilling and aligned with the organizational purpose; *efficient* – tools, resources, and policies that empower; *embracing* – sense of belonging, community and connectedness; and *empathetic* – support, caring and flexibility. The multifaceted and dynamic nature of the employee experience requires both leaders and HR teams to demonstrate sincere and sustainable commitment to the entire employee journey.

There is compelling evidence that investing in employee experience is good for business. As shown in an MIT study, the return on investment (ROI) to organizations that have high employee experience ratings is reflected by higher engagement, twice the innovation and customer satisfaction, four times the profitability and a stronger brand compared to their lower-rated peers (Dery & Sebastian, 2017).

Integrating Customer and Employee Experience

As companies increasingly compete on customer experience, integrating employee experience and customer experience programs and platforms becomes necessary to provide better organizational clarity, commitment and actionability. This requires cross-functional collaboration between HR, marketing and analytics teams for effective customer and employee journey mapping, and the design, development and adoption of appropriate engagement strategies, tools and metrics.

Organizations that are customer-centric and brand-centric can benefit from the virtuous circle by focusing on improving the end-to-end journeys of both employees (recruitment, onboarding, development and retention) and customers (consideration, evaluation, purchase and post-purchase). This involves identifying and evaluating critical touchpoints of their respective journeys, as well as taking actions to eliminate pain points and improve gain points that enhance the experiences of both employees and customers. Organizations can further leverage big data and AI-based platforms to perform reliable people and customer analytics to generate valuable insights for diagnostics, decision-making and interventions. A data-driven approach supported by internal branding activities will enable and empower organizations to deliver great employee and customer experiences which in turn contribute to greater loyalty, higher satisfaction and stronger advocacy.

Figure 6.1 presents a framework that highlights the importance of organizations in adopting a holistic approach to integrating the management of employee and customer journeys and experiences while leveraging on technology and digitalization to enhance the desired outcomes of satisfaction, loyalty and advocacy that strengthen internal and external brand value.

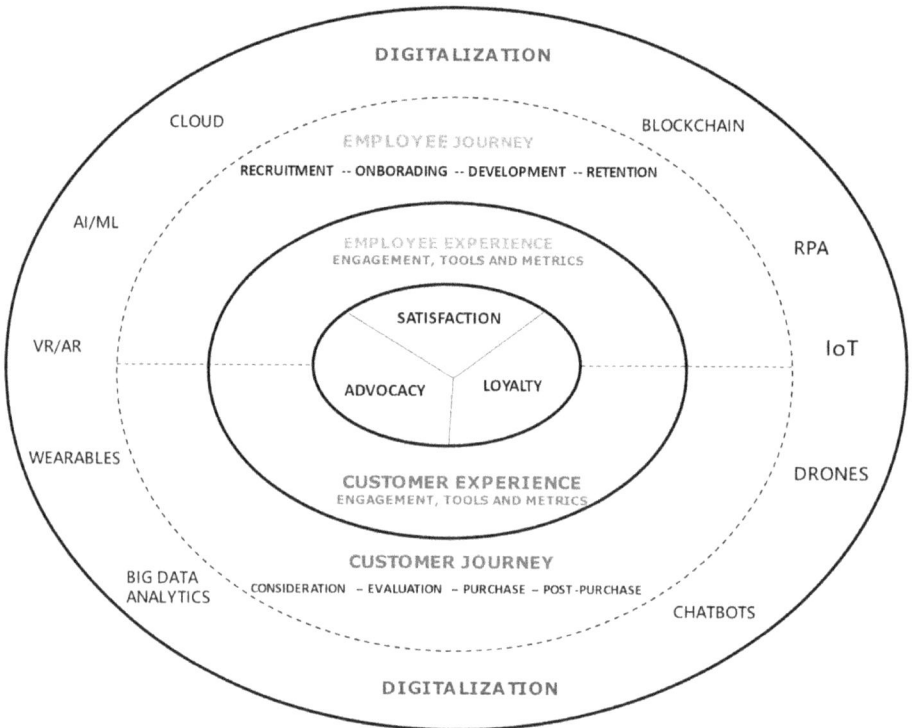

Figure 6.1: Integrating Employee and Customer Experience in the Age of Digitalization. Source: Author.

Morgan (2018) reports the close relationship and benefits of integrating employee and customer experience to the organization from various studies. Some noteworthy findings include: (1) companies that excel in customer experience have 1.5 times more engaged employees than companies with poor customer experience; (2) companies with highly engaged employees outperform the competition by 147 percent; (3) companies that invest in employee experience are four times more profitable than those that do not; and (4) 89 percent of companies expect to compete on customer experience. In summary, the benefits of integrating employee and customer experience are stronger employee engagement, higher customer satisfaction, stronger brand affinity, better profitability and higher growth.

Internal Branding in the Age of Digitalization and Uncertainty

In the age of digitalization and hyper-connectivity, leaders need to also recognize the value of leveraging technologies such as the cloud, artificial intelligence (AI), internet of things (IoT), blockchain, big data and analytics, virtual and augmented reality, chatbots, wearables, drones and robotic process automation (RPA) to enhance and enable the organization's value chain and eco-system to consistently deliver seamless and connected user experiences for both employees and customers. Important benefits to the internal and external stakeholders include higher productivity, more transparency, better scalability, stronger engagement and more personalized or tailored user experiences.

According to Harvard Business School's sponsored study (2018) of senior business leaders, 87 percent indicated that digitalization is now an important priority, with two-thirds expecting to change their business model in the next three years and 62 percent reporting that their organizations have embarked on digital transformation programs. Given that this is a long-term corporate imperative, the transformation must be an inclusive, engaging and empowering process involving every employee to ensure success from both an employee experience and business performance point of view.

However, digital transformation led by AI and automation is creating a great deal of anxiety about job redundancies, diminished roles and responsibilities and dehumanization of the work culture and environment. In the book *Leadership by Algorithm*, De Cremer (2020) provides insightful perspectives of the challenges leaders face in delicately balancing the role of machines (robots) and people as organizations embrace digital transformation and operate in data-rich environments to drive decision-making and improve employee and customer engagement supported by AI.

Will the current best practices of internal branding that help leaders to align their organizations with the values and brand promise be impacted as decision making, engagement, processes and communications are increasingly driven by AI? In other words, will AI-driven leadership and decision-making create a more efficient, transparent but dehumanized organizational climate? What unique challenges do Asian companies, who are already behind the internal branding curve, face as they undergo digital transformation and prepare for a hyper-competitive future for talent and customers?

At the time of writing of this chapter, the world is facing an unprecedented economic and human crisis brought about by the COVID-19 pandemic. This has resulted in millions of employees being furloughed or laid off and disrupting not only their livelihoods but also deeply affecting their morale, productivity and sense of well-being. Mercer's Global Talent Trends study (2020) reports that the business impacts of the COVID-19 pandemic in the medium term and the ongoing impacts and opportunities of AI and technology are creating a great deal of fear and anxiety among employees. In their survey, 34 percent of the employees expect their jobs to disappear in the next three years, and 55 percent trust their companies to provide the skills, training and development to cope with the changes or disappearances of their jobs altogether.

Seventy-seven percent of companies strongly believe that their employee benefits reflect their brand values. However, there is a compelling need to rethink and recalibrate to demonstrate a greater responsibility toward employees as companies embark on digitalization programs, including automation, that may erode health and other employee benefits. This is evident from Mercer's survey (2020), which revealed that 99 percent of the organizations will embark on digital transformation in 2020 and only 29 percent will pull back in the event of a downturn, while acknowledging the huge skills gap and the need for workforce learning and reskilling to ensure business success.

The Mercer study also found that one of the top priorities for leadership and HR in 2020 is to deliver on the employee experience, with more than half of the executives reporting that they are redesigning their organizational structures to become more people-centric. The COVID-19 pandemic has created new and pressing challenges globally, as employees have to fulfill their roles and responsibilities while navigating social distancing, quarantine, site closures and working remotely.

More so than ever, leaders need to step up their efforts at internal branding with empathy, flexibility and inclusiveness to energize the employee experience and restore a sense of optimism and purpose in these challenging times. By taking greater ownership of the brand and creating the appropriate culture defined by purpose-driven brand values that resonate with both employees and customers, Asian leaders can aspire to build resilient and agile organizations and deliver differentiated and sustainable global brand experiences. Asian global leadership in a VUCAH world will increasingly be measured by leaders' abilities to effectively align the organizational purpose with the brand values, which in turn will influence and shape both employee and customer experiences.

References

Berry, L. L. & Parasuraman, A. (1991). *Marketing Services: Competing Through Quality*. The Free Press (New York, NY).

Brand Finance (2020). Brand Finance Global 500 2020. Retrieved on 3 April 2020, from https://brandfinance.com/images/upload/brand_finance_global_500_2020_preview.pdf

Davis, S. M. & Dunn, K. (2002). *Building the Brand-Driven Business: Operationalize Your Brand to Drive Profitable Growth*. Josey-Bass (San Francisco, CA).

Davis, S. M. (2009). *The Shift: The Transformation of Today's Marketers into Tomorrow's Growth Leaders*. Josey-Bass (San Francisco, CA).

Davis, J. (2018). Brand of gold. *Dialogue Review*. Retrieved from https://dialoguereview.com/brand-gold/.

De Chernatony, L. & Segal-Horn, S. (2001). Building on services characteristics to develop successful services brands. *Journal of Marketing Management, 17*(7/8), 645–691.

De Cremer, D. (2020). *Leadership by Algorithm: Who Leads and Who Follows in the AI Era*. Harriman House (United Kingdom).

Dery, K. & Sebastian, I. (2017). Building business value with employee experience. MIT Sloan CISR Research Briefing, *XVII*(6). Retrieved on 3 April 2020, from https://cisr.mit.edu/publication/2017_0601_EmployeeExperience_DerySebastian.

Doland, A. (2014). Branding lessons for China's Alibaba. AdAge. Retrieved on 3 April 2020, from https://adage.com/article/global-news/alibaba-teach-chinese-brands/295115.

Foster, C., Punjaisri, K. & Cheng, R. (2010). Exploring the relationship between corporate, internal and employer branding. *Journal of Product & Brand Management, 19*(6), 401–409.

Harvard Business Review (2018). Every organizational function needs to work on digital transformation. Retrieved on 3 April 2020, from https://hbr.org/sponsored/2018/11/every-organizational-function-needs-to-work-on-digital-transformation.

Interbrand (2010–2019). Retrieved from https://www.interbrand.com/best-brands/best-global-brands/2010-2019/ranking/.

Lee Yohn, D. (2018). 2018 will be the year of the employee experience. *Forbes*. Retrieved on 3 April 2020, from https://www.forbes.com/sites/deniselyohn/2018/01/02/2018-will-be-the-year-of-employee-experience/#66d6df991c8f.

Liker, J. K. (2004). *The Toyota Way: 14 Management Principles from the World's Greatest Manufacturer*. McGraw-Hill (New York, NY).

Marshall, J. F. (2013). How Starbucks, Walmart and IBM launch brands internally and what you can learn from them. *Forbes*.

Mckoy, Deb (2014). Peppergrain. Retrieved on 3 April 2020, from https://peppergrain.com/richard-branson-branding-quote/.

Mercer (2019a). Building a better employee experience. Retrieved on 3 April 2020, from https://www.mercer.com/our-thinking/career/voice-on-talent/building-a-better-employee-experience.html.

Mercer (2019b). Mercer, Global Talent Trends Study 2019. Retrieved on 3 April 2020, from https://www.mercer.us/our-thinking/career/global-talent-hr-trends.html.

Mercer (2020). Mercer, Global Talent Trends Study 2020. Retrieved on 3 April 2020, from https://www.mercer.us/content/dam/mercer/attachments/private/us-2020-global-talent-trends-2020-report.pdf.

Mitchell, C. (2002). Selling the brand inside. *Harvard Business Review*, January, *80*(1), 99–105.

Morgan, B. M. (2018). The un-ignorable link between employee experience and customer experience. *Forbes*. Retrieved on 3 April 2020, from https://www.forbes.com/sites/blakemorgan/2018/02/

23/the-un-ignorable-link-between-employee-experience-and-customer-experience/
#788dc3c148dc.

Mosley, R. W. (2007). Customer experience, organizational culture and the employer brand. *Brand Management*, *15*(2), 123–134.

Roll, M. (2015). *Asian Brand Strategy: Building and Sustaining Strong Global Brands in Asia*. Palgrave Macmillan (London, UK).

Part III: **Asian Global Leadership in Action**

Alison R. Eyring and James D. Eyring
Chapter 7
Collective Leadership Capacity for Growth

Introduction

In today's global business environment, sustained business growth is a key indicator of success and a driver of share price and company valuations (Gebhardt, Lee & Swaminathan, 2001; Penman, Zhu & Wang 2019). Achieving and sustaining growth in today's complex, interconnected and ever-evolving world requires new collective leadership capabilities that not only span functions across a business, but also across entire business ecosystems. Over the past 40 years, rapid market expansion and business growth has characterized most of the Asia region and nearly two generations of business leaders have led growth or worked in expanding organizations throughout their career in Asia. Thus, global perspectives on leading growth can be enriched by this perspective. This chapter builds on the emerging paradigm of collective leadership and links the core tenets of collective leadership to capabilities required for sustained business growth and by incorporating Asian values and experience. In this way, we contribute to forming a more global perspective on the collective leadership capacity for growth.

In the global business environment, sustained growth is a key indicator of business success. Growth drives share price and company valuations (Gebhardt, Lee & Swaminathan, 2001), which impact a firm's ability to attract capital. Increased capital allows firms to invest in new capabilities such as product innovations, market expansions and human capital acquisition and development (Penman, Zhu & Wang 2019). Achieving and sustaining business growth is challenging as it requires complex organization-level capabilities such as market orientation (Bahadir, Bharadwaj & Parzen, 2009), ambidexterity (Junni et al., 2013) and entrepreneurial orientation (Wales, 2016). Building and leveraging these organization-level capabilities for growth is a key leadership imperative.

Nowhere in the world is there more of a need to build capabilities to achieve and sustain business growth than in Asia. Since the 1970s, the world's economic center of gravity has shifted from the West towards the East (Mahbubani, 2009; Quah, 2011). Over this time, countries such as China, India, Indonesia and Singapore have been transformed by market expansion, modernization and rising prosperity. Asian corporations also have become more competitive and now account for almost 40 percent of *Fortune*'s Global 500 list (*Fortune* Global 500, 2019). Sustained business and economic growth across Asia have attracted both foreign and domestic investment. Due to high levels of economic and business growth, many firms in

https://doi.org/10.1515/9783110671988-007

Asia have experienced higher growth rates relative to their counterparts in more established markets in North America and Western Europe.

While Asia has sustained uniquely high levels of growth and transformation, it is not unique in experiencing a faster pace change, increased volatility, and greater complexity in the business environment. Over the past ten to fifteen years, a growing number of leadership scholars (e.g., Carson 2005; Denis, Langley & Sergi, 2012) have argued that increased complexity and the rapidly changing nature of work make it difficult for a single leader to successfully perform all leadership functions. This thinking has expanded the view of leadership beyond traits of an individual leader towards a model of collective leadership – a dynamic process in which multiple team members take up elements of the leadership role (Friedrich et al., 2009; Carson, Tesluk & Marrone, 2007). In this paradigm, leadership is viewed as a collective achievement that is brought about by all participants of the leadership process (Contractor et al., 2012). While a significant body of research on collective leadership has emerged, there is no cohesive framework, language or common definition of "collective leadership." In the private sector, the study of collective leadership tends to focus on shared leadership within teams (Carson et al., 2007), while education or public sector scholars focus on distributed leadership (Tian, Risku & Collin, 2016). A growing number of leadership scholars focus on collective leadership for complex and adaptive systems and emphasize the emergent nature of leadership (Alexy et al., 2018).

While the world's economic center of gravity has shifted towards the East, scholarly writing around collective leadership has remained largely in the West. However, the construct of collective leadership is particularly relevant for Asia, where high growth, complex supply chains and rapidly changing markets place heavy demands on leaders whose role may change faster than they are able to change or learn. For example, at Huawei, the Chinese global telecommunications leader, a rotating CEO structure employs a form of collective leadership to address high complexity and market dynamism (Tao, De Cremer & Chunbo, 2018). Western multinationals such as Mastercard and Dell also have used "co-CEOs" to oversee their Asia Pacific region as a means of addressing the complexity of managing by a single leader.

While the dynamic and complex external environments in Asia make collective leadership more necessary, the core tenets of collective leadership seem to be more consistent with individualistic and egalitarian cultural norms which characterize North America and much of Northwestern Europe (Taras, Kirkman & Steel, 2010). The tenets may require some adaptation to translate to the majority of countries of the world – not just those of Asia.

Cross-cultural research has demonstrated that cultural norms and values such as collectivism, power-distance and uncertainty avoidance play an important role in shaping leadership behaviors, organizational practices and relationships (House et al., 2004; Northouse, 2007). For example, Confucian Asian and South Asian cultures value and accept power-differentiated relationships between managers and their team members. This will impact the emergence of collective leadership among individuals not formally sanctioned to lead. At the same time, leaders in collectivistic cultures are more likely to prioritize the good of the many over the needs of the individual, and leaders in collectivistic cultures are more likely to encourage the collective distribution of resources and collective action (Koo & Park, 2018). A global perspective on collective leadership that reflects both the East and the West will benefit leaders, followers and the broader business community.

Globalizing the Perspective on Collective Leadership

While the body of literature on collective leadership is incredibly diverse, it is founded on three underlying tenets: (1) leadership is an emergent property of a group or network of interacting individuals; (2) leadership responsibilities are distributed among formal and informal leaders; and (3) expertise is distributed across the many, not the few. These core tenets are consistent with Western cultural norms and market practices (Taras, Kirkman & Steel, 2010) and require some adaptation to translate into the majority of countries of the world. This section suggests how we can globalize the three core tenets of collective leadership by incorporating Asian cultural values as well.

The first tenet of collective leadership is that leadership is an emergent property of a group or network of interacting individuals. The idea that leadership is an emergent property of a group or network of interacting individuals is one that is well-suited to egalitarian Western cultures that downplay or minimize hierarchy or power-distance in the workplace. Asian national cultures, on the other hand, understand roles and responsibilities that are ascribed to power-differentiated relationships and use these to provide social order. The role of the leader is both valued and respected. More importantly, many actions within an organization will not emerge unless sanctioned by formal authority. This is relevant to the emergence of collective leadership. We suggest that formal leaders need to sanction and encourage emergent leadership within their organizations.

While most research on collective leadership is focused on leadership within a single work group (Contractor et al., 2012), the practice of collective leadership is even more important across functions or geographies, as complex problems typically require leaders from different parts of the organization for resolution. Collective leadership across functions or geographies is less likely to emerge when poor collaboration or interdepartmental interactions impede the development of shared priorities, resolution of conflict and improved practice. Thus, a more global restatement of the first tenet of collective leadership is: Leadership emerges within or across groups or networks of interacting individuals when sanctioned and supported by senior leaders. In other words, the role of formal, senior leaders in sanctioning emergent leadership and encouraging cross-organization collaboration can be a powerful enabler of collective leadership.

The second tenet of collective leadership is that leadership responsibilities are distributed among formal and informal leaders. The idea that some leadership responsibilities will be distributed to informal or emergent leaders fits well with the values of egalitarianism and individualism in which individuals are encouraged to stand out and express their thoughts freely. Across Asia, it is typically the expectation of leaders and followers alike that a formal leader will provide clarity of roles and responsibilities. This clarity minimizes ambiguity and uncertainty in the organization, which is an important cultural value. Collectivistic cultures also support and encourage the distribution of resources and collective action. For example, in Japan, change efforts are typically implemented after formal and informal leaders are thoroughly engaged and provide inputs to the new direction. This engagement increases the amount of time needed to gain alignment within the organization, but it also increases the speed of execution once an agreement has been attained. This approach ensures that individuals with specific expertise are included and avoids the dynamic of individual personalities determining who is heard. If a company relies purely on an emergent form of distributed leadership, some leaders with required expertise may be excluded, leading to suboptimal results. Worse, leaders who are historically excluded from the leadership process may continue to be excluded. Thus, a more global restatement of the second tenet is: leadership responsibilities should be proactively distributed among formal and informal leaders. In other words, a more purposeful distribution of power ensures that individuals with the right expertise are involved in key decisions impacting the organization.

The final tenet of collective leadership is that expertise is distributed across the many, not the few. Because growth rates in Asia are often three to five times higher than that experienced by more developed markets in the West, businesses in Asia often face significant gaps in expertise. These businesses must proactively build individual, team and organization knowledge and capabilities faster than do more mature or slower growing businesses. For example, while a pharmaceutical company in the US must build sales capabilities for multiple sales channels, in Asia, it must determine suitable channel strategies and partners in each market at the same time that it is building sales capabilities for each of those channels. In Asia, success is only achieved when leaders aggressively build expertise and capabilities across the organization. Thus, a more global perspective on this third tenet of collective leadership is that expertise is distributed unevenly, and core capabilities must be developed across the many, not the few. In other words, collective leadership must proactively build the organization and leader capabilities required for growth.

Globalizing these core tenets of collective leadership (shown in Table 7.1) shifts the view from leadership as spontaneous and emergent to one that is spontaneous and emergent while simultaneously purposeful and proactive. This view does not undervalue the importance of emergent, spontaneous or informal leadership – rather, it

Table 7.1: Global Perspective on Collective Leadership.

Core Tenet	Global Perspective
Leadership is an emergent property of a group or network of interacting individuals.	Leadership emerges in a group or network of interacting individuals when sanctioned and supported by more senior leaders.
Leadership responsibilities are distributed among formal and informal leaders.	Leadership responsibilities should be intentionally and actively distributed among formal and informal leaders.
Expertise is distributed across the many, not the few.	Expertise is distributed unevenly, and core capabilities must be developed across the many, not the few.

elevates the value and importance of leadership to encourage and guide the formation of collective leadership and the development of crucial capabilities across the organization. In this way, collective leadership can be a critical enabler of business performance and growth.

Organization Capabilities for Growth

Research across disciplines of marketing, economics and strategic management have identified strategic capabilities that drive business growth (e.g., Chang et al., 2014; Rauch & Hatak, 2016; Rauch & Frese, 2007). Unlike attributes such as learning agility (De Meuse, 2017) or growth mindset (Dweck, 2017) which are embedded within individuals, these capabilities are organization-level constructs that are embedded across process, people and technology. These capabilities must be developed across the organization in sufficient quantity to drive growth. Collective leadership can aid in the development and activation of these growth capabilities. In the following section, we explore three of these capabilities needed for growth and the collective leadership required to build and activate these capabilities.

Market Orientation

Market Orientation is the ability of an organization to understand and anticipate external trends and to translate this into impactful action within the organization. Market orientation is often operationalized as a customer-centered culture and as a set of norms or practices for gathering, disseminating and acting upon market intelligence (Gauzente, 1999). Companies that have greater market orientation experience greater innovation, higher levels of customer loyalty and satisfaction, higher quality products and ultimately greater financial performance (Chang et al., 2014).

Several factors contribute to a company's market orientation, including interdepartmental connectiveness, top team focus, market-based reward systems and a customer-centered culture (Kirca, Jayachandran & Bearden, 2005). The most significant of these factors is interdepartmental connectiveness. Companies with increased levels of cross-departmental communication and interaction experience lower interdepartmental conflict and increased knowledge sharing. Lower interdepartmental conflict and increased knowledge sharing, in turn, leads to better coordination to serve customers and better dissemination of important market information. The impact of national culture on market orientation has been mixed. Some research shows that market orientation is stronger in collectivistic cultures (Brettel, Engelen, & Heinemann, 2009) while other research has found no difference in effect sizes (Cano, Carrillat, & Jaramillo, 2004).

Collective leadership enables market orientation by driving interdepartmental connectiveness and creating an external focus. By focusing on the market and customers, top leadership teams send signals to the organization that leaders are responsible for understanding and acting upon customer and market input. By encouraging cross-departmental collaboration and sharing of information, they sanction and encourage collective leadership. Eyring and Consuegra (2017) provide an example of cross-functional collective leadership from a global retail company. In this organization, global leaders from the HR and Marketing departments partnered to share consumer data with staff to help them understand changing customer needs and profiles. This information sharing facilitated employee behavioral change and motivated informal leadership to act on the consumer data. By sharing information, the leaders built knowledge and capabilities across many individuals, making collective leadership in this area more likely.

Ambidexterity

Organization ambidexterity (OA) is an organization's ability to efficiently manage its current business demands while simultaneously adapting to changes in the environment (Raisch & Birkinshaw, 2008). Ambidextrous organizations implement two types of innovation: exploration of new growth opportunities (e.g. new products, channels, customers or geographies); and exploitation of existing assets (i.e. facilities, brands, technologies and so on) to improve productivity and efficiency. Explore innovation has a greater impact on revenue growth and exploit innovation has a greater impact on profit growth, while the combination of the two has a multiplicative effect on growth in revenue and profits (Junni et al., 2013).

Conducting exploit and explore innovation simultaneously is challenging and can create tensions in the organization (Koryak et al., 2018). In addition, many distinct factors contribute to a firm's OA, including firm strategy, organization structure, continuous improvement programs, top team composition, firm maturity and financial slack (Josephson, Johnson & Mariadoss, 2016; Raisch & Birkinshaw, 2008). Some companies keep exploit and explore activities separate. For example, Cisco acquires firms with emerging technologies while its existing internal teams focus on refining and exploiting established products (Stettner & Lavie, 2014). In Singapore, DBS bank built a separate leadership team to pursue new digital innovations and then migrated this new business entity into its core business to drive transformation. At the same time, the entire bank exploited technology to transform the customer experience and lower back office transition costs (Kien et al., 2015).

Companies also can drive both exploit and explore innovation simultaneously through the top leadership team (Havermans et al., 2015). For example, top leadership focus that helps their team converge (execute priorities) and diverge (create new opportunities) and builds routines that support both processes drives both exploit and explore innovation. This leadership focus impacts team behaviors, communication and decision-making. These factors, in turn, drive team innovation and an overall increase in organization ambidexterity (Mihalache et al., 2014; Zacher & Rosing, 2015).

Team capabilities also impact organization ambidexterity. For example, cohesive teams share and use knowledge and technical expertise in ways that increase innovation (Jansen et al., 2016). Building a shared sense of cohesion and efficacy within a team depends on strong interpersonal relationships and a common belief among team members that they are collectively capable of achieving their goals. Team discipline, support and trust enable team members to combine exploit and explore innovation efforts (Stettner & Lavie, 2014).

The relationship between cohesion and knowledge sharing that has been observed in teams also may occur at an organization level. Yang, Zhou and Zhang (2015) found that companies with more collectivistic cultures experienced greater ambidexterity. They attributed this to greater organization citizenship behaviors and greater knowledge dissemination in the organization.

Samsung provides a good example of collective leadership intentionally building capabilities that increased both exploit and explore innovation and thus build organization ambidexterity (Eyring, 2017). In the 1980s, its CEO famously told employees, "Change everything except your wives and children." In the highly collectivistic and hierarchical culture of Korea, this translated into radical changes, including a partnership with the Russia Academy of Science for access to basic research, a structured approach and process for innovation and extensive training across the organization at all levels on how to innovate and how to improve existing processes to be more cost competitive. Greater innovation emerged, and the business transformed itself and grew to become a global electronics powerhouse over the ensuing decades. This collective approach to innovation is much different from Western firms that historically have relied on individual-driven innovation.

Collective leadership enables OA as it builds the capabilities that organizations need to drive innovation and change. Top leadership teams that purposefully focus on and set routines around ambidexterity send signals on the importance of both exploit and explore innovation to the broader organization. This context encourages leadership for innovation to emerge broadly. These same leaders ensure that expertise needed for exploit (e.g., process improvement) and explore (e.g., new product design) activities is developed and distributed across the organization.

Entrepreneurial Orientation

Entrepreneurial orientation (EO) is a strategic firm-level strategy-making process that enables firms to make entrepreneurial decisions such as risk-taking and exploring new business opportunities. EO is defined and measured through three factors: innovativeness, proactivity and risk-taking. These areas have been operationalized through surveys of manager perceptions, review of firm behavior (e.g., new product announcements) and review of resource allocation (e.g., R&D investments) (Lyon, Lumpkin & Dess, 2000). Companies with higher levels of EO deliver higher levels of performance, revenue growth and profit compared to similar companies with lower EO (Wales, 2016). Firms with high EO also are more likely to innovate and take risks. They have better firm-level learning processes and are more open to change. These results are similar for small and large companies.

Little research has been conducted on precedents and drivers of EO. Some research suggests that firm management and founder involvement in governance impacts EO (Deb & Wiklund, 2017). Other research has examined national cultural dynamics. For example, Kreiser et al. (2010) have examined cultural factors that predicted EO in SMEs. They have found that SMEs in cultures with high uncertainty avoidance and power-distance (many cultures in Asia) had lower risk-taking behavior and proactiveness. Countries high in individualism (e.g., the US) also were less proactive. They also found that some company factors (e.g., firm size, industry) and country-level factors (e.g., GDP, economic and political risk) influenced risk-taking and proactiveness. In line with these country-level factors, other research suggests that the impact of culture on EO depends upon the level of development of the country (Pinillos & Reyes, 2011).

Founder-led organizations are shaped by their founder's personality and risk tolerance. However, as companies grow and scale, their culture evolves. Collective leadership that motivates and rewards innovation, risk-taking and proactivity enables EO. As companies become older and more established, they will attract, select and retain leaders who fit well with the existing culture. To build or maintain EO, top leaders must intentionally hire and promote formal and informal leaders who drive innovation, take risks and shape or encourage proactive behavior in others. To many leaders, this is uncomfortable.

Conclusion

In this chapter, we have suggested ways to "globalize" the perspective on collective leadership by reflecting values from both the East and the West. We have presented the case that that collective leadership requires formal leadership to model, sanction and support collective leadership. We have described formal, senior leadership responsibilities and collective leadership responsibilities needed to build important organization-level capabilities for growth. These capabilities are collective assets that benefit stakeholders inside and outside of the business, such as employees, top management, investors and customers.

Leading and sustaining business growth is not for the faint of heart, nor is it the responsibility of a single leader at the top of the organization. Collective leadership is needed to build critical organization, team and individual capabilities required to achieve and sustain business growth. This collective leadership is both purposeful and emergent. It is both formal and informal. It is proactive in building capabilities and supportive of the emergence of the expertise required for growth. Building a collective leadership capacity for growth is an imperative for leaders everywhere and requires perspectives from both the West and the East.

References

Alexy, N., Hazy, J., D'Innocenzo, L., Erogul, M. S., Fairhurst, G., Raelin, J., Seers, A., Spillane, J. & Sweet, T. (2018). Studying collective leadership as a complex, dynamic and co-created phenomenon. Academy of Management Symposium.

Bahadir, S. C., Bharadwaj, S. & Parzen, M. (2009). A meta-analysis of the determinants of organic sales growth. *International Journal of Research in Marketing, 26*(4), 263–275.

Brettel, M., Engelen, A. & Heinemann, F. (2009). New entrepreneurial ventures in a globalized world: The role of market orientation. *Journal of International Entrepreneurship, 7*(2), 88–110.

Cano, C. R., Carrillat, F. A. & Jaramillo, F. (2004). A meta-analysis of the relationship between market orientation and business performance: evidence from five continents. *International Journal of Research in Marketing, 21*(2), 179–200.

Carson, J. B. (2005). Shared leadership and culture: Potential emergence and global application. In N.S. Huber, M.C. Walker (Eds.), *Emergent Models of Global Leadership: A Volume in Building Leadership Bridges*, 1–16.

Carson, J. B., Tesluk, P. E. & Marrone, J. A. (2007). Shared leadership in teams: An investigation of antecedent conditions and performance. *Academy of Management Journal, 50*(5), 1217–1234.

Chang, W., Franke, G. R., Butler, T. D., Musgrove, C. F. & Ellinger, A. E. (2014). Differential mediating effects of radical and incremental innovation on market orientation-performance relationship: A meta-analysis. *Journal of Marketing Theory and Practice, 22*(3), 235–250.

Contractor, N. S., DeChurch, L. A., Carson, J., Carter, D. R. & Keegan, B. (2012). The topology of collective leadership. *The Leadership Quarterly, 23*(6), 994–1011.

Deb, P. & Wiklund, J. (2017). The effects of CEO founder status and stock ownership on entrepreneurial orientation in small firms. *Journal of Small Business Management, 55*(1), 32–55.

De Meuse, K. P. (2017). Learning agility: Its evolution as a psychological construct and its empirical relationship to leader success. *Consulting Psychology Journal: Practice and Research, 69*(4), 267.

Denis, J. L., Langley, A. & Sergi, V. (2012). Leadership in the plural. *The Academy of Management Annals, 6*(1), 211–283.

Dweck, C. (2017). *Mindset-updated edition: Changing the way you think to fulfil your potential.* Hachette UK.

Eyring, A. (2017). *Pacing for Growth: Why Intelligent Restraint Drives Long-term Success.* Berrett-Koehler Publishers.

Eyring, A. & Consuegra, J. (2017). How HR and Marketing Can Partner for Growth. *People & Strategy, 40*(4), 14–20.

Fortune Global 500 (2019). Retrieved on 26 April 2020 from https://fortune.com/global500/

Friedrich, T. L., Vessey, W. B., Schuelke, M. J., Ruark, G. A. & Mumford, M. D. (2009). A framework for understanding collective leadership: The selective utilization of leader and team expertise within networks. *The Leadership Quarterly, 20*(6), 933–958.

Gauzente, C. (1999). Comparing market orientation scales: A content analysis. Marketing Bulletin-Department of Marketing Massey University, 10, 76–82.

Gebhardt, W. R., Lee, C. M. & Swaminathan, B. (2001). Toward an implied cost of capital. *Journal of Accounting Research, 39*(1), 135–176.

Havermans, L. A., Den Hartog, D. N., Keegan, A. & Uhl-Bien, M. (2015). Exploring the role of leadership in enabling contextual ambidexterity. *Human Resource Management, 54*(S1), 179–200.

House, R. J., Hanges, P. J., Javidan, M., Dorfman, P. W. & Gupta, V. (Eds.). (2004). *Culture, leadership, and organizations: The GLOBE study of 62 societies.* Sage Publications.

Jansen, J. J., Kostopoulos, K. C., Mihalache, O. R. & Papalexandris, A. (2016). A socio-psychological perspective on team ambidexterity: The contingency role of supportive leadership behaviours. *Journal of Management Studies, 53*(6), 939–965.

Josephson, B. W., Johnson, J. L. & Mariadoss, B. J. (2016). Strategic marketing ambidexterity: Antecedents and financial consequences. *Journal of the Academy of Marketing Science, 44*(4), 539–554.

Junni, P., Sarala, R. M., Taras, V. & Tarba, S. Y. (2013). Organizational ambidexterity and performance: A meta-analysis. *Academy of Management Perspectives*, 27(4), 299–312.

Kien, S. S., Soh, C, Weill, P. & Ching, Y. (2015). Rewiring the enterprise for digital innovation: the case of DBS Bank. Case study. HBP No. NTU071. Publication No.:ABCC-2015-004. Published in the Asian Business Case Centre. Nanyang Technological University.

Kirca, A. H., Jayachandran, S. & Bearden, W. O. (2005). Market orientation: A meta-analytic review and assessment of its antecedents and impact on performance. *Journal of Marketing, 69*(2), 24–41.

Koo, H. & Park, C. (2018). Foundation of leadership in Asia: Leader characteristics and leadership styles review and research agenda. *Asia Pacific Journal of Management, 35*(3), 697–718.

Koryak, O., Lockett, A., Hayton, J., Nicolaou, N. & Mole, K. (2018). Disentangling the antecedents of ambidexterity: Exploration and exploitation. *Research Policy, 47*(2), 413–427.

Kreiser, P. M., Marino, L. D., Dickson, P. & Weaver, K. M. (2010). Cultural influences on entrepreneurial orientation: The impact of national culture on risk taking and proactiveness in SMEs. *Entrepreneurship Theory and Practice, 34*(5), 959–984.

Lyon, D. W., Lumpkin, G. T. & Dess, G. G. (2000). Enhancing entrepreneurial orientation research: Operationalizing and measuring a key strategic decision-making process. *Journal of Management, 26*(5), 1055–1085.

Mahbubani, K. (2009). *The new Asian hemisphere: The irresistible shift of global power to the East.* Public Affairs.

Mihalache, O. R., Jansen, J. J., Van den Bosch, F. A. & Volberda, H. W. (2014). Top management team shared leadership and organizational ambidexterity: A moderated mediation framework. *Strategic Entrepreneurship Journal, 8*(2), 128–148.

Penman, S. H., Zhu, J. & Wang, H. (2019). The Implied Cost of Capital: Accounting for Growth. Available at SSRN 3470619.

Pinillos, M. J. & Reyes, L. (2011). Relationship between individualist–collectivist culture and entrepreneurial activity: evidence from Global Entrepreneurship Monitor data. *Small Business Economics, 37*(1), 23–37.

Quah, D. (2011). The global economy's shifting centre of gravity. *Global Policy, 2*(1), 3–9.

Raisch, S. & Birkinshaw, J. (2008). Organizational ambidexterity: Antecedents, outcomes, and moderators. *Journal of Management, 34*(3), 375–409.

Rauch, A. & Frese, M. (2007). Let's put the person back into entrepreneurship research: A meta-analysis on the relationship between business owners' personality traits, business creation, and success. *European Journal of Work and Organizational Psychology*, 16(4), 353–385.

Rauch, A. & Hatak, I. (2016). A meta-analysis of different HR-enhancing practices and performance of small and medium sized firms. *Journal of Business Venturing, 31*(5), 485–504.

Stettner, U. & Lavie, D. (2014). Ambidexterity under scrutiny: Exploration and exploitation via internal organization, alliances, and acquisitions. *Strategic Management Journal, 35*(13), 1903–1929.

Taras, V., Kirkman, B. L. & Steel, P. (2010). Examining the impact of culture's consequences: A three-decade, multilevel, meta-analytic review of Hofstede's cultural value dimensions. *Journal of Applied Psychology, 95*(3), 405.

Tao, T., De Cremer, D., & Chunbo, W. (2018). *Huawei: Leadership, culture and connectivity.* Sage Publishing.

Tao, T., De Cremer, D., & Chunbo, W. (2016). *Huawei: Leadership, Culture, and Connectivity.* SAGE Publications, India.

Tian, M., Risku, M. & Collin, K. (2016). A meta-analysis of distributed leadership from 2002 to 2013: Theory development, empirical evidence and future research focus. *Educational Management Administration & Leadership*, 44(1), 146–164.

Wales, W. J. (2016). Entrepreneurial orientation: A review and synthesis of promising research directions. *International Small Business Journal, 34*(1), 3–15.

Yang, Z., Zhou, X. & Zhang, P. (2015). Discipline versus passion: Collectivism, centralization, and ambidextrous innovation. *Asia Pacific Journal of Management, 32*(3), 745–769.

Zacher, H. & Rosing, K. (2015). Ambidextrous leadership and team innovation. *Leadership & Organization Development Journal.*

Kai Chi Yam, Jamie L. Gloor and Lucy Liu

Chapter 8
Humor and Its Effects for Leaders in the East and West

In 2008, a journalist threw a shoe at George W. Bush, former United States president. Bush quickly fended off the incident with a joke. "If you want the facts," he laughed, "it was a size 10 shoe that he threw" (Myers & Rubin, 2008). A few months later, the same incident happened in China, when a student threw a shoe at Chinese Prime Minister Wen Jiabao. The prime minister's reaction to this incident, however, was distinctively different from President Bush's reaction – he denounced it as "despicable behavior" (Burns, 2009).

These examples juxtapose two prominent world leaders – one from the West and one from the East – who, when faced with very similar situations, responded with polar reactions. These events illustrate a divergent understanding of humor across cultures: while the US president responded with light-heartedness and humor, the Chinese prime minister responded with utter seriousness. In this chapter, we highlight these culturally embedded attitudes toward humor, including how they can facilitate – or falter – effective global leadership.

A History of Humor in the East and West

Cooper (2004) defines humor as "a social communication intended to be amusing." Although leaders may use humor as a strategic tool to achieve various organizationally-relevant goals (for example, to build relationships with followers, as seen in Cooper, Kong & Crossley, 2018; to create a pleasant atmosphere, as in Cooper, 2004; and to reduce stress and promote a community spirit, as in Romeo & Cruthirds, 2006), like any tool in a toolbox, the instrument is only effective when it fits the situation. Although leaders often have sufficient power and status to guide follower sensemaking at work, including setting the tone for humor expression and reactions (Cooper, 2004; Yam et al., 2018), they may also lose face if ill-fitting tools are used. Thus, we compare humor in Western and Eastern (specifically, Chinese) cultures, grounded in three theoretical perspectives and focused on leadership.

The Chinese understanding of humor has been undeniably shaped by Confucianism. Confucius (551–479 BC) was a Chinese philosopher who created a system in which political, moral and social principles determined life in China. This philosophy has since extended to many neighboring Asian countries (Wang et al., 2005), promoting the conviction that humor is not valued in society (Jiang, Li & Hou, 2019). In fact,

https://doi.org/10.1515/9783110671988-008

Confucius once stated that "a man has to be serious to be respected" (Liao, 2007). Statements like this and their grounding in a pervasive ideology have deeply shaped people's appreciation of humor, leading them to deem it inappropriate and associate it with intellectual frivolity and social nonchalance (Yue, 2010).

The Western understanding of humor can be traced back to the ancient Greeks. In the era of Plato (428/427–424–423 B.C.) and Aristotle (384–322 B.C), humor was cherished as a form of natural expression of amusement, promoting fun and pleasure in social activities (Grant, 1980). Democritus, a Greek philosopher also known as "the laughing philosopher" (Bremmer, 1997), was one of the first people to coin the term "humor" to denote mirth. Even today, people with humorous personalities in more Western civilizations are regarded as more extroverted and socially desirable, while people who lack humor are often confronted with negative attitudes and regarded as grouchy or overly serious (Allport, 1961).

Although this discussion might paint a picture of a rather humorless East, this is not entirely accurate. Indeed, research has demonstrated the presence and effectiveness of leader humor in countries such as China (e.g., Yam et al., 2018). However, varying levels of humor appreciation in both cultures may shape leaders' enactment and effectiveness of humor use in professional settings (Yang, Kitchen & Bacouel-Jentjens, 2017).

Humor as a Skill in the Global Leadership Toolbox

The three main processes through which leader humor affects organizationally relevant outcomes include social exchange, stress relief and positive emotion (Cooper et al., 2018). Although the vast majority of humor research has been conducted in Western contexts such as the US, and empirical, cross-cultural comparisons of leader humor use are rare (see Yang et al., 2017, for a review), we largely ground our arguments in these three theoretical frameworks, outlining how each process might differ in the East and the West.

The social exchange function of humor relies on the Social Exchange Theory, which explains human interactions as exchanges of goods and services (Cropanzano & Mitchell, 2005). Whereas low-quality relationships largely comprise transactional and economic exchanges, high-quality relationships also comprise social exchanges that generate a sense of gratitude, obligation, and trust, in addition to respect, liking and loyalty. However, higher-quality exchanges and relationships are inherently less hierarchical, which may trigger divergent effects in Eastern versus Western contexts.

In the East, for example, Confucian mentalities are regarded as a precious element of social order. Because humor is considered a form of private enjoyment (Xu, 2011) which also shapes and reduces hierarchies (Cooper, 2005; Cooper et al., 2018),

Chinese people may be afraid that humor might affect their social status, and therefore renounce humor to reduce their stress (Yue, 2011). For these reasons, in China as well as in other Asian countries, humor may not be seen as a form of valued social exchange that generates higher-quality relationships.

In the West, however, hierarchies are seemingly less essential for social order and are viewed as being more permeable, while the people tend to be more egalitarian (e.g., see Hofstede, Hofstede & Minkov, 2010). For these reasons, humor may be perceived more positively, and thus may also be a more effective leadership tool in the West than in the East via these social exchange processes.

The stress-reduction function of humor is based on the theory of conservation of reservations. Within this framework, Hobfoll (1989) explains the psychological experience of stress as a potential or actual loss of resources, or an insufficient gain of new resources following a resource investment. Resources can take on a number of forms, with leader humor being an interpersonal, socioemotional resource most relevant to this discussion. Because work inherently involves stress, leader humor may help employees reappraise this stress or even directly alleviate it by boosting employees' socioemotional resources. However, the culturally embedded evaluations of humor as private versus public (or shared) may trigger divergent effects in Eastern versus Western contexts, since these forces alter humor's status as a resource.

In the East, for example, Chinese people report using less humor to cope with stress (Chen & Martin, 2007), even though this coping strategy is an internal process completely invisible to others. Indeed, shared humor in more formal contexts such as classrooms may be associated with more – not less – stress and anxiety (Zhang, 2005). However, in the West, psychoanalysts such as Sigmund Freud (1905) have long proclaimed the broad-reaching stress-reduction functions of humor as a defense mechanism to reject reality and protect oneself from suffering. Indeed, many studies have argued and shown that humor is associated with less tension and lower stress in Western workplaces (e.g., Lang & Lee, 2010). For these reasons, humor may be perceived more positively, and thus may also be a more effective leadership tool in the West than in the East via these stress-reduction processes.

Finally, the third function of humor refers to its ability to increase positive emotions, based on the broaden-and-build theory. In this framework, Fredrickson (2004) highlights the potential of positive emotions in expanding people's creativity and openness. Because positive attitudes and humor tend to breed more of the same, leaders then can trigger more positive emotions in their employees by using humor (Cooper et al., 2018) while also stimulating their employees' creativity and productivity (Cooper, 2008; Huang, Gino & Galinsky, 2015). However, the culturally embedded evaluations of humor as distracting versus facilitative may trigger divergent effects in Eastern versus Western contexts, as these forces may alter the valence of emotions that humor incites.

For example, Chinese undergraduates tend to associate humor with negative adjectives (e.g., unpleasantness), whereas the opposite is true for American undergraduates (e.g., pleasantness; Jiang, Que & Lu, 2011). These patterns are apparent long before ever entering the workplace, since Chinese children already link humor to negative connotations and motivations such as aggression and disruption (Chen, Rubin & Sun, 1992). In contrast, Freud (1928) vocally propagated humor as a powerful and effective defense mechanism against negative emotions, thereby facilitating everyday life at home *and* at work. For these reasons, humor may be perceived more positively, and thus may also be a more effective leadership tool in the West than in the East via these emotion-based processes.

For a review, we juxtapose China (i.e., the East) and the West (i.e., most often relying on studies from the US, as well as philosophers and psychoanalysts from Europe), with a brief summary of each of the three dominant theories of humor in Figure 8.1.

	BACK GROUND	SOCIAL EXCHANGE	STRESS RELIEF	POSITIVE EMOTION
CHINA	A man has to be serious to be respected. Liao, 2007	Proper humor is private. Xu, 2011	Useless humor to cope with stress. Chen and Martin, 2005	Humor is associated with seriousness and unpleasantness. Jiang et al, 2011
WEST	Natural expression of amusement, fun and delight. Grant, 1924/1970	Humorous leaders are more socially desirable. Allport, 1961	Humor relieves stress. Freud, 1950/1960	Humor removes negative emotions. Freud, 1928

Figure 8.1: A Cross-Cultural Comparison of Humor from Three Theoretical Perspectives.

Is Leader Humor Effective Across Cultures?

After reviewing major differences in the use of and perception of humor between the East and the West, a critical question remains. Is humor a useful tool for global leadership across cultures? Lay beliefs and research suggest that leaders in the West who use humor tend to be charismatic. But is leader humor effective in the East? Some suggest that it is not. Yang and colleagues (2017), for example, cautioned against "the blind adaption or convergence of leader behaviors (e.g., humor)." To answer this question, we turn to benign violation theory (BVT) to understand what makes things funny in the first place (McGraw & Warren, 2010).

Benign violation theory (BVT) makes three interrelated predictions about the generation of humor. First, a norm violation must occur. The violation can be physical (e.g., tickling someone), symbolic (e.g., sarcasm), or linguistic (e.g., puns). Second, the violation must be perceived as benign. For example, tickling quickly turns weird or even offensive if the target is not a close friend or a loved one; jokes that violate gender norms might offend others. Third, the first two conditions must occur simultaneously, otherwise humor is lost in translation (McGraw & Warren, 2010). Critically, McGraw and colleagues suggested that BTV should apply cross-culturally. Yet, humor is always said to be in the eye of the beholder. We suggest that the East and the West differ on the second critical dimension of BVT – namely, what constitutes a malign versus a benign norm violation.

For example, in the West, dirty jokes are relatively common and constitute benign norm violation and are hence funny (especially among men). The same dirty jokes, however, are considered malign in the East where talking about sex, even in the form of jokes, is often considered a taboo. Similarly, it is common for Westerners to make jokes toward disgraceful political figures whereas it is obviously a taboo among many Easterners who tend to endorse the collective and authority in society. All in all, it is not whether leader humor works or not in global leadership, but *how* it is being used. No one would expect the same jokes to be funny to both Westerners and Easterners, but the effectiveness of leader humor should hold across cultures.

In one study where followers could freely conceptualize what constitutes leader humor behaviors, they rated the leader as higher on leader-member exchange and reported greater work engagement when the leader often used humor at work in both China and the United States (Yam et al., 2018). Likewise, in another study with a similar research methodology, followers again rated humorous leaders as more likeable in both China and the United States (Yam et al., 2019). Although cross-cultural comparisons on the effective use of leader humor are limited, extant research does provide preliminary support to the proposition that leader use of humor can be an effective tool for successful global leadership. With these findings in mind, we offer the following broad recommendations for leaders who manage culturally-diverse teams:

1. Leaders must be mindful of the cultural norms of different group members. Avoid violations of sensitive norms (even in the most benign way) such as politics in China or sexuality in the Middle East.
2. Humor should only be used with close subordinates in the East as norm violations are more likely to be viewed as benign when the violator shares a close relationship with the perceiver, whereas it can be useful toward most subordinates in the West.
3. Humor directed toward younger subordinates might be more effective in the East than their older counterparts, due to globalization and cultural convergence.
4. Differences in the receptivity of humor might be greater between industries than between cultures. For example, start-ups and tech firms might have a more playful culture (partly due to a greater number of younger employees) compared to other more established industries (such as government agencies, consulting firms, and so on).

Conclusion

It is ever more important for the increasingly boundary-less leaders of global businesses to take caution when using humor in mixed cultural company or in an entirely different culture. Although humor is often touted as a reliable tool for effective leadership, various cultural forces – three of which we have reviewed here – may meaningfully alter employees' humor appreciation and the effects of leaders' humor. However, as with many social group comparisons, the focus is often on differences than on similarities. Thus, we also caution readers and leaders from overinterpreting the suggestions we highlighted here, because there is often more diversity within – rather than between – groups, including the East and the West (see Gelfand & Denison, 2020; Lu, Nisbett & Morris, 2020). Overall, we do believe that humor can be an effective tool for a global leader, if the leader possesses cultural intelligence and uses humor under the right contexts, with the right people, and at the right time.

References

Allport, G. W. (1961). *Pattern and Growth in Personality*. Holt: Reinhart & Winston.

Bremmer, J. N. (1997). Jokes, jokers and jokebooks in Ancient Greek culture. *A Cultural History of Humor*, 11–28.

Burns, J. F. (2009). Shoe is thrown at Chinese premier. *The New York Times*. Retrieved from: www.nytimes.com/2009/02/03/world/asia/03shoe.html

Chen, G.-H. & Martin, R. A. (2007). A comparison of humor styles, coping humor, and mental health between Chinese and Canadian university students. *Humor – International Journal of Humor Research*, *20*(3), 215–234.

Chen, X., Rubin, K. H. & Sun, Y. (1992). Social reputation and peer relationships in Chinese and Canadian children: A cross-cultural study. *Child Development*, *63*(6), 1336–1343.

Cooper, C. D. (2004). Did you hear the one about humor and leadership? A field study of supervisor humor and leader–member exchange quality. *Academy of Management Proceedings*.

Cooper, C. D. (2008). Elucidating the bonds of workplace humor: A relational process model. *Human Relations*, *61*(8), 1087–1115.

Cooper, C. D., Kong, D. T. & Crossley, C. D. (2018). Leader humor as an interpersonal resource: integrating three theoretical perspectives. *Academy of Management Journal*, 769–796.

Cropanzano, R., & Mitchell, M (2005). Social Exchange Theory: An Interdisciplinary Review. Journal of Management, 31, 874–900.

Decker, W. H. (1987). Managerial humor and subordinate satisfaction. *Social Behavior and Personality: An International Journal*, *15*(2), 225–232

Decker, W. H. & Rotondo, D. M. (2001). Relationships among gender, type of humor, and perceived leader effectiveness. *Journal of Managerial Issues*, 450–465.

Eid, M. & Diener, E. (2001). Norms for experiencing emotions in different cultures: Inter- and intranational differences. *Journal of Personality and Social Psychology*, 869–885.

Fredrickson, B. L. (2004). The broaden-and-build theory of positive emotions. *The Royal Society*, *359*, 1367–1378.

Freud, S. (1905). *Der Witz und seine Beziehung zum Unbewussten*. Wien: Internationl Psychoanalytic University.

Freud, S. (1928). Humor. *The International Journal of Psychoanalysis*.

Gelfand, M. J. & Denison, E. E. (2020). Moving beyond the West vs. the rest: Understanding variation within Asian groups and its societal consequences. *Proceedings of the National Academy of Sciences, 117*(1), 5100–5102.

Grant, M. A. (1980). *The Ancient Rhetorical Theories of the Laughable: The Greek Rhetoricians and Cicero*. U.M.I.

Guess, D. C. (2004). Decision making in individualistic and collectivistic cultures. *General Psychological Issues in Cultural Perspective, 4*(1).

Hobfoll, S. E. (1989). Conservation of resources: A new attempt at conceptualizing stress. *The American Psychologist, 44*, 513–524.

Hofstede, G., Hofstede, G. J. & Minkov, M. (2010). *Cultures and Organizations: Software of the Mind*. New York: McGraw-Hill.

Homans, G. C. (1958). Social behavior as exchange. *American Journal of Sociology, 63*, 597–606.

Huang, L., Gino, F. & Galinsky, A. D. (2015). The highest form of intelligence: Sarcasm increases creativity for both expressers and recipients. Or*ganizational Behavior and Human Decision Processes, 131*, 162–177.

Jiang, F., Que, X. D. & Lu, S. (2011). Different attitudes toward humor between Chinese and American students: Evidence from the Implicit Association Test. *Psychological Reports, 109*(1), 99–107.

Jiang, T., Li, H. & Hou, Y. (2019). Cultural Differences in Humor Perception, Usage, and Implications. *Frontiers Psychology, 10*, 123.

Lang, J. C. & Lee, C. H. (2010). Workplace humor and organizational creativity. *The International Journal of Human Resource Management, 21*(1), 46–60.

Liao, C.-c. (2007). One aspect of Taiwanese and American sense of humour: attitudes toward pranks. *Internation Journal of Research in Humanities, 2*, 25–46.

Lin, L., Ho, Y. & Lin, W. E. (2013). Confucian and Taoist work values: An exploratory study of the chinese transformational leadership behavior. *Journal of Business Ethics, 113*, 91–103.

Lu, J. G., Nisbett, R. E. & Morris, M. W. (2020). Why East Asians but not South Asians are underrepresented in leadership positions in the United States. *Proceedings of the National Academy of Sciences, 117*(9), 4590–4600.

Myers, S. L. & Rubin, A. J. (2008). Iraqi journalist hurls shoes at Bush and denounces him on TV as a "dog." *The New York Times*. Retrieved December 2008, from: www.nytimes.com/2008/12/15/world/middleeast/15prexy.html.

McGraw, P., & Warren, C. (2010). Benign violations: Making immoral behavior funny. Psychological Science, 21, 1141–1149.

Priest, R. F. & Swain, J. E. (2002). Humor and its implications for leadership effectiveness. *Humor – International Journal of Humor Research, 15*(2), 169–189.

Romero, E. J. & Cruthirds, K. W. (2006). The use of humor in the workplace. *Academy of Management Perspectives, 20*(2), 58–69.

Unteregger, F. (2019). Funny Business "insights from comedy". Zürich.

Wachturm. (2001). *Die Suche der Menschheit nach Gott*. Wachturm-Gesellschaft.

Wang, J., Wang, G. G., Ruona, W. E. & Rojewski, J. W. (2005). Confucian values and the implications for internationl HRD. *Human Resource Development International, 83*(3), 311–326.

Xu, W. (2011). The classical Confucian concepts of human emotion and proper humour. *Humour in Chinese Life and Letters*.

Yam, K. C., Barnes, C., Leavitt, K., Wei, W., Lau, T. C. & Uhlmann, E. (2019). Why so serious? A laboratory and field investigation of the link between morality and humor. *Journal of Personality and Social Psychology, 117*, 758–772.

Yam, K. C., Christian, M., Wei, W., Liao, Z. & Nai, J. (2018). The mixed blessing of leader sense of humor: Examining costs and benefits. *Academy of Management Journal*, *61*, 348–369.

Yang, I., Kitchen, P. J. & Bacouel-Jentjens, S. (2015). How to promote relationship-building leadership at work? A comparative exploration of leader humor behavior between North America and China. *The International Journal of Human Resource Management*, *28*(10), 1454–1474.

Yang, I., Kitchen, P. J. & Bacouel-Jentjens, S. (2017). How to promote relationship-building leadership at work? A comparative exploration of leader humor behavior between North America and China. *The International Journal of Human Resource Management*, *28*. 1454–1474.

Yue, X. D. (2010). Exploration of Chinese humor: Historical review, empirical findings, and critical reflections. *International Journal of Humor Research*, *23*(3), 403–420.

Yue, X. D. (2011). The Chinese ambivalence to humor: Views from undergraduates in Hong Kong and China. *International Journal of Humor Research*, *24*(4), 463–480.

Zhang, Q. (2005). Immediacy, humor, power distance, and classroom communication apprehension in Chinese college classrooms. *Communication Quarterly*, *53*(1), 109–124.

Sandy Lim and Jingxian Yao
Chapter 9
The Role of Leaders in Shaping a Civil and Respectful Workplace

To keep up with today's fast-growing, ever-changing and competitive economy, organizations have increasingly focused on how to improve speed and efficiency and benchmark their performance. To this end, organizations have attempted to equip their workers with up-to-date skill sets, emphasized radical innovation that helps to save costs or enhance productivity, adopted new communication channels such as social media platforms and smartphone applications, and integrated artificial intelligence tools to assist in decision making (Gordon, 2013; MacCormick, Dery & Kolb, 2012; O'Leary, 2013; Zhou & Li, 2012). Asian countries are generally at a higher rate of economic growth and information technology adoption, and thus are likely to engage in the aforementioned endeavors to a larger extent. Despite the evident benefits or potential values of these approaches to the bottom line, an overemphasis on speed and efficiency has caused the "human touch" to decline in organizational communications or processes. For example, instead of making the effort to greet and engage in face-to-face interactions with coworkers, employees may prefer to send an abrupt email or text message to get things done quickly. This is compounded by the urge to multi-task in order to save time (e.g., sending text messages to others during meetings).

As a result, important values such as respect and civility appear to be eroding in the workplace. Indeed, Cortina et al. (2001) found that more than 70 percent of employees have experienced workplace incivility, defined as "low-intensity deviant behavior with ambiguous intent to harm the target, in violation of workplace norms for mutual respect" (Andersson & Pearson, 1999). Thirty percent workers in the United States reported being bullied (i.e., belittled, humiliated or threatened) at work (U.S. Workplace Bullying Survey, 2021). Similar disrespectful behaviors have also become rising problems in Asia, with 77 percent of employees identifying themselves as targets of uncivil behaviors (Yeung & Griffin, 2008).

The prevalence of uncivil and disrespectful behaviors in the workplace is disturbing, especially with a growing body of evidence over the past two decades showing that being treated uncivilly and disrespectfully leads to negative work and personal outcomes (e.g., Hershcovis, 2011; Schilpzand, De Pater & Erez, 2016). As such, it seems that a narrow focus on promoting bottom-line performance may yield an unwanted byproduct – an unfriendly and disrespectful work environment – that can backfire to impair organizational functioning and thriving.

https://doi.org/10.1515/9783110671988-009

Leaders in organizations play an important role in shaping a civil and respectful workplace. However, more often than not, leaders themselves are caught up with the organizational pursuit for speed and efficiency in a never-ending bid to increase productivity and competitiveness. It is thus not surprising that organizational research has tended to focus on bottom-line performance as a key indicator of effective leadership (Lieberson & O-Connor, 1972; Wang, Tsui & Xin, 2011). While the focus on economic gain is important, we argue that a good leader should also create a conducive social environment for employees in order to sustain the long-term growth and functionality of the organization. When interpersonal civility is sacrificed for speed and efficiency, employees develop many negative reactions, including increased intentions to quit and counterproductive work behaviors (Boswell & Olson-Buchanan, 2004; Rahim & Cosby, 2016; Sliter, Sliter & Jex, 2012), such that any immediate economic gain becomes short-term and unsustainable. Leaders, with their formal positions and personal influences in the workplace, are in a particularly powerful position to discourage uncivil and disrespectful behaviors. Such efforts are necessary to inculcate the right values and attitudes in employees so that the appropriate norms are set in place to sustain the long-term health of the organization.

Unfortunately, incivility seems prevalent not just in Western cultures where individual rights and freedom of expression are encouraged, but also in Asian societies where social harmony is valued (e.g., Lim & Lee, 2011; Li & Lim, 2017). This suggests that different values characterizing Western and Eastern cultures might serve to promote and sustain uncivil behaviors in different ways. Consequently, measures used to reduce incivility and promote civility have to be adapted to the cultural context in order for them to work effectively.

In this chapter, we introduce some of these nuances to guide leaders in building a respectful and supportive workplace. First, we review the existing literature and reveal some of the most common consequences of incivility and disrespectful behaviors. We then highlight the important role of leaders and explain a number of ways through which leaders can counter uncivil behaviors. Next, we illustrate the cultural differences between Western and Eastern cultures with regard to how these behaviors take place and how people respond to uncivil treatment. Taking the cultural nuances of the incivility phenomenon into consideration, we conclude by discussing how leaders in Western and Eastern cultures can focus on some differential and unique aspects of the cultural context when they attempt to create a civil and respectful environment.

The Negative Consequences of Incivility and Disrespectful Behaviors

Experiences of uncivil and disrespectful treatment trigger affective, cognitive, attitudinal and behavioral responses that are generally detrimental for both employees themselves and their organizations. Over the last two decades, scholars have widely examined and substantiated the harmful impact of incivility, particularly on its victims (e.g., Hershcovis, 2011; Schilpzand, De Pater & Erez, 2016). We recently conducted a meta-analysis to synthesize this body of research comprehensively by including a large number of empirical studies and examining the most commonly studied outcomes in the existing literature (Yao, Lim, Guo, Ou, & Ng, in press). Our findings clearly show that experiencing incivility has negative implications on a wide range of work-related outcomes. For example, employees who are treated uncivilly tend to reduce their effort at work and display lower productivity. When employees experience uncivil and disrespectful treatment, they become less satisfied with their job, less committed to their organization and more inclined to quit. As such, the failure to cultivate a conducive and civil social environment may leave organizations with less motivated and loyal employees. In more severe cases, employees may retaliate against their experiences of mistreatment by engaging in deviant behaviors, such as sabotaging organizational properties, disclosing business secrets or cheating in work tasks, all of which are costly to organizations.

Beyond work outcomes, our research also suggests that employees' personal well-being suffers when they are treated uncivilly. In particular, they can experience a whole range of negative emotions such as anger, anxiety and sadness (e.g., Lim et al., 2018) after being disrespected. When such experiences accumulate over time, their psychological and physical well-being will likely take a turn for the worse. These include experiencing symptoms of anxiety and depression, as well as somatic health issues and illnesses (e.g., Lim et al., 2008). When employees' health suffers, organizational functioning will eventually be negatively impacted because of reduced productivity, increased sick leave, unanticipated disruptions to work operations and a higher risk of workplace accidents.

Although most uncivil and disrespectful acts in organizations appear minor and of low intensity (thus are seemingly not so serious), they can, in fact, escalate to more severe mistreatment and become collective and normative. In Andersson and Pearson's (1999) terms, this escalation process is called "the spiralling effect of incivility in the workplace." When small incidents of incivility and rudeness accumulate, they may evolve to more deliberate, aggressive or even physically violent forms of mistreatment, especially when it involves tit-for-tat revenge between people. Moreover, if various forms of interpersonal mistreatment are not suppressed in time and spiral out of control, the organization as a whole may become an uncivil entity (Kamp & Brooks, 1991). In that case, uncivil and disrespectful behaviors become a collective action and a norm, and employees, being both instigators and victims of mistreatment, will suffer even more severe work and health consequences.

The Role of Leaders in Countering Incivility and Disrespectful Behaviors

Given the detrimental consequences of incivility, it is essential for organizations and their leaders to address such problematic behaviors and shape a civil and respectful workplace. In particular, with their legitimate reward and sanction power as well as personal influence, leaders are at a powerful position and play a key role in curbing interpersonal misbehaviors. Even with the high demand for speed and efficiency in today's business world, a good leader should not only pursue bottom-line performance and immediate economic gains, but also utilize their unique capabilities to cultivate a conducive social environment. They can do so in a number of ways.

First, leaders can serve as role models who treat their subordinates respectfully. From a social learning perspective (Bandura & Walters, 1977), individuals capture and interpret cues from their social environment to understand the desirability of certain behaviors. In the organizational context, a convenient and straightforward way of social learning is to mimic the behaviors of leaders at higher levels of the organizational hierarchy. Employees tend to follow their leaders' behaviors, with the belief that similar behaviors will be appreciated by leaders. Research has widely examined such trickle-down processes and found that ethical, servant and justice-oriented leadership exert positive influence on employees and trigger their ethical behaviors, service performance and adherence to fairness, respectively (Frazier & Tupper, 2018; Masterson, 2001; Mayer et al., 2009). Applying the notion of trickle-down processes to the context of interpersonal behaviors, we expect that leaders who treat their subordinates with dignity and respect will promote positive social interactions among employees, whereas rude and abusive leaders will result in the prevalence of uncivil behaviors. In support, Mawritz et al. (2012) found that abusive supervision by managers and team leaders was related to increased interpersonal deviance of team members. Hence, in order to minimize incivility and disrespectful behaviors, leaders should behave respectfully themselves and serve as role models for employees.

Second, leaders have the power and resources to establish policies against incivility, reward appropriate behaviors and sanction uncivil conduct. Scholars have called for formalized organizational policies that detail norms and regulations for interpersonal behaviors (Ferris, Chen & Lim, 2017; Lim, Cortina & Magley, 2008; Skarlicki & Kulik, 2004). Specifically, existing monetary rewards for task performance or task-related behaviors should be supplemented by policies that regulate social behaviors. After organizational-level policies are in place, leaders at different levels will need to actively monitor and consistently reinforce the relevant rewards and sanctions. The successful implementation of these policies links employees' interpersonal behaviors closely with rewards or sanctions. To achieve this, leaders must make the rewards and sanctions explicit and clearly attributable to interpersonal behaviors. The rewards and sanctions for employees must also be timely to achieve its intended effect. Managers and team leaders should also assess the efficacy of the measures periodically and seek to improve these policies when necessary.

Third, leaders can promote respectful norms more implicitly by providing employees with subtle cues for social learning. In addition to directly modeling leaders' behaviors, employees may also observe how leaders react to them or other subordinates' behaviors and understand whether certain behaviors are desired or frowned upon by leaders (James et al., 1978). When leaders give verbal acknowledgment to employees who are respectful to others, or simply become more approving of such employees, they send cues signaling that civility is encouraged.

Last but not least, leaders must be mindful not to become incivility instigators. The power possessed by leaders is a double-edged sword – it is an effective tool to counter uncivil conduct, but also makes employees more vulnerable when they are mistreated by leaders. Indeed, when employees experience uncivil mistreatment by their leaders, they are less willing and less able to strike back and may choose to suffer the mistreatment in silence (Tavanti, 2011). The inability of employees to defend themselves against their leaders, coupled with the notion that people conveniently select less powerful people to direct their mistreatment (Cortina, Rabelo & Holland, 2018), highlights an unfortunate situation in which leaders readily display uncivil behaviors to their vulnerable subordinates. Hence, to cultivate a positive social environment, leaders should not only devote attention to incivility and disrespectful behaviors among employees, but also be mindful not to abuse their power and become instigators of mistreatment themselves.

Taken together, leaders play a key role in countering interpersonal mistreatment and cultivating civil and respectful interpersonal behaviors among employees, primarily by serving as role models, establishing and executing formalized policies, accrediting positive interpersonal behaviors informally, and avoiding the misuse of power and the convenient choice of subordinates as targets of mistreatment.

Cultural Differences in Incivility and Disrespectful Behaviors

The preceding discussions on the phenomenon of incivility and disrespectful behaviors, as well as the ways through which leaders can counter these behaviors, are relevant to most cultures. However, given the significant cultural differences around the globe and the important roles of cultural influences on people's social perceptions and behaviors (Bond, 2004; Cohen, 1998; Smith and Bond, 1999), understanding the cultural nuances in incivility and disrespectful behaviors are essential for scholars and practitioners alike. Even within a local context, the growing number of multinational companies and the increasing ethnic diversity in the workforce require organizations and their leaders to understand how the dynamics of interpersonal mistreatment vary across cultures (Li & Lim, 2017). Unfortunately, the vast majority of research in this area has been conducted in the Western context. This, coupled with the trend that many Asian countries, including China, India, Korea, Japan and Singapore, are becoming increasingly influential economies in the world, highlights an unfortunate gap in understanding how workplace incivility in the Western context is different from that in the Eastern context. In this chapter, we discuss several important aspects of such cultural nuances, focusing on individualism as a potential driver of uncivil conduct in the Western context and power distance as a potential driver in the Eastern context, and different manifestations of and response to uncivil behaviors (i.e., active or passive forms) across the two cultures.

Western individualistic cultures emphasize self-identity and place less importance on social awareness and the development and maintenance of interpersonal bonds with others (Schwartz, 1990). Therefore, in Western organizations, employees tend to see themselves as independent individuals, downplay their identity as a team or organizational members and are less attentive in social interactions. Although it is not necessary that employees intend to disregard or harm others, they may act in more self-centred, disrespectful, and inconsiderate manners due to a lower need to demonstrate social cohesion. As such, individualism may be an important underlying cause of incivility and disrespectful behaviors in the Western context. In support, Liu et al. (2009) found that collectivism, as a cultural value opposite of individualism, predicted lower workplace incivility.

In addition, when employees from Western cultures conduct uncivil behaviors, these behaviors are likely to take active and explicit forms. This is because they tend to express themselves in direct ways (Kim et al., 2010) and because they feel less awkward about engaging in explicit conflicts with others. One potential problem with direct and explicit interpersonal conflicts is that if these conflicts are not managed timely and properly and evolve with retaliatory acts, they may escalate to serious problems and cause hostility and resentment among employees.

Asian collective cultures seem to inhibit incivility by highlighting the collective self and norms of interpersonal harmony, yet research has shown that incivility is also prevalent in the Asian context (Lim & Lee, 2011). Therefore, there may be some characteristics in the Asian culture that potentially foster uncivil conduct. Power distance, which refers to the acceptance of power asymmetry among individuals (Hofstede, Hofstede & Minkov, 2010), is such a characteristic and particularly promotes uncivil behaviors by organizational members toward their counterparts with lower power. Many Western cultures such as the US are characterized by low power distance, thus employees expect to be treated with equal respect and dignity regardless of the power and status of the other party. In contrast, many Asian cultures such as Japan and Singapore are characterized by high power distance, and as such, employees are more likely to internalize disrespectful and aggressive behaviors of powerholders (e.g., leaders) as normative and become more acceptive and less confrontational toward these behaviors (House et al., 2004). Lending support to this argument, Lian et al. (2012)

showed that the relationship between experienced abusive supervision and perceived interpersonal injustice was mitigated by power distance orientation, such that when compared to their counterparts with lower power distance orientation, employees with higher power distance orientation regarded leader-to-subordinate mistreatment as more acceptable and perceived lower interpersonal injustice subsequent to experiencing abusive supervision. In a similar vein, Vogel et al. (2015) conducted a country-level examination and found that employees in Asian cultures (Singapore and Taiwan), as compared to those in Western cultures (the United States and Australia), were less reactive to abusive supervision. From the perspective of leaders, because their disrespectful and aggressive behaviors toward subordinates are widely accepted, they may spend less effort in regulating their negative interpersonal behaviors and care less about treating their subordinates with dignity and respect.

Although this discussion mainly concerns formal power in organizations and leader-subordinate relationships, there is a wider range of indicators of informal power that may also make the powerless party vulnerable to mistreatment and free the powerful party of the need to regulate their interpersonal behaviors. Such indicators of informal power include gender, race, tenure, expertise and even proximity to formal authorities (Berger, Cohen & Zelditch Jr, 1972; Zhang, Waldman & Wang, 2012). Given the abundant cues through which employees can generate power and status evaluations and consequently adjust their interpersonal attitudes and behaviors (i.e., aggressive for the powerful and submissive for the powerless), it is possible that incivility driven by power distance is rather prevalent in the Asian context.

In contrast to employees from Western cultures who conduct uncivil behaviors and respond to them in active and direct forms, employees from Asian cultures are likely to behave in passive and indirect forms. This is largely due to the high importance placed on saving face and maintaining harmony in Asian cultures (Xu & Huang, 2012). The passive and indirect behavioral patterns seemingly help to prevent the escalation of disrespectful behaviors to intense conflicts; however, the superficial harmony resulting from these behavioral patterns may create an illusion that there is no issue with the social environment. In this case, leaders may be less attentive to the occurrence of incivility and disrespectful behaviors and the victims who have suffered from these behaviors. As a result, the issue of interpersonal deviance may be hidden and left unresolved, thereby resulting in lingering negative consequences on employees' work and health.

Cultural-Specific Leadership against Incivility and Disrespectful Behaviors

The cultural differences driving incivility and disrespectful behaviors offer leaders useful insights on how to counter them in a specific cultural context. In the Western context, leaders can focus on nurturing collective identity and goals to counter individualistic behaviors that show disrespect to others, as well as dedicating efforts to prevent the escalation of minor uncivil conduct to severe conflicts. As outlined earlier, leaders can do so by serving as role models and providing implicit cues for social learning. Policies discouraging uncivil interactions can be introduced into organizational training protocols early in the socialization process of new employees and built into existing regulations so that leaders can intervene early, before minor forms of uncivil interactions or interpersonal conflicts among employees spiral out of control. For example, in parallel to performance goals, organizations may specify protocols of interpersonal behaviors that specifically inhibit rudeness, exclusion and aggression among employees.

In the Asian context, leaders should be aware that organizations characterized by high power distance can easily become nesting grounds for incivility to take place. To curb this, several measures can be put in place. First, there is a need to caution leaders against the abuse of power. In collectivistic societies where power distance is high, deviant or abusive behaviors that originate from more powerful individuals are likely to be tolerated by silent victims, giving rise to a superficial impression of harmony within the organization. Channels should be created so that abusive behaviors from higher-ranking employees can be safely reported and sanctioned (e.g., via independent third parties). Management workshops may be given by external trainers to enhance leaders' self-consciousness of their interpersonal behaviors. Second, it will be useful for leaders to bear in mind a set of indicators of informal power beyond formal rank (e.g., gender, majority versus minority) and focus on the occurrence of incivility between power-imbalanced parties. Close attention should be paid to indirect and passive forms of disrespectful behaviors because they can easily be brushed aside as unintentional or seemingly harmless acts. These organizational interventions are particularly important in the Asian context, because high power distance cultures may often normalize disrespectful behaviors toward junior employees. However, organizations should be cautious about the potential downsides of "overcorrecting" interpersonal behaviors, such as discouraging formal or informal power holders from giving constructive criticism. There is thus a need for organizations to draw a clear line between negative (yet sensible) feedback and interpersonal disrespect.

Concluding Thoughts

In this chapter, we have focused on some key cultural differences between many Western and Asian cultures and have highlighted the areas that leaders can pay attention to when working with different cultures. However, this is not to say that all individuals in the West are highly individualistic or that high power distance exists in all organizations in the East. On the contrary, a great amount of diversity exists in most cultures, and it is important to observe the interpersonal dynamics in each cultural setting and test one's assumptions before attempting any interventions.

Notwithstanding, good leaders in the East are those who know how to refrain from abusing their power and have learned how to detect and address interpersonal mistreatment in the workplace. Many organizations, irrespective of their geographic location, are characterized by high power distance (e.g., uniformed services, health-care) and suffer from practices that tolerate incivility, especially when the perpetrators are top performers and higher-ranking employees. Dealing with such challenges is not easy but is necessary, and we believe that lessons learned from addressing these issues can offer valuable insights to managers around the globe.

References

Andersson, L. M. & Pearson, C. M. (1999). Tit for tat? The spiraling effect of incivility in the workplace. *Academy of Management Review*, *24*(3), 452–471.

Bandura, A. & Walters, R. H. (1977). Social learning theory (Vol. 1). Prentice-Hall (Englewood Cliffs, NJ).

Berger, J., Cohen, B. P. & Zelditch Jr, M. (1972). Status characteristics and social interaction. *American Sociological Review*, *37*(3), 241–255.

Bond, M. H. (2004). Culture and aggression – From context to coercion. *Personality and Social Psychology Review*, *8*(1), 62–78.

Boswell, W. R., Olson-Buchanan, J. B. & LePine, M. A. (2004). Relations between stress and work outcomes: The role of felt challenge, job control, and psychological strain. *Journal of Vocational Behavior*, *64*(1), 165–181.

Cohen, D. (1998). Culture, social organization, and patterns of violence. *Journal of Personality and Social Psychology*, *75*(2), 408–419.

Cortina, L. M., Magley, V. J., Williams, J. H. & Langhout, R. D. (2001). Incivility in the workplace: Incidence and impact. *Journal of Occupational Health Psychology*, *6*(1), 64–80.

Cortina, L. M., Rabelo, V. C. & Holland, K. J. (2018). Beyond blaming the victim: Toward a more progressive understanding of workplace mistreatment. *Industrial and Organizational Psychology*, *11*(1), 81–100.

Hershcovis, M. S. (2011). "Incivility, social undermining, bullying . . . oh my!": A call to reconcile constructs within workplace aggression research. *Journal of Organizational Behavior*, *32*(3), 499–519.

Ferris, D. L., Chen, M. & Lim, S. (2017). Comparing and contrasting workplace ostracism and incivility. *Annual Review of Organizational Psychology and Organizational Behavior*, *4*(1), 315–338.

Frazier, M. L. & Tupper, C. (2018). Supervisor prosocial motivation, employee thriving, and helping behavior: A trickle-down model of psychological safety. *Group & Organization Management*, *43*(4), 561–593.

Gordon, E. E. (2013). Future jobs: Solving the employment and skills crisis: Solving the employment and skills crisis. ABC-CLIO.

Hofstede, G. H., Hofstede, G. J. & Minkov, M. (Eds.). (2010). Cultures and organizations: Software for the mind. McGraw-Hill (New York, NY).

House, R. J., Hanges, P. J., Javidan, M., Dorfman, P. W. & Gupta, V. (Eds.). (2004). Culture, leadership, and organizations: The GLOBE study of 62 societies. Sage Publications.

James, L. R., Hater, J. J., Gent, M. J. & Bruni, J. R. (1978). Psychological climate: Implications from cognitive social learning theory and interactional psychology. *Personnel Psychology, 31*(4), 783–813.

Kamp, J. & Brooks, P. (1991). Perceived organizational climate and employee counterproductivity. *Journal of Business and Psychology, 5*(4), 447–458.

Kim, Y. H., Chiu, C. Y., Peng, S., Cai, H. & Tov, W. (2010). Explaining East-West differences in the likelihood of making favorable self-evaluations: The role of evaluation apprehension and directness of expression. *Journal of Cross-Cultural Psychology, 41*(1), 62–75.

Li, X. & Lim, S. (2017). Cross-cultural differences in workplace aggression. In *Research and Theory on Workplace Aggression*. (Eds.). Bowling, N. A. & Hershcovis, M. S., pp. 245–268. Cambridge University Press.

Lian, H., Ferris, D. L. & Brown, D. J. (2012). Does power distance exacerbate or mitigate the effects of abusive supervision? It depends on the outcome. *Journal of Applied Psychology, 97*(1), 107–123.

Lieberson, S. & O'Connor, J. F. (1972). Leadership and organizational performance: A study of large corporations. *American Sociological Review, 37*(2), 117–130.

Lim, S., Cortina, L. M. & Magley, V. J. (2008). Personal and workgroup incivility: impact on work and health outcomes. *Journal of Applied Psychology, 93*(1), 95–107.

Lim, S., Ilies, R., Koopman, J., Christoforou, P. & Arvey, R. D. (2018). Emotional mechanisms linking incivility at work to aggression and withdrawal at home: An experience-sampling study. *Journal of Management, 44*(7), 2888–2908.

Lim, S. & Lee, A. (2011). Work and nonwork outcomes of workplace incivility: Does family support help?. *Journal of Occupational Health Psychology, 16*(1), 95–111.

Liu, W., Steve Chi, S. C., Friedman, R. & Tsai, M. H. (2009). Explaining incivility in the workplace: The effects of personality and culture. *Negotiation and Conflict Management Research, 2*(2), 164–184.

MacCormick, J. S., Dery, K. & Kolb, D. G. (2012). Engaged or just connected? Smartphones and employee engagement. *Organizational Dynamics, 41*(3), 194–201.

Masterson, S. S. (2001). A trickle-down model of organizational justice: relating employees' and customers' perceptions of and reactions to fairness. *Journal of Applied Psychology, 86*(4), 594–604.

Mawritz, M. B., Mayer, D. M., Hoobler, J. M., Wayne, S. J. & Marinova, S. V. (2012). A trickle-down model of abusive supervision. *Personnel Psychology, 65*(2), 325–357.

Mayer, D. M., Kuenzi, M., Greenbaum, R., Bardes, M. & Salvador, R. B. (2009). How low does ethical leadership flow? Test of a trickle-down model. *Organizational Behavior and Human Decision Processes, 108*(1), 1–13.

O'Leary, D. E. (2013). Artificial intelligence and big data. *IEEE Intelligent Systems, 28*(2), 96–99.

Rahim, A. & Cosby, D. M. (2016). A model of workplace incivility, job burnout, turnover intentions, and job performance. *Journal of Management Development, 35*(10), 1255–1265.

Schilpzand, P., De Pater, I. E. & Erez, A. (2016). Workplace incivility: A review of the literature and agenda for future research. *Journal of Organizational Behavior, 37*, S57–S88.

Schwartz, S. H. (1990). Individualism-collectivism: Critique and proposed refinements. *Journal of Cross-Cultural Psychology, 21*(2), 139–157.

Skarlicki, D. P. & Kulik, C. T. (2004). Third-party reactions to employee (mis) treatment: A justice perspective. *Research in Organizational Behavior, 26*(1), 183–229.

Sliter, M., Sliter, K. & Jex, S. (2012). The employee as a punching bag: The effect of multiple sources of incivility on employee withdrawal behavior and sales performance. *Journal of Organizational Behavior, 33*(1), 121–139.

Smith, P. B. & Bond, M. H. (1999). Social psychology: Across cultures. Allyn & Bacon.

Tavanti, M. (2011). Managing toxic leaders: Dysfunctional patterns in organizational leadership and how to deal with them. *Human Resource Management*, *6*(1), 127–136.

U.S. Workplace Bullying Survey (2021). Retrieved from https://workplacebullying.org/wp-content/uploads/2021/03/2021-Full-Report.pdf

Vogel, R. M., Mitchell, M. S., Tepper, B. J., Restubog, S. L., Hu, C., Hua, W. & Huang, J. C. (2015). A cross-cultural examination of subordinates' perceptions of and reactions to abusive supervision. *Journal of Organizational Behavior*, *36*(5), 720–745.

Wang, H., Tsui, A. S. & Xin, K. R. (2011). CEO leadership behaviors, organizational performance, and employees' attitudes. *The Leadership Quarterly*, *22*(1), 92–105.

Xu, E. & Huang, X. 2012. Ostracism, Chinese style. In *Handbook of Chinese Organizational Behavior: Integrating Theory, Research and Practice* (Eds.). Huang, X. & Bond, M. H., pp. 258–271. Edward Elgar (Cheltenham, UK).

Yao, J., Lim, S., Guo, C. Y., Ou, A. Y. & Ng, J. W. X. (in press). Experienced incivility in the workplace: A meta-analytic review of its construct validity and nomological network. *Journal of Applied Psychology*.

Yeung, A. & Griffin, B. (2008). Workplace incivility: Does it matter in Asia? *People and Strategy*, *31*(3), 14–19.

Zhang, Z., Waldman, D. A. & Wang, Z. (2012). A multilevel investigation of leader–member exchange, informal leader emergence, and individual and team performance. *Personnel Psychology*, *65*(1), 49–78.

Zhou, K. Z. & Li, C. B. (2012). How knowledge affects radical innovation: Knowledge base, market knowledge acquisition, and internal knowledge sharing. *Strategic Management Journal*, *33*(9), 1090–1102.

Ke Michael Mai

Chapter 10
Crying Out Creativity via Asian Global Leadership

Creativity is just connecting things. When you ask creative people how they did something, they feel a little guilty because they didn't really do it, they just saw something. It seemed obvious to them after a while. — Steve Jobs, *The Next Insanely Great Thing*

Globally, creativity has been identified as an essential factor to facilitate economic growth and social reform at the macro level (Florida, 2004; Zhou & Shalley, 2011) and enhance individual performance and competitiveness at the micro level (Amabile, 1988, 1996; Oldham & Cummings, 1996; Zhou, 1998). We have witnessed the success of automobile giants, such as Ford and Tesla, and the accomplishments of the telecommunication firms, such as Cisco and Alcatel-Lucent Enterprise, as well as all the pioneering companies in the technology and IT industry, such as Apple and Google, in Silicon Valley. As you may have noticed, many of these drastic innovations incubated in the Western context. According to the Global Innovation Index (GII, 2019), a global index measuring the level of innovation of a country, produced jointly by Cornell University, INSEAD and the World Intellectual Property Organization (WIPO), US and European nations indeed dominate the top innovation ranking over the past five years, with only Singapore being the geographical outlier on the list.[1] However, the same report also pointed out that continuous innovation performance improvements are now primarily happening in Asia, catching up with North America and Europe.

Anecdotal evidence seems to provide us with support to such findings. In 1913, Henry Ford invented a modern, fast and efficient way to manufacture automobiles in America and roughly two decades later, Eiji Tyoda further refined and perfected his system. A series of innovators across the Western world developed the television – and the tech specialists at Sony, Toshiba and Samsung, along with a host of other Asian companies, found ways to make TVs better, cheaper and more efficient. Steve Jobs, iconic leader of technological invention, invented a company that made a phone smart in California, and computer engineer Lei Ju made the phone cheap, powerful and accessible to everyone in China. All this anecdotal evidence points to the pattern that although Asia may be the harbor of some of the world's most popular economies,

---

[1] Comparing with other Western nations on the top 10 list, such as, Switzerland (1st), the Netherlands (4th), and Sweden (2nd), effectively translate their innovation inputs into a higher level of outputs, Singapore (8th) produces lower levels of output relative to their innovation inputs (Global Innovation Index, 2019).

https://doi.org/10.1515/9783110671988-010

it is still not the incubator of the world's leading innovations and inventions. Lee Kuan Yew, the pioneer who designed and engineered the modern Singapore, once told *Time* (2013) that as the biggest economic entity in Asia, "China will inevitably catch up to the US in GDP, but its creativity may never match America's because its culture does not permit a free exchange and contest of ideas."

Although most of the economic entities in Asia are still behind Western peers, individual creativity and industry innovation are now necessary. This is because many Asian countries are suffering diminishing returns from capital investment, cheap labor and natural resources, and are having to re-evaluate economic growth strategies as a result. The transition from resource-driven, export-led economies to more sustainable growth models based on human capital development, new technology and innovation will be a key challenge for many Asian countries over the next decade.

In more advanced economies, long-term economic growth is ultimately sustained through innovation and creativity. Developing Asian countries must cultivate creativity and innovation if they are to achieve a sustainable high-income status.[2] So if creation is as easy as what Steve Jobs described in the opening quote, why are companies in Asian countries less likely to initiate the leading innovations and inventions? How can people in Asia be more creative? What does it take to lead employees in Asia to effectively generate creative outcomes? To answer these questions, we have to first take a look at what factors contribute to the creative output discrepancies between Eastern and Western countries.

Different Creativity Processes Across Diverse Cultures

For Nobel Laureate Albert Szent-Györgyi, "Discovery is seeing what everyone else has seen and thinking what no one else has thought." In the creativity literature, creativity has been understood as a process that results in ideas that are both *novel* and *useful* (Amabile, 1983). Novelty refers to a unique discovery in shape, process or composition and expresses an unusual state of uncommon effectiveness (Runco & Jaeger, 2012), while usefulness refers to the attachment of appropriateness, practical fit and thus its fundamental value (Amabile, 1988). Scholars have begun to examine the critical notion that an individual's creativity can be closely linked to the cultural

---

2 In the literature, innovation is traditionally defined as the successful implementation of creative ideas. Based on Ford (1996), creativity plays a critical role in the entire innovation process. Therefore, although I focused on creativity in the latter part of the chapter, similar to Ford's (1996) stance, I don't necessarily restrict creativity to any specific stage of innovation.

environment in which the individual is embedded (e.g., Lubart, 1990; Chiu & Kwan, 2010; De Dreu, 2010; Leung & Morris, 2010; Morris & Leung, 2010; Varsakelis, 2001; Wang, 2011). We can understand culture as a set of shared knowledge, values, norms and beliefs that shape a collective entity, such as a nation (Doney, Cannon, & Mullen, 1998) or an organization (Schein, 1990). It helps to further build the cognition and motivation and consequently help to answer to the question about how members within the entity should approach the creative process (Chiu & Kwan, 2010; Chua, Roth & Lemoine, 2015; Leung et al., 2008; Morris & Leung, 2010).

Research is still developing on understanding how people engage in the creative process and how they produce creative outcomes differently given their various cultural backgrounds. Early research took a country comparison approach to document cultural differences in creative performance, often finding individuals from Asia (e.g., Japan and China) to be less creative than those from the West (e.g., the U.S. and Europe) using a variety of laboratory tasks (Torrance, 1969; Niu & Sternberg, 2001, 2002, 2003; Noriko, Fan & Van Dusen, 2001). Another stream of research used a values-based approach to conceptualize culture (e.g., Bechtoldt et al., 2010; Erez & Nouri, 2010; Hofstede, 2001; Rank, Pace & Frese, 2004; Schwartz, 1999; Shane, 1992). Such research points to the focus on the value-based constructs, such as individualism/collectivism (Bechtoldt et al., 2010; Shane, 1992) and uncertainty avoidance (Shane, 1995). However, research in this stream failed to provide a consistent and conclusive answer (see Leung & Morris, 2010).

Recent developments in cross-cultural psychology have started to pivot attention to social norms related to shared expectations about the "appropriate" way of thinking and acting (Zou et al., 2009). Following this logic and presenting an initial theoretical framework, Gelfand and colleagues (2006) suggest that *cultural tightness*, as a particular cultural dimension that portrays the extent to which a society is regulated by strong social norms and a low tolerance for deviant behavior, is the antecedent to creativity because it socializes people to develop psychological adaptations characterized by caution, predictability and discipline. In other words, tight cultures could contribute to promoting convergent thinking by socializing individuals to think and act in line with social norms and rules. It has been shown that convergent thinking could restrict creativity by limiting one "within the box" rather than providing the cognitive framework to encourage cognitive reflexibility. But some scholars have also proposed that it can also be beneficial to creativity, for example, in facilitating the selection of creative ideas to suit a given context (Corpley, 2006; Duguid & Goncalo, 2012).

In the more recent work, Chua and colleagues (2015) propose a new theoretical model to also take into account the audience country's culture – the locale for which an innovation or creative idea is intended (e.g., the difference between the innovator's and the audience country's culture), and they coined this model as the Cultural Alignment Modal of Global Creativity (CAMGC). They emphasized three relevant cultural characteristics: (a) the innovator's country's level of cultural tightness; (b) the audience/client country's level of cultural tightness; and (c) the extent to which the client country's cultural content is close to that of the innovator's country (i.e., cultural distance). Based on the CAMGC framework, we need to understand the culture tightness of both the innovator's and the client's origin. The model argues that the tighter the culture of an individual's country, the less likely the individual will be to engage in a foreign creative task, because a tight culture discourages deviation and change. Furthermore, when the cultural distance between one's own country and client's country is wide, individuals from tight cultures might feel uncertain of succeeding there because the local context embodies knowledge, values, norms, preferences and other conditions that differ sharply from their own. This further lowers their creative self-efficacy, making them less likely to engage in the creative task. However, when the culture gap is small, tight cultures promote the likelihood of engaging in creativity tasks and heighten the likelihood of success.

Asia is a vastly diverse region, and thus, I would be careful about lumping all the Asian countries together, but many of them do share similar cultural characteristics. For example, many Asian countries focus on a hierarchical structure, emphasizing collective interests over individual gains, and promoting collective harmony and further avoiding any conflicts. These features are closely related to cultural tightness. In general, Asia is a pretty culturally "tight" continent. In a ranking of 33 countries in terms of cultural tightness, the research found that the five tightest countries were all in Asia (Gelfand et al., 2011). China and Japan, the region's two economic powerhouses, ranked in the top 10 (out of 33). The only Asian locale to qualify as more culturally "loose" was Hong Kong, which was long a British colony (see Figure 10.1). Therefore, based on the aforementioned research, it is hard for Asian people to engage in divergent thinking, given that the tight culture encourages a strong social norm with a low tolerance for any deviations. People from Asia are prevention-focused and are very cautious and concerned about not making any mistakes. Similarly, culturally "tight" Asians could be less receptive to foreign ideas, as they tend to think more narrowly and less globally. In addition, "tight" countries tend to create their own obstacles to innovation – regulations and rules that conflict with the creative process. It is not easy to innovate in such a place because there could be many rules and norms regulating individuals' behaviors and mindsets. For example, politically sensitive topics such as homosexuality and religion are carefully monitored and sanctioned in artistic productions. The benefit of cultural tightness is that it promotes local innovations, generating major success within the region. For example, Alibaba took over eBay in China via a creative localization strategy, and similarly, Grab bought Uber in Southeast Asia due to the novel business operations they embrace locally in Malaysia and Singapore.

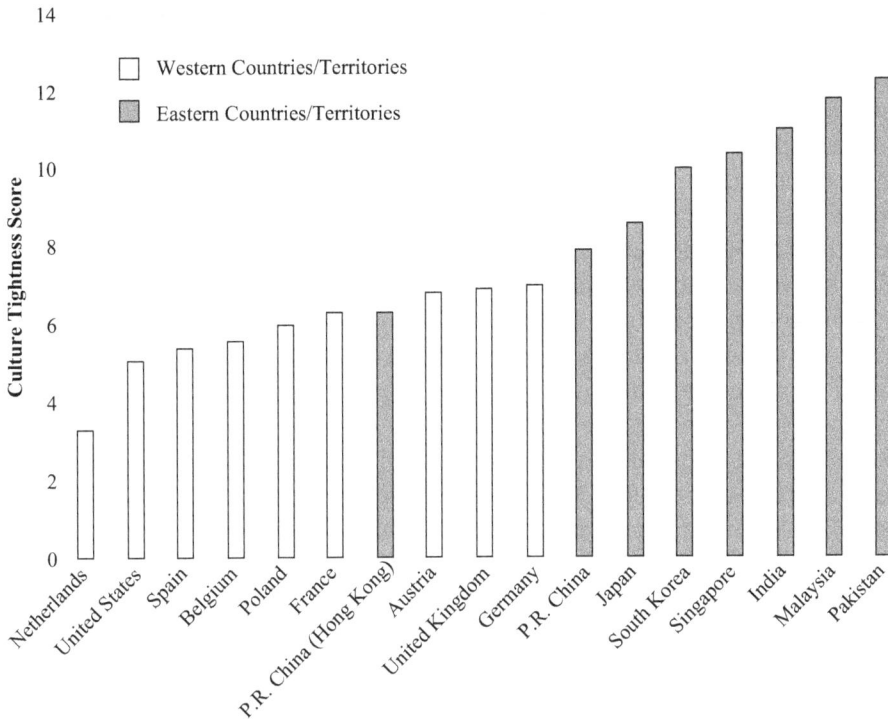

Figure 10.1: Culture Tightness Score for 17 Countries/Territories.

Different Perceptions of Creativity

Another account for the different outputs between the East and the West is that there could be a drastically different understanding of creativity in these two regions. The distinction between the two components of idea novelty and idea usefulness is necessary for understanding the variation in cultural effects on creativity. Researchers generally found that there is a stronger emphasis on usefulness and practicality in the East and a stronger emphasis on novelty and originality in the West (Noriko, Fan & Van Dusen, 2001). According to Amabile (1996), the major antecedents of creativity are: (a) domain-relevant skills; (b) mental processes of breaking perceptual and habitual sets; (c) task motivation; and (d) context, namely the specific situation and social environment. In a given task executed in different culture backgrounds, Erez and Nouri (2010) propose that it is likely that both task motivation and social context may vary across cultures and cultural values.

For task motivation, we can look at how value attributes, such as power distance, collectivism and uncertainty avoidance can in fact direct individuals to usefulness and appropriateness of their ideas, which restrain the novelty direction. Collectivism culture corresponds with tradition, security and conformity (Hofstede, 2001; House et al.,

2004), which were shown to be negatively related to creativity (Dollinger et al., 2007; Kasof et al., 2007). Power distance reflects the extent to which power is equally or differentially distributed among members of a society, and highlights the acceptance for compliance and discipline (Hofstede, 1980; Schwartz & Bilsky, 1990). Subordinates in societies high on power distance are accustomed to depending on their supervisors for direction and decision-making (House et al., 2004), and communication in high power distance cultures is mostly top-down (Javidan & House, 2001). As a result, individuals rarely think independently and try to generate their own creative solutions, especially when they are different from the orders they received from the top. Lastly, being creative and exploring something new need to tolerate uncertainty and potential risk. A culture that prefers to avoid uncertainty severely limits the opportunities to allow individuals to explore the deviant options and consequently confines their chance to seek anything new. For example, a high tolerance for uncertainty is associated with risk-taking, tolerance for mistakes, and low bureaucracy, which encourage exploration and novel ideas (Cummings, 1965; Miron, Erez & Naveh, 2004; O'Reilly, Chatman & Caldwell, 1991). In contrast, a high power-distance culture significantly restricts deviations from normative behaviors (Jansen, Van Den Bosch & Volberda, 2006). Taken together, individuals from collectivism, high power distance and low uncertainty avoidance (tends to be Asian countries; Hofstede, 2001) cultures are more likely to prefer ideas that are more appropriate and useful, rather than novel and original.

Additionally, the social context in which a creative task is performed is also crucial (Zhou & Su, 2010). Sensitivity to the social context may vary across cultures. Among East Asians, there is a greater sensitivity to the social context compared with Americans (Morris & Peng, 1994). Furthermore, given the importance of "face" in East Asian culture, people tend to adhere to existing social norms, whereas concern with self-esteem tends to lead Westerners to adhere to one's own internal standards (Heine et al., 2008). Based on the social facilitation theory (Sanders, 1981), the presence of other dissimilar cultures could enhance the effect of cultural values on creative focus. Therefore, when there are individuals from individualistic, low power distance, and low uncertainty avoidance cultures present (e.g., Westerners), Asians are more likely to be promoted to seek for more appropriate and useful solutions and ideas. This account highlights the importance of taking into consideration the social impact from either a leader or a client, particularly how a different dimension of creativity is judged and preferred in the presence of dissimilar cultures.

How to Lead Creativity in Asia?

Now that we have walked through the literature to understand the cultural influence on creativity, I propose the following question: What does it take to lead employees in Asia to effectively generate both novel and useful ideas and solutions? In the following section, I elaborate on how to develop leadership with a global perspective that can help individuals and organizations boost creativity in an Asian context.

First of all, leaders need to start with a realization that tolerance needs to be developed. As I presented earlier, many cultural factors related to uncertainty and risk tolerance could drag down creativity, especially the novelty dimension. Almost two decades ago, in his bestselling book *The Rise of the Creative Class*, Richard Florida ranked tolerance as one of the "three T's" that are key to creativity, the others being talent and technology. Tolerance is key to attract talent, allowing employees to make mistake and enhance workplace autonomy. Furthermore, it opens up the possibility to challenge the Asian culture of avoiding risk and the fear of making mistakes, and liberates individuals' minds by enabling them to think more freely. As an example, Huawei promotes a culture of tolerance for creativity and innovation that enables the organization to be the global leader of 5G technology, as Ren Zhengfei, the CEO of Huawei, firmly believes that innovation is only possible with tolerance (Tao, De Cremer & Wu, 2016).

Second, leaders should also embrace cultural diversity in the workplace, given that more and more talents coming from different cultural origins are working in Asia. In such highly globalized economic entities, organizations should take full advantage of the trend. The notion that working across cultural boundaries can promote creativity is not exactly new (Perry-Smith & Shalley, 2003; Perry-Smith & Mannucci, 2017), but it is not easy to accomplish such a goal. Nonetheless, there are still a few ways that can help make this happen. At the individual level, people can actively try to cultivate culturally diverse social networks. In a study conducted at a professional press club in the United States, Chua (2018) found that maintaining a culturally diverse network of professional contacts was particularly helpful when one needed to creatively solve global challenges that require drawing on knowledge and ideas from multiple cultures. The most diverse network connections are built via weak ties (Granovetter, 1973). However, in a sharp contrast to Western countries, where weak ties of infrequent interaction and low intimacy are more frequently used than stronger ties, networks in Asia, especially East Asia, social connections and contacts (e.g., *guanxi*) were predominantly relatives and friends of high intimacy to network users (Bian & Ikeda, 2017). As a leader, one should promote and encourage his or her employees to try to build and maintain ties with associates and colleagues from diverse countries and cultural backgrounds, creating as many opportunities as possible for those infrequent encounters. This strategy would provide many useful, diverse ideas, giving a trusted team member the "thumbs-up" and responsibility to say "No" to an opinion or idea, even when it is endorsed by the majority.

Third, a leader in an Asian context could easily throw the followers – who are comfortable staying in the current cultural environment – off guard, if he or she constructively challenges the followers at every turn. Employees should be informed that they could be challenged and should expect the disagreement while being comfortable with it. Asian leaders should also create a safe environment and encourage their followers to voice different ideas. Such an organizational culture (or departmental culture) can overwrite the country's culture to motivate individuals to think differently. Of course, doing so also requires the leader to (a) recruit the right individuals who are not afraid of challenging the status quo; (b) promote the current employees to challenge each other's ideas in a non-competitive setting; and (c) implement the appropriate performance appraisal system that further rewards these dissenting voices and challenging suggestions.

Regarding leadership behavior, Bass (1997) proposes that the transformational leadership paradigm is sufficiently broad to provide a basis for understanding leadership in all situations and settings, and transformational leadership has been found to enhance the creative potential of individual employees (e.g., Shin & Zhou, 2003). Mumford and colleagues (Mumford, 2000; Mumford et al., 2002) conceptually propose that transformational leadership could facilitate the introduction of new ideas and creative potential by providing vision, motivation and intellectual stimulation to followers. Similarly, in the Asian context, transformational leadership can further unleash the power of dialectical thinking – the willingness to accept change as a fact of life and to tolerate contradiction (Paletz & Peng, 2009). Interestingly, Asians tend to be more prone to dialectical thinking than Westerners, thanks to the influence of Eastern concepts such as the yin/yang dynamic of Taoism and the Buddhist precept that everything is temporary and nothing is permanent. This is an Eastern strength to harnessing creativity. However, due to power distance and social hierarchy, Asian leaders tend to favor an authoritative approach towards managing followers. This top-down and directive approach, focusing on compliance and rules, limits individuals' ability to change the status quo (Zhang, Tsui & Wang, 2011). To release the power of dialectical thinking among Asian employees, Asian leadership should further engage in *intellectual stimulation* (i.e., questioning followers' assumptions and inspiring them to achieve higher goals besides quarterly key performance indicators), individualized consideration (i.e., recognizing the unique growth and developmental needs of followers as well as offering coaching and consulting to followers), establishing *charism* or *idealized influence* (i.e., setting up a clear sense of purpose to the team that energizes and builds identification with the leader), and setting up *inspirational motivation* (e.g., setting clear, ambitious and meaningful goals).

In sum, to stimulate creativity, one should understand the cultural cause of the creativity discrepancies between "East" and "West." Governments and organizations need to promote creativity by providing more resources, but what is arguably more important is that the Asian leaders should engage in Asian global leadership by exerting a higher level of tolerance, embracing and encouraging cultural diversity, establishing a psychologically safe environment for suggestions and challenges, and really practicing transformational leadership at work.

References

Amabile, T. M. (1983). The social psychology of creativity: A componential conceptualization. *Journal of Personality and Social Psychology*, *45*(2), 357–377.

Amabile, T. M. (1988). A model of creativity and innovation in organizations. In B. M. Staw, & L. L. Cummings (Eds.), *Research in Organizational Behavior*, *10*, 123–167. JAI Press (Greenwich, CT).

Amabile, T. M. (1996). *Creativity in context*. Westview Press (Boulder, CO).

Bass, B. M. (1997). Does the transactional–transformational leadership paradigm transcend organizational and national boundaries? *American Psychologist*, *52*(2), 130–139.

Bechtoldt, M. N., De Dreu, C. K. W., Nijstad, B. A. & Choi, H.-S. (2010) Motivated information processing, social tuning, and group creativity. *Journal of Personality and Social Psychology*, *99*(4), 622–637.

Bian, Y. & Ikeda, K. (2017). East Asian social networks. In R. Alhajj & R. J. Springer (Eds.), *The Encyclopedia of Social Network Analysis and Mining*. Springer Science (New York, NY).

Chiu, C.-Y. & Hong, Y. Y. (2013). *Social Psychology of Culture*. Psychology Press (New York, NY).

Chiu, C.-Y. & Kwan, L. Y.-Y. (2010). Culture and creativity: A process model. *Management and Organization Review*, *6*(3), 447–461.

Chua, R. Y. J. (2018). Innovating at cultural crossroads: How multicultural social networks promote idea flow and creativity. *Journal of Management*, *44*(3), 1119–1146.

Chua, R. Y. J., Roth, Y. & Lemoine, J. F. (2015). The impact of culture on creativity: How cultural tightness and cultural distance affect global innovation crowdsourcing work. *Administrative Science Quarterly*, *60*(2), 189–227.

Cropley, A. (2006). In praise of convergent thinking. *Creativity Research Journal*, *18*(3), 391–404.

Cummings, L. (1965). Organizational climates for creativity. *Academy of Management Journal*, *8*(3), 220–227.

De Dreu, C. K. W. (2010). Human creativity: Reflections on the role of culture. *Management and Organization Review*, *6*(3), 437–446.

Dollinger, S. J., Burke, P. A. & Gump, N. W. (2007). Creativity and values. *Creativity Research Journal*, *19*(2–3), 91–103.

Doney, P. M., Cannon, J. P., & Mullen, M. R. (1998). Understanding the influence of national culture on the development of trust. *Academy of management review*, *23*(3), 601–620.

Duguid, M. M. & Goncalo, J. A. (2012). Living large: The powerful overestimate their own height. *Psychological Science*, *23*(1), 36–40.

Erez, M. & Nouri, R. (2010). Creativity: The Influence of Cultural, Social, and Work Contexts. *Management and Organization Review*, *6*(3), 351–370.

Florida, R. (2004). America's looming creativity crisis. *Harvard Business Review*, *82*, 122–136.

Ford, C. M. (2000). Creative developments in creativity theory. *The Academy of Management Review*, *25*(2), 284–287.

Gelfand, M. J., Nishii, L. H. & Raver, J. L. (2006). On the nature and importance of cultural tightness-looseness. *Journal of Applied Psychology*, *91*(6), 1225–1244.

Gelfand, M. J., Raver, J. L., Nishii, L., Leslie, L. M., Lun, J., Lim, B. C., . . . & Aycan, Z. (2011). Differences between tight and loose cultures: A 33-nation study. *Science, 332*(6033), 1100–1104.

Global Innovation Index (2019). Creating Healthy Lives–The Future of Medical Innovation (12th Ed). Cornell University, INSEAD, and the World Intellectual Property Organization.

Granovetter, M. S. (1973). The strength of weak ties. *American Journal of Sociology*, *6*, 1360–1380.

Heine, S. J., Takemoto, T., Moskalenko, S., Lasaleta, J. & Henrich, J. (2008). Mirrors in the head: Cultural variation in objective self-awareness. *Personality and Social Psychology Bulletin*, *34*(7), 879–887.

Hofstede, G. (1980). Motivation, leadership, and organization: Do American theories apply abroad? *Organizational Dynamics*, *9*(1), 42–63.

Hofstede, G. (2001). *Culture's consequences: Comparing values, behaviors, institutions, and organizations across nations*. Sage Publications (Thousand Oaks, CA).

House, R. J., Hanges, P. J., Javidan, M., Dorfman, P. W. & Gupta, V. (Eds.). (2004). *Culture, leadership, and organizations: The GLOBE study of 62 societies*. Sage Publications.

Jansen, J. J., Van Den Bosch, F. A. & Volberda, H.W. (2006). Exploratory innovation, exploitative innovation, and performance: Effects of organizational antecedents and environmental moderators. *Management Science*, *52*(11), 1661–1674.

Javidan, M. & House, R. J. (2001). Cultural acumen for the global manager: Lessons from project GLOBE. *Organizational Dynamics*, *29*(4), 289–305.

Kasof, J., Chen, C., Himsel, A. & Greenberger, E. (2007). Values and creativity. *Creativity Research Journal*, *19*(2–3), 105–122.

Lee, K.-Y. (2013). Late Singapore Leader Lee Kuan Yew Had Opinions on Everything. Times. Retrieved on 9 January 2021 from: https://time.com/3748654/singapore-lee-kuan-yews-opinions/

Leung, A. K. Y., Maddux, W. W., Galinsky, A. D. & Chiu, C. (2008). Multicultural experience enhances creativity: The when and how. *The American Psychologist, 63*(3): 169–181.

Leung, K. & Morris, M. W. (2010). Culture and creativity: A social psychological analysis. In D. D. Carmer, J. K. Murnighan & R. van Dick (Eds). *Social psychology and organizations*. Routledge (New York, NY).

Lubart, T. I. (1990). Creativity and cross-cultural variation. *International Journal of Psychology*, *25*, 39–59.

Miron, E., Erez, M. & Naveh, E. (2004). Do personal characteristics and cultural values that promote innovation, quality, and efficiency compete or complement each other? *Journal of Organizational Behavior*, *25*(2), 175–199.

Morris, M. W. & Leung, K. (2010). Creativity East and West: Perspectives and parallels. *Management and Organization Review*, *6*(3), 313–327.

Morris, M. W. & Peng, K. (1994). Culture and cause: American and Chinese attributions for social and physical events. *Journal of Personality and Social Psychology*, *67*(6), 949–971.

Mumford, M. D. (2000). Managing creative people: Strategy and tactics for innovation. *Human Resource Management Review*, *10*, 313–351.

Mumford, M. D., Scott, G. M., Gaddis, B. & Strange, J. M. (2002). Leading creative people: Orchestrating expertise and relationships. *The Leadership Quarterly*, *13*, 705–750.

Niu, W. & Sternberg, R. J. (2001) Cultural influences on artistic creativity and its evaluation. *International Journal of Psychology*, *36*, 225–241.

Niu, W. & Sternberg, R. J. (2002) Contemporary Studies on the Concept of Creativity: The East and the West. *Contemporary Studies*, *36*(4), 269–288.

Niu, W. & Sternberg, R. J. (2003) Societal and school influences on student creativity: The case of China. *Psychology in the Schools*, *40*(1), 103–114.

Noriko, S., Fan, X. & Van Dusen, L. (2001) A comparative study of creative thinking of American and Japanese college students. *Journal of Creative Behavior*, *35*(1), 24–36.

Oldham, G. R. & Cummings, A. (1996). Employee creativity: Personal and contextual factors at work. *Academy of Management Journal*, *39*, 607–634.

O'Reilly III, C. A., Chatman, J. & Caldwell, D. F. (1991). People and organizational culture: A profile comparison approach to assessing person-organization fit. *Academy of Management Journal*, *34*(3), 487–516.

Paletz, S. B. & Peng, K. (2009). Problem finding and contradiction: Examining the relationship between naive dialectical thinking, ethnicity, and creativity. *Creativity Research Journal*, *21*(2–3), 139–151.

Perry-Smith, J. E. & Shalley, C. E. (2003). The social side of creativity: A static and dynamic social network perspective. *Academy of Management Review*, *28*(1), 89–106.

Perry-Smith, J. E. & Mannucci, P. V. (2017). From creativity to innovation: The social network drivers of the four phases of the idea journey. *Academy of Management Review*, *42*(1), 53–79.

Rank, J., Pace, V. L. & Frese, M. (2004). Three Avenues for Future Research on Creativity, Innovation, and Initiative. *Applied Psychology*, *53*(4), 518–528.

Runco, M. A. & Jaeger, G. J. (2012). The standard definition of creativity. *Creativity Research Journal*, *24*(1), 92–96.

Sanders, G. S. (1981). Driven by distraction: An integrative review of social facilitation theory and research. *Journal of Experimental Social Psychology*, *17*(3), 227–251.

Schein, E. H. (1990). *Organizational Culture*, *45*(2), 109. American Psychological Association.

Schwartz, S. H. (1999). A theory of cultural values and some implications for work. *Applied Psychology: An International Review*, *48*, 23–47.

Schwartz, S. H. & Bilsky, W. (1990). Toward a theory of the universal content and structure of values: Extensions and cross-cultural replications. *Journal of Personality and Social Psychology*, *58*(5), 878–891.

Shane, S. A. (1992). Why do some societies invent more than others? *Journal of Business Venturing*, *7*(1), 29–46.

Shane, S. (1995). Uncertainty avoidance and the preference for innovation championing roles. *Journal of International Business Studies*, *26*, 47–68.

Shin, S. J. & Zhou, J. (2003). Transformational leadership, conservation, and creativity: Evidence from Korea. *Academy of Management Journal*, *46*(6), 703–714.

Spencer-Rodgers, J., Boucher, H. C., Mori, S. C., Wang, L. & Peng, K. (2009). The dialectical self-concept: Contradiction, change, and holism in East Asian cultures. *Personality and Social Psychology Bulletin*, *35*(1), 29–44.

Tao, T., De Cremer, D. & Chunbo, W. (2016). *Huawei: Leadership, Culture, and Connectivity*. SAGE Publications India.

Torrance, E. P. (1969). What is honored: Comparative studies of creative achievement and motivation. *Journal of Creative Behavior*, *3*(3), 149–154.

Varsakelis, N. C. (2001). The impact of patent protection, economy openness and national culture on R&D investment: A cross-country empirical investigation. *Research Policy*, *30*(7), 1059–1068.

Wang, A. Y. (2011). Contexts of creative thinking: A comparison on creative performance of student teachers in Taiwan and the United States. *Journal of International and Cross-Cultural Studies*, *2*(1), 1–14.

Zhang, A. Y., Tsui, A. S. & Wang, D. X. (2011). Leadership behaviors and group creativity in Chinese organizations: The role of group processes. *The Leadership Quarterly*, *22*, 851–862.

Zhou, J. (1998). Feedback valence, feedback style, task autonomy, and achievement orientation: Interactive effects on creative performance. *Journal of Applied Psychology*, *83*(2), 261–276.

Zhou, J. & Shalley, C. E. (2011). Deepening our understanding of creativity in the workplace: A review of different approaches to creativity research. In Z. Sheldon (Ed.), *APA handbook of industrial and organizational psychology. Vol 1: Building and developing the organization*. (pp. 275–302). American Psychological Association (Washington, DC).

Zhou, J. & Su, Y. (2010). A missing piece of the puzzle: The organizational context in cultural patterns of creativity. *Management and Organization Review*, *6*(3), 391–413.

Zou, X., Tam, K. P., Morris, M. W., Lee, S. L., Lau, I. Y. M. & Chiu, C. Y. (2009). Culture as common sense: Perceived consensus versus personal beliefs as mechanisms of cultural influence. *Journal of Personality and Social Psychology*, *97*(4), 579–597.

Irene E. De Pater and Gareth S. X. Ting

Chapter 11
Leadership Development: Challenging Work Experiences in Singapore

Leadership development refers to the expansion of organization members' capacities "to be effective in leadership roles and processes" (McCauley, Van Velsor & Ruderman, 2010, p. 2), where leadership roles can come with or without formal authority (Day, 2000) and leadership processes refer to those "that facilitate setting direction, creating alignment, and maintaining commitment in groups of people who share common work" (McCauley, Van Velsor et al., 2010, p. 2). The most common purposes of leadership development are improving leaders' performance, expanding their capacities for higher-level positions, fostering innovation and creative thinking, succession planning and organizational change (e.g., McCauley, Kanaga & Lafferty, 2010; Prokopeak, 2018).

Leadership development is an urgent and challenging issue for organizations around the globe (e.g., Beer, Finnström & Schrader, 2016; Moldoveanu & Narayandas, 2019) and especially for organizations in Asia. Here, economic growth remains high and business opportunities are abundant (Chin et al., 2015). Moreover, more and more organizations operating in Asia prefer to develop their leaders internally rather than recruiting them from other parts of the world, as Asian leaders are thought to have culturally relevant leadership styles and a better understanding of the Asian context (see Economic Development Board, 2017; Puri, Zhao & Chandrasekar, 2018). Yet, there is a shortage of strong Asian leaders in the region, which makes leadership development a particularly pressing issue (Chin et al., 2015; Deloitte, 2015).

Although organizations use a variety of methods for leadership development, such as coaching and stretch assignments, they invest most in classroom-based leadership programs carried out by established educational institutions (e.g., Deloitte, 2019; Prokopeak, 2018). While individuals who take part in such programs often benefit from them in terms of enhanced career prospects (Moldoveanu & Narayandas, 2019), organizations are disappointed with their effectiveness for the organization as a whole and thus the return on their investments (Beer et al., 2016; Deloitte, 2019; Glaveski, 2019; Iordanoglou, 2018; Moldoveanu & Narayandas, 2019). For instance, research has shown that although classroom training is the most popular tool for leadership development among organizations in Asia (used by 87 percent of organizations), only 9 percent of the organizations rated it as very effective, whereas 73 percent rated it as moderately effective (Mercer, 2013).

There are several reasons for the disappointing effectiveness of classroom-based leadership development efforts. First, most leaders who come back from a leadership development program are well-trained and highly motivated, yet back in their

https://doi.org/10.1515/9783110671988-011

organizational context, they often lack opportunities to transfer their acquired knowledge, skills and abilities to their jobs. This not only results in a low return on investment for the organization, but may also result in frustration and voluntary turnover (Beer et al., 2016; Ford et al., 1992). Second, developmental needs arise whenever leaders encounter situations for which they lack the necessary skills, knowledge or experiences, whereas classroom-based leadership development programs take place at a set moment in time. Hence, leaders may not be able to acquire knowledge, skills and abilities when they need it. Moreover, employees are most motivated to learn and develop best when their work requires them to do so (Glaveski, 2019; McCall, 2004; McCall, Lombardo & Morrison, 1988), whereas new skills and knowledge that are not applied soon will be forgotten (Glaveski, 2019; Murre & Dros, 2015). Third, although the often standardized content of classroom-based leadership development programs could serve as an indicator of its standards, it has been acknowledged that leadership development should not be a one-size-fits-all endeavor, because different leaders have different needs for development, and different organizational contexts have different competency requirements (Mercer Mettl, 2019). Therefore, it has been suggested that organizations should emphasize leadership development in the context of their work rather than focusing on leadership development that takes leaders away from their work (Beer et al., 2016; Day, 2000, 2007; Deloitte, 2019; McCauley, McCall et al., 2014).

Indeed, it has been recognized that individuals' work experiences are among the most important facilitators of leadership development, especially when work experiences are challenging (DeRue & Wellman, 2009; Dragoni et al., 2009; McCall et al., 1988; McCauley et al., 1994). Research has shown that 48 percent of organizations in Asia consider challenging job experiences as very effective, whereas 42 percent consider them to be moderately effective. A study the Center for Creative Leadership conducted among leaders in the public sector in Singapore corroborates these findings (P. Y. Ong, 2008): 92 percent of the respondents highlighted challenging work experiences as being significant for their leadership development, whereas only 11 percent of the respondents indicated that classroom training was effective for leadership development.

Challenging Work Experiences

Challenging work experiences refer to "work activities for which existing tactics and routines are inadequate and that require new ways of dealing with work situations" (De Pater et al., 2009, p. 299). They provide leaders with the opportunity and motivation to learn (McCauley et al., 1994) and facilitate the development of a wide range of skills, knowledge, abilities and insights that increase leaders' capacities for effective leadership (DeRue & Wellman, 2009; Dragoni et al., 2009; McCall et al.,

1988; Seibert et al., 2017). Challenging work experiences come in many forms, yet they "have one thing in common: they create disequilibrium – an imbalance between current skills and demands that calls for people to move out of their comfort zone" (Frankovelgia & Riddle, 2010, p. 128).

Based on interviews with successful executives in the United States, McCauley and colleagues (McCauley, Ohlott & Ruderman, 1999; McCauley et al., 1994) have developed a taxonomy of challenging job components that are especially potent for leadership development. It encompasses five clusters of challenging job components: job transitions, creating change, high levels of responsibility, managing boundaries and dealing with diversity (see Table 11.1). This taxonomy not only facilitates

Table 11.1: Clusters of Challenging Job Components.

Clusters	Description	Leadership development occurs because
Job transitions	– Any change in employment status or job content that causes unfamiliar situations.	– Leaders have to develop new strategies to deal with problems and opportunities because they are confronted with situations in which their existing tactics and routines are inadequate. – Leaders are motivated to prove themselves to their (new) superiors, peers and subordinates.
Creating change	– Taking decisions and actions that steer the organization in a new direction. – Solving any problem that may occur.	– Leaders have a clear goal and the freedom to determine how to accomplish the goal. – Leaders have to develop new behaviors and attitudes to deal with the demands of the situation.
High levels of responsibility	– Increased visibility. – Opportunity to make a significant impact. – Dealing with broader and more complex problems and higher stakes.	– Leaders are motivated to enhance their skills and abilities because they are in the spotlight and have the opportunity to make a difference. – Leaders have to develop their skills and abilities to address problems of increased complexity. – Leaders have to integrate different perspectives.

Table 11.1 (continued)

Clusters	Description	Leadership development occurs because
Managing boundaries	– Work across lateral boundaries within or external to the organization.	– Leaders have to develop strategies for influencing people over whom they have no direct authority and gaining their cooperation. – Leaders have to balance demands and priorities of various internal and external parties.
Dealing with diversity	– Leading people with different backgrounds, values, needs and experiences.	– Leaders are challenged to learn and understand business and workplace issues from other perspectives.

systematic research on on-the-job leadership development, but it also serves as a framework for assessing and optimizing the developmental potential of work roles.

In this chapter, we examine the challenging job components of leaders in Asia. It is timely to do so, because leadership in the 21st century has new and unique requirements that are important for leadership effectiveness and organizations' success (Deloitte, 2019). Yet, this study is not only important because it will allow us to update our insights in on-the-job experiences that facilitate leadership development, but also because it is conducted in Asia. That is, the existing taxonomy of challenging job components (McCauley et al., 1999) is based on the experiences of successful executives in the West, and research suggests that – due to cultural differences – leading in the East requires different behaviors, skills, knowledge and abilities than leading in the West. For instance, research has suggested that leaders in Asia are especially valued for qualities such as humility, cultural adaptability and VUCA-friendliness (Deloitte, 2012; Puri et al., 2018; The Conference Board, 2013). Hence, in order to be able to optimize leadership development in the context of their work in Asia, it is important to gain insight in the unique challenges Asian leaders encounter in their work.

Method

Participants

Trained research assistants conducted 46 structured interviews with leaders in Singapore to acquire in-depth information regarding the challenging experiences leaders encounter in their work. These leaders were identified and selected by the research assistants and came from a wide variety of industries (e.g., oil and gas, hospitality, education, entertainment, banking and manufacturing), where they fulfilled a wide variety of roles (e.g., CEO, director, operations manager, branch manager and project manager). For reasons that we describe in the following sections, we only used 39 of the interviews in our analyses. Most of the leaders in our final sample were male (74 percent). Their average age was 44.88 (SD = 10.66) years and, on average, they worked in their current leadership position for 7.22 years (SD = 5.82).

Interview Procedure

The in-depth interviews probed into the challenging experiences leaders have at work. Leaders were asked to think back and remember a work situation that happened within the past six months in which they were really challenged. We intentionally did not define the term "challenge" because we aimed to study work experiences that leaders lived through that they perceived to be challenging (i.e., a person-centric approach; Weiss & Rupp, 2011). After the leaders described the challenging work situation in general, they were asked more detailed questions. With these questions, we aimed to gain insight into what characteristics make work situations challenging (i.e., "Why was this situation a challenge for you?"; "What characteristics of the tasks you engaged in in this situation made it challenging?"). Each interview was conducted individually and lasted between 30 and 60 minutes. The interviews were audio-recorded and transcribed to facilitate the analyses.

Coding

To develop a coding scheme, the authors reviewed all interview transcripts to extract all possible exemplars of challenging job components (i.e., units of analysis). Based on this information, the first author developed a coding scheme and both authors coded all units of analysis. The authors agreed 90.29 percent of the time and all discrepancies were resolved through discussions and consultations of the transcripts.

We excluded 7 interviews from the analyses in order to maintain a certain level of homogeneity. These interviews described challenging experiences respondents had in general, whereas the aim of the interviews was to gather information about a specific challenging situation that respondents had experienced in the past six months. Combining characteristics from these general challenges with those of the specific challenges described by the majority of the respondents may have contaminated the data (Glomb, 2002).

Results

Preliminary Analysis

Although we did not specifically ask the respondents if (and if so, what) they had learned from the challenging situations they described in the interviews, several of them volunteered such information:

> This project has been on for quite some time. It's definitely challenging . . . and I should say that it is an ongoing learning process. [Respondent 5]

> You basically learn from experience. Of course I make mistakes and I risk getting scolded. I do bear consequences now and then. But it is part of the learning process. [Respondent 14]

Challenging work experiences not only result in leadership development at the individual level, but they also result in leadership development at the team and organizational levels:

> Having gone through this challenge . . . actually this challenge has lifted [the department] to another level of competencies. You see in the past, they worked to support the local plant, now they extended their support to the international level. So this is a typical example of what one can do if one is willing to take challenges at a higher level of responsibility. And the additional capabilities resulted in higher market value of the organization. [Respondent 26]

Hence, the interview data corroborate previous research that established relationships between challenging work experiences and leadership development.

General Themes

In Table 11.2, we present the general themes of the challenging situations that the respondents reported. In order to illuminate these themes and in light of the small sample size, the analyses were limited to descriptive statistics.

Challenging Job Components

With reference to the question of why the respondents considered the situations challenging, the challenging job components they mentioned fell into several major categories. Table 11.3 reports the broad categories of challenging job components: challenges related to people (others and the self), challenges related to tasks (the content and the load of work), and challenges related to situations (inside and outside the organization). Respondents often mentioned more than one specific challenging job component within a broad category. The subcategories of the challenging job

Table 11.2: General Themes.

Theme	Proportion	Examples
Arising problems	6/46	– Dealing with an angry customer (Technical Service Manager) – Equipment breakdown (Project Manager)
Decision making	5/46	– Deciding (with three partners) about launching a new business (Partner) – Deciding (with five branch managers) which three get an extra staff member (Branch Manager)
Developing something new	2/46	– Opening a restaurant overseas for a Singaporean brand (Franchise Officer) – Creating a tailor made fund order processing system (Director and Head of Fund Administration)
Expanding the business	3/46	– Expanding the number of branches from 1 to 3 (Business Owner) – Growing a start-up at a fast pace (Partner)
Managing a big project/event	6/46	– Build an offshore oil and rig platform overseas (Engineering Procurement Manager) – Repair a damaged airplane (COO and Executive Director)
Organizational change	10/46	– Reorganizing the production floor to optimize production processes (Talent Acquisition and Development Manager) – Implementing a new IT system (Assistant Vice President Procurement Department)
Problems with boss	1/46	– Dealing with a superior who interferes in the responsibilities of the department head (Head of Housekeeping Department)
Problems with employees	6/46	– Managing a CEO who wants to fire a subordinate (Head Human Resources) – Having to fire an underperforming employee (Senior Advising Group Manager)
General[1]	7/46	– Dealing with clients (Trust Relationship Manager) – Managing people (Operations Manager)

Note: General challenges are excluded from the analyses.

components are reported in Table 11.4 (challenges related to people), Table 11.5 (challenges related to tasks), and Table 11.6 (challenges related to situations).

Challenges Related to People

One of the first observations was the large proportion of challenging job compo-nents that refer to people-related challenges. In fact, the majority of the challenging job components were people-related (228 out of a total of 443). Several respondents underlined that people can create major challenges:

Table 11.3: Challenging Job Components.

Challenging Job Components					
Challenges related to people	228/443	Challenges related to tasks	172/443	Challenges related to situations	43/443
Challenges related to others	163/228	Challenges related to the content of work	111/172	Challenges related to situations inside the organization	17/43
Challenges related to the self	65/228	Challenges related to the load of work	61/172	Challenges related to situations outside the organization	26/43

Most of the time the challenges don't come from the task itself – they come from the people surrounding the task; they are the ones giving the problems.   [Respondent 23]

With the correct framework, with a steady outline, you know the boundary set, it is not difficult to maneuver right, but it's dealing with people that sometimes makes it challenging.
[Respondent 27]

Challenges related to people not only refer to challenges related to others (163 out of a total of 228) but also refer to challenges related to the self (65 out of a total of 228). The substantial proportion of challenges related to the self is noteworthy, as previous research did not highlight such challenges. Table 11.4 provides an overview of these challenges.

Table 11.4: Challenging Job Components Related to People.

Challenges related to others (163/228)		Challenges related to the self (65/228)	
Influencing others (e.g., convincing external parties, motivating employees, overcoming resistance to change, managing conflict, managing others' emotions)	40	Changing mindset (e.g., adapting to change, overcoming demotivation, convincing the self, keeping an open mind)	12
Managing misalignment (e.g., goal misalignment between departments, misalignment of interest of employees and organization)	27	Intrinsic emotion regulation (i.e., managing one's own emotions)	11
Dealing with diversity (e.g., age diversity; cross-cultural diversity; diversity in experience, educational level)	19	Impression management (e.g., proving oneself, keeping face)	10

Table 11.4 (continued)

Challenges related to others (163/228)		Challenges related to the self (65/228)	
Dealing with people problems (e.g., subordinates, colleagues, superiors, clients, other stakeholders)	18	Lack of confidence (e.g., in the self, in others)	8
Coordinating and creating collaboration (between people, teams, departments, organizations)	16	Anticipating problems (e.g., being cautious, walking on eggshells)	7
Performance pressure (from superiors, top management, stakeholders outside the organization)	10	High visibility (i.e., being in the spotlight)	4
High expectations (from subordinates, superiors, top management, clients, other stakeholders)	9	Being underqualified (i.e., having a lack of SKAs)	4
Lack of support (from subordinates, superiors, top management, external stakeholders)	8	Performance pressure (i.e., internal pressure to perform)	4
Underqualified employees (i.e., employees lack SKAs)	7	Managing misalignment (i.e., misalignment between interest of the self and interests of the organization)	3
Interdependence (being dependent on other departments, external stakeholders)	5	High personal risk (i.e., high stakes for the self)	2
Bringing bad news	4		

Challenges Related to Others

As shown in Table 11.4, the three most mentioned challenges related to others are influencing others (40 out of 163), managing misalignment (27 out of 163) and dealing with diversity (19 out of 163). The subcategory *influencing others* encompasses, among others, influencing without authority, overcoming resistance to change, changing others' mindset, managing others' emotion, negotiation and motivating others. Examples are:

> Obviously some of them were friends, they worked together, they ate together and they sometimes even spent time together on the weekends. So when the person was being let go, there were some emotions among the team members and we had to make them understand why we needed to do so, why that decision was being made and why it was important to do so.
>
> [Respondent 45]

> We need to reposition our entire workforce and get them to work cohesively with one another. Our plant has been here for like 20 years and everybody is very used to the area that they work in. They will feel that whatever they are doing is actually the right thing, so why is there a need to change? So the challenge is really to get people to understand the big picture behind the entire changes.   [Respondent 5]

The subcategory *managing misalignment* contains challenges stemming from goal misalignment between departments, misalignment between the interests of employees and the interests of the organization, and misalignment between the interests of colleagues or business partners. Examples are:

> Top management wants to go ahead with the change, but I also need to listen to my people. I can't ignore their concerns and their feedback. But I must also try to see how I could meet the directions of top management. So I guess I have to balance both interests and try to make an objective decision.   [Respondent 29]

> Some people really just work for themselves. They don't work for the company. To them, their own interest is more important.   [Respondent 23]

> Sometimes a simple process can be a nightmare, especially when different departments have different key performance indicators.   [Respondent 27]

The subcategory *dealing with diversity* encompasses challenges such as age diversity and cross-cultural differences. Examples are:

> I think for our team, almost everyone is from a different country. And I think the hardest thing to do is motivation. I actually never thought about this, but people from different countries will have different, very different motivations.   [Respondent 40]

> So this is also a challenge. We have a lot of people that we employed for less than three years, and we have a core group of staff that has been here between seven and eighteen years. I think the ratio is close to 1:2. Although we see value in the work habits of the aged, there is a difference between the younger staff and the older staff. It causes a lot of friction.   [Respondent 35]

Challenges Related to the Self

As shown in Table 11.4, the three most mentioned challenges related to the self are changing one's mindset (12 out of 65), intrinsic emotion regulation (11 out of 65) and impression management (10 out of 65). The subcategory *changing one's mindset* includes challenges such as keeping an open mind, adapting to change and convincing the self. Examples are:

> The whole process of generating new thoughts can only be meaningful if you start removing some of the other old thoughts that were hindering it. So basic assumptions need to be reconsidered and discarded if they are not relevant.   [Respondent 4]

> First of all, you have to really convince yourself that the whole thing will work out for the better before you can convince your staff to actually accept the changes and move forward.
>
> [Respondent 41]

The subcategory *intrinsic emotion regulation* encompasses all instances where respondents had to actively manage their own emotions in order to function effectively. Examples are:

> I also worry. But I must remain positive. If I show my pessimistic attitudes, how can I manage my employees, how do I motivate my subordinates and ask them to remain positive? It cannot be done! That's one of the major challenges I faced. I really need to remain positive about the company, about the situation. But in my heart, I'm not positive.   [Respondent 33]

> You know, it's kind of a crappy feeling when you feel that you have done a lot of work, but you don't feel acknowledged or recognized and appreciated for what you have done . . . So I think the hard part of the situation is to not take it personally. It's very difficult to not take something personally when it happens. And I did take it personally when it happened, I was pretty pissed off.
>
> [Respondent 7]

The subcategory *impression management* includes challenges such as proving oneself to others, keeping face and emotional labor. Examples are:

> Your behaviors, what you say, your attitudes, will cast significant influence on your subordinates. They can take some words to elaborate and to imply certain things. Because this is a sensitive period, people are very sensitive to what you say. We have to be very cautious.
>
> [Respondent 33]

> Unfortunately, the higher management does not understand our problems and they continue to insist that we make a profit. I cannot speak up against that, as I do not wish to be considered as being pessimistic and seen as having no motivation to achieve their standards.
>
> [Respondent 22]

Challenges Related to Tasks

Of the 443 challenging job components that we extracted from the interviews, 172 were related to the tasks the respondents performed to deal with the challenging situation. Table 11.5 provides an overview of these challenges. Although the majority of these challenging job components relate to the quality or content of work (111 out of 172), a considerable proportion of these challenges stem from the quantity or load of work (61 out of 172).

Challenges Related to the Content of Work

As shown in Table 11.5, the three most frequently mentioned challenges related to the content of work are high responsibility (46 out of 111), novelty (15 out of 111) and

Table 11.5: Challenging Job Components Related to Tasks.

Challenges related to the content of work (111/172)		Challenges related to the load of work (61/172)	
High responsibility (e.g., high impact, high stakes, high risk, high responsibility)	46	High volume of work (i.e., high workload, working on a large scale)	25
Novelty (e.g., first time one encounters a task or situation, first time the organization encounters a task or situation)	15	Time pressure (i.e., having to work at a high pace, deadlines, urgency)	21
Cognitive complexity (e.g., many task components, not knowing what to do, high level of cognitive processing)	13	Long working hours	15
Individual decision making (e.g., how to expand the business, choosing among options, choosing between two negatives, prioritizing, making recruitment decisions)	11		
Large scope (i.e., having a variety of responsibilities, working with different stakeholders, fulfilling multiple roles)	8		
Implementing change (e.g., implementing new systems, implementing new procedures, customizing, optimizing)	6		
Developing new strategies (e.g., looking for new directions, looking for new ways to address issues)	5		
Dealing with adversity (e.g., things do not work out, closing down a line of business)	4		
Develop things from scratch (i.e., developing something that does not yet exist)	3		

cognitive complexity (13 out of 111). The subcategory *high responsibility* encompasses challenges such as high impact, high stakes, high risk and high responsibility:

> This problem creates a huge challenge because completion of this task is a critical milestone and other tasks are dependent on the completion of this task. If we cannot complete it on time, the project will come to a halt and obviously that will affect the quality, the timeline and the budget. [Respondent 12]

> As head of the company, I felt very responsible for the livelihood and the happiness of the employees as well as their families. [Respondent 12]

The subcategory *novelty* consists of challenges related to doing something for the first time (as an individual, team, or organization) and encountering issues/situations for the first time. Examples are:

One day, I received a phone call from one of our customers. He said that our technician dam-aged their server while repairing their multi-function machine. I was in fact shocked to hear that, and the customer sounded very angry. In my eight years in this job, this was the first time that I encountered a situation like this. So it took me a while to see how to deal with this issue.
[Respondent 6]

We were the first company in the global business to undertake this development. You know, the transition to this new system. So it was actually quite a, I would say, very pressuring mo-ment.
[Respondent 29]

The subcategory *cognitive complexity* encompasses challenges that involve many components, require a high level of information processing, and where there is un-certainty regarding the efficiency or effectiveness of potential ways to reach desired outcomes. Examples are:

This job includes several components and we have to liaise with various organizations to com-plete the job. It is even more complex because many components are uncertain. [Respondent 8]

There are a lot of things that go on at the same time, and I have to connect with people from different departments, to leverage, to mentor, to simplify the processes. So it needs a lot of thought processing.
[Respondent 27]

Challenges Related to the Load of Work

As shown in Table 11.5, challenges related to the load of work are a high volume of work (25 out of 61), time pressure (21 out of 61) and working long hours (15 out of 61).

The subcategory *high volume of work* encompasses challenges related to the amount and scale of work. Examples are:

Six months ago, my company organized the [event]. The most challenging aspect of it was to manage the registration area. We had very little manpower, a lot of the volunteers did not turn up, and we had only 20 people to manage 5,000 registrants a day. That was really challenging.
[Respondent 17]

I have to put together the data, information and activities, and relative performance of each of the eighty programs, all within the timeline for six weeks. That's a great challenge. Completing eighty program reviews within six weeks. That is definitely a great challenge.   [Respondent 9]

The subcategory time pressure includes challenges related to having to work at a fast pace, deadlines and urgency. Examples are:

For this particular project, we would need to achieve our goals in six months without incurring additional resources, so that is challenging.
[Respondent 26]

I guess what made it challenging is that we needed to make the deadline. The two partners were visiting from the US and they were only here for four days. We ran out of time and we needed to make a decision.
[Respondent 7]

The subcategory *long working hours* encompasses challenges related to having to spend a lot of time at work. Examples are:

> Sometimes we were not able to work from 8 to 5. Sometimes we even worked until 8pm or 9pm. Sometimes it would be later. So our family or personal time was much affected.
> [Respondent 18]

> Growing a company is already super hard when you need to put 14–18 hours every day . . . when you also start fundraising, it is like another full time job.   [Respondent 40]

Challenges Related to the Situation

Of the 443 challenging job components that we extracted from the interviews, 43 were related to a situation inside (17 out of 43) or outside (26 out of 43) of the organization. Table 11.6 provides an overview of these challenges.

Table 11.6: Challenging Job Components Related to the Situation.

Challenges related to situations inside the organization (17/43)		Challenges related to situations outside the organization (26/43)	
Lack of control (e.g., lack of authority; chaotic work environment; rules and regulations)	7	Lack of control (working across organizational boundaries, rules and regulations, geo-political situations)	8
Ambiguity (e.g., not knowing what exactly happened, not knowing why, lack of information)	5	Uncertainty (i.e., not knowing what will happen outside the organization)	8
Dealing with adversity (e.g., financial setbacks, poor performance)	2	Dealing with diversity (e.g., working across time-zones, differences in rules and regulations)	4
Uncertainty (i.e., not knowing what will happen within the organization)	2	Ambiguity (e.g., not knowing what happened, lack of information)	3
Unforeseen circumstances (i.e., sudden events)	1	Dealing with adversity (e.g., increased competition, geo-political crises)	2
		Unforeseen circumstances (i.e., sudden events)	1

Challenges Related to Situations Inside the Organization

As can be seen in Table 11.6, the most common challenges related to a situation inside the organization are lack of control (7 out of 17) and ambiguity (5 out of 17).

The subcategory *lack of control* includes components such as lack of authority and organizations' rules and regulations. Examples are:

> A very simple principal of management is that the manager must have direct control and com-mand over the subordinates. Here, the arrangement is very funny. The arrangement is that the manager does not have that. It is the so called senior manager who has the control.
> [Respondent 23]

> They always feel that my unit imposes on them, but we are not. The organization implemented certain policies and procedures. It is not up to us. But some don't really understand, so that makes the whole task even more challenging. [Respondent 9]

The subcategory *ambiguity* includes components such as a lack of information, lack of clarity, not knowing what exactly happened or not knowing why things (have to) happen. Examples are:

> There were multiple ways of interpretating how things were to be done. Each department viewed it in light of their own key performance indicators. [Respondent 27]

> I couldn't get the report, I didn't get the full data and I didn't get the correct data. That created friction. [Respondent 35]

Challenges Related to Situations Outside the Organization

As can be seen in Table 11.6, the most common challenges related to a situation out-side the organization are lack of control (8 out of 26) and uncertainty (8 out of 26).

The subcategory *lack of control* includes components such as working across orga-nizational boundaries, rules and regulations and geopolitical situations. Examples are:

> Another challenge was that we could not control our supplier. The supplier sometimes had some delay in delivering their raw materials. And at the same time our client expected us to deliver in time. So we were sandwiched between the client and the supplier. [Respondent 18]

> Either success or failure was not so much depending on our own efforts. Rather, our life, our fate, was very much depending on external factors. The geopolitical situation. [Respondent 33]

The subcategory *uncertainty* includes challenges stemming from not knowing what will happen in the environment. Examples are:

> I struggled. Basically, I asked myself how the company was going to be. Will it go bankrupt? Will we be retrenched or even lose our jobs, or will the company survive and become more prosperous? I would say it could be half-half, it's very hard to say. [Respondent 33]

> We run at a very tight schedule. Any delay will cause further delay downstream. But there are four stations involved. The client might change the concept, might change what they want. And then the engineer and the designer may change the design. Supplies might be late, delay-ing the fabrication. [Respondent 18]

Discussion

We conducted 46 interviews with leaders in Singapore to investigate the challenging experiences leaders have at work and the job components that make work challenging. The data are unique in that they look at specific challenging situations rather than at challenging job experiences in general, using existing, aggregate measures of job challenge. Analysis of the data provides support for previously proposed challenging job components (McCauley et al., 1999; McCauley et al., 1994) and identifies several additional subcategories of challenging job components.

Of note is that challenges evolve over time and never occur alone. On average, respondents identified about 11 unique challenging job components in the situation they described during their interview. As one of them noted:

> We identified problems and tried to find a solution to these issues, which led to many other issues. [Respondent 29]

An important finding is the prevalence of people-related challenging job components. Most interviews that we analyzed comprised one or more challenging job components related to other people (38 out of 39) and the self (26 out of 39). Although existing research on challenging job components includes several challenges relates to others (see Table 11.1), this study is the first to highlight the magnitude and scope of people-related challenges. Existing research has, so far, largely overlooked challenges related to the self. Yet our data reveal that such challenges are common.

People-related challenges may be more common in the East than in the West. Research suggests that people engagement; building relationships and collaborations; being courageous, assertive and proactive; concise and clear communication; and cultural sensitivity are among the most important leadership skills in Asia (P. Ong & Avolio, 2008; Puri et al., 2018; The Conference Board, 2013). Yet, Asian leaders are likely to be more inclined to focus on harmony and to avoid failure, they are behaviorally more reserved and their communication style is more indirect (Puri et al., 2018).

The prevalence of people-related challenges and the fact that both other-related and self-related challenges stem from unique individuals may partly explain why organizations and leaders consider learning from experiences more effective for leadership development than in-class training. Classroom settings may not be optimal for learning how to deal with such individual challenges. However, further research on the nature and occurrence of challenges related to others and the self may be fruitful in providing insight into how we can support leaders in the development of such skills.

Another important finding is that the task-related challenges our respondents identified included challenges related to both the content and the load of work. Previous research that identified challenging job components predominantly focused on challenges related to the content of work (e.g., McCall et al., 1988; McCauley et al., 1999; McCauley et al., 1994) and largely considered challenges related to the load of work to be work stressors (e.g., Cavanaugh et al., 2000; LePine, Podsakoff & Lepine, 2005). It should be noted though that we did not specifically ask our respondents to report challenges that supported their leadership development. It is thus unclear whether workload-related challenges stimulate leadership development as much as other types of challenges. Future research on the developmental outcomes of workload-related challenges may be fruitful in providing insight into this matter. Further, it may be beneficial to examine the combined effects of challenges related to the content of work and challenges related to the load of work.

The findings of this study provide an overview of challenges that Asian leaders encounter in their work. Respondents selected and described one challenging situation among many challenging situations. Hence, we do not know why they chose the one they reported on. It may have been the most severe, memorable or recent one (Glomb, 2002). Furthermore, some of the challenges we identified may be unique to leaders in Asia. That is, due to cultural norms and values that underline, among others, the importance of humility, avoiding failure and establishing and maintaining harmony (e.g., Lewis, 2010; The Conference Board, 2013), leaders in the East may encounter more people-related challenges than leaders in the West. Yet, given the increasing diversity of the workforce, the strong economic development in Asia (e.g., Chin et al., 2015; Economic Development Board, 2017), and the continuing globalization of Asian organizations, it is highly likely that leaders worldwide will face similar challenges in the near future. Hence, although this study has illustrated a wide range of challenges Asian leaders encounter in their work, we suggest that the framework we developed for analyzing leadership challenges will be applicable to leaders in both the East and the West.

This framework may be helpful in the development of effective leadership development programs. For instance, organizations may redesign jobs to include more challenging work experiences and provide their (future) leaders with coaches or mentors to help them deal with the challenges they encounter. Business schools may incorporate challenging work experiences in their curriculum, and classroom-based leadership programs may prepare current and future leaders for the challenges they are likely to encounter in their jobs and help them to develop adequate strategies to do so.

References

Beer, M., Finnström, M. & Schrader, D. (2016). Why leadership training fails – and what to do about it. *Harvard Business Review*, *94*(10), 50–57. Retrieved on 29 January 2020 from: https://hbr.org/2016/10/why-leadership-training-fails-and-what-to-do-about-it.

Cavanaugh, M. A., Boswell, W. R., Roehling, M. V. & Boudreau, J. W. (2000). An empirical examination of self-reported work stress among U.S. managers. *Journal of Applied Psychology, 85*, 65–74. doi:10.1037//0021-9010.85.1.65.

Chin, V., Dayal, R., Meyer, M., Nettesheim, C., Waltermann, B. & Yong, J. T. (2015). Overcoming Asia's obstacles to growth: How leading companies are reshaping their environment. Retrieved on 18 March 2020 from: https://www.bcg.com/publications/2015/globalization-growth-overcoming-asia-obstacles-growth.aspx.

Day, D. V. (2000). Leadership development:: A review in context. *The Leadership Quarterly, 11*, 581–613. doi:10.1016/S1048-9843(00)00061-8.

Day, D. V. (2007). Developing leadership talent. Retrieved on 20 March 2020 from: https://www.shrm.org/foundation/ourwork/initiatives/resources-from-past-initiatives/Documents/Developing%20Leadership%20Talent.pdf.

De Pater, I. E., Van Vianen, A. E. M., Bechtoldt, M. N. & Klehe, U. C. (2009). Employees' challenging job experiences and supervisors' evaluations of promotability. *Personnel Psychology, 62*, 297–325. doi:10.1111/j.1744-6570.2009.01139.x.

Deloitte (2012). Fuelling the Asian growth engine: Talent challenges, strategies and trends. Retrieved on 20 March 2020 from: https://www2.deloitte.com/content/dam/Deloitte/global/Documents/HumanCapital/dttl-hc-fuellingtheasiangrowth-8092013.pdf

Deloitte (2015). SEA human capital trends 2015: Leading in the new world of work. Retrieved on 20 March 2020 from: https://www2.deloitte.com/content/dam/Deloitte/au/Documents/human-capital/deloitte-au-hc-global-human-capital-trends-2015-301115.pdf

Deloitte (2019). 2019 Global Human Capital Trends. Retrieved on 20 March 2020 from: https://www2.deloitte.com/us/en/insights/focus/human-capital-trends.html.

DeRue, D. S. & Wellman, N. (2009). Developing leaders via experience: The role of developmental challenge, learning orientation, and feedback availability. *Journal of Applied Psychology, 94*, 859–875. doi:10.1037/a0015317.

Dragoni, L., Tesluk, P. E., Russell, J. E. A. & Oh, I.-S. (2009). Understanding managerial development: Integrating developmental assignments, learning orientation, and access to developmental opportunities in predicting managerial competencies. *Academy of Management Journal, 52*, 731–743. doi:10.5465/AMJ.2009.43669936.

Economic Development Board (2017). *Talent: Investing in leadership development for Asia*. Singapore: Economic Development Board Singapore. Retrieved on 18 March 2020 from: https://www.edb.gov.sg/en/news-and-events/insights/talent/investing-in-leadership-development-for-asia.html

Ford, J. K., Quinones, M. A., Sego, D. J. & Sorra, J. S. (1992). Factors affecting the opportunity to perform trained tasks on the job. *Personnel Psychology, 45*, 511–527. doi:10.1111/j.1744-6570.1992.tb00858.x.

Frankovelgia, C. C. & Riddle, D. D. (2010). Leadership coaching. In E. Van Velsor, C. D. McCauley & M. N. Ruderman (Eds.), *The Center for Creative Leadership Handbook of Leadership Development* (3rd ed., pp. 125–146). Jossey-Bass (San Francisco, CA).

Glaveski, S. (2019). Where companies go wrong with learning and development. *Harvard Business Review*. Retrieved on 26 February 2020 from: https://hbr.org/2019/10/where-companies-go-wrong-with-learning-and-development.

Glomb, T. M. (2002). Workplace anger and aggression: Informing conceptual models with data from specific encounters. *Journal of Occupational Health Psychology, 7*, 20–36. doi:10.1037//1076-8998.7.1.20.

Iordanoglou, D. (2018). Future trends in leadership development practices and the crucial leadership skills. *Journal of Leadership, Accountability and Ethics, 15*, 118–129. doi: 10.33423/jlae.v15i2.648

LePine, J. A., Podsakoff, N. P. & Lepine, M. A. (2005). A meta-analytic test of the challenge stressor-hindrance stressor framework: An explanation for inconsistent relationships among stressors and performance. *Academy of Management Journal, 48*, 764–775. doi:10.5465/AMJ.2005.18803921.

Lewis, R. D. (2010). *When Cultures Collide: Leading across Cultures*. Nicholas Brealey Publishing (London, UK).

McCall, M. W. (2004). Leadership development through experience. *The Academy of Management Executive, 18*, 127–130. doi:10.2307/4166101.

McCall, M. W., Lombardo, M. M. & Morrison, A. M. (1988). *The Lessons of Experience: How Successful Executives Develop on the Job*. Lexington Books (Lexington, MA).

McCauley, C. D., Kanaga, K. & Lafferty, K. (2010). Leadership development systems. In E. Van Velsor, C. D. McCauley & M. N. Ruderman (Eds.), *The Center for Creative Leadership Handbook of Leadership Development* (3rd ed., pp. 29–61). Jossey-Bass (San Francisco, CA).

McCauley, C. D., McCall, M. W., Kraut, A. I., Nagrath, M. & Thulin, I. G. (2014). *Using Experience to Develop Leadership Talent: How Organizations Leverage On-the-Job Development*. Jossey-Bass (San Francisco, CA).

McCauley, C. D., Ohlott, P. J. & Ruderman, M. N. (1999). *Job Challenge Profile*. Jossey-Bass/Pfeiffer (New York, NY).

McCauley, C. D., Ruderman, M. N., Ohlott, P. J. & Morrow, J. E. (1994). Assessing the developmental components of managerial jobs. *Journal of Applied Psychology, 79*, 544–560. doi:10.1037/0021-9010.79.4.544.

McCauley, C. D., Van Velsor, E. & Ruderman, M. N. (2010). Introduction: Our view of leadership development. In E. Van Velsor, C. D. McCauley & M. N. Ruderman (Eds.), *The Center for Creative Leadership Handbook of Leadership Development* (3rd ed., pp. 1–28). Jossey-Bass (San Francisco, CA).

Mercer Mettl (2019). Leadership development trends 2019. Retrieved on 25 February 2020 from: https://www.mmc.com/content/dam/mmc-web/insights/publications/2019/sep/Leadership.Development.Trends.2019.pdf.

Mercer (2013). Asia Pacific leadership development practices study report. Retrieved on 25 February 2020 from: www.mercer.com › Talent › Develop-APLdrshpDevPractStudyRpt.

Moldoveanu, M. & Narayandas, D. (2019). The future of leadership development. *Harvard Business Review, 97*(2), 40–48. Retrieved on 29 January 2020 from: https://hbr.org/2019/03/the-future-of-leadership-development

Murre, J. M. J. & Dros, J. (2015). Replication and analysis of Ebbinghaus' forgetting curve. *PLoS ONE, 10* (7). doi:10.1371/journal.pone.0120644.

Ong, P. & Avolio, B. J. (2008). Accelerating the growth of the Asian leader. *Ethos*. Retrieved from: https://www.csc.gov.sg/articles/accelerating-the-growth-of-the-asian-leader.

Ong, P. Y. (2008). Leadership development in the Singapore public service. *Ethos*. Retrieved on 20 March 2020 from: https://www.csc.gov.sg/articles/leadership-development-in-the-singapore-public-service.

Prokopeak, M. (2018). Follow the leader(ship) spending. Retrieved on 20 March 2020 from: https://www.chieflearningofficer.com/2018/03/21/follow-the-leadership-spending/.

Puri, S., Zhao, S. & Chandrasekar, N. A. (2018). The global Asian leader: From local star to global CXO. Retrieved on 18 March 2020 from: https://www.ccl.org/wp-content/uploads/2018/02/The-Global-Asian-Leader-Research-Report.pdf.

Seibert, S. E., Sargent, L. D., Kraimer, M. L. & Kiazad, K. (2017). Linking developmental experiences to leader effectiveness and promotability: The mediating role of leadership self-efficacy and mentor network. *Personnel Psychology, 70*, 357–397. doi:10.1111/peps.12145.

The Conference Board. (2013). Fast track: Accelerating the leadership development of high potentials in Asia. Retrieved on 18 March 2020 from: https://www.rightmanagement.ch/wcm/connect/right-ch-en/home/thoughtwire/categories/thought-leadership/fast-track-accelerating-the-leadership-development-of-high-potentials-in-asia

Weiss, H. M. & Rupp, D. E. (2011). Experiencing work: An essay on a person-centric work psychology. *Industrial and Organizational Psychology: Perspectives on Science and Practice, 4*, 83–97. doi:10.1111/j.1754-9434.2010.01313.x.

Sooyeol Kim

Chapter 12
The Role of Leadership on Employees' Recovery in an Asian Context

"Recovery" refers to those processes, whether activities or experiences, by which employees relieve their stress and obtain the resources they need to maintain their levels of well-being and performance (Sonnentag & Geurts, 2009). As modern-day employees increasingly face heavy work-related demands and long working hours, the topic of recovery has garnered heightened research attention by those who seek opportunities to mitigate the effects of occupational stress. Various researchers have examined the benefits of recovery on employees' psychological well-being (Hunter & Wu, 2016; Kim et al., 2017; Kühnel et al., 2017; Zacher et al., 2014) and sales performance (Kim, Park & Headrick, 2018). Their studies have supported the idea that employee recovery helps reduce the costs of stress while supplying resources needed to achieve work-related outcomes. The benefits of recovery are important for today's employees, who work in a competitive globalized market.

The world's most accelerated economic growth and fiercest market competition are occurring in Asia. According to World Bank statistics (World Bank, n.d.), even amid the challenging global economic environment of the 2010s, certain East Asian countries (China, Japan, South Korea and Taiwan) and Association of Southeast Asian Nations (ASEAN) countries (Singapore, Indonesia, Malaysia and Vietnam) consistently showed rapid expansion and economic growth. However, this economic success made harsh demands on employees, whether in the form of long working hours, customer complaints or work pressure. Because interest in work–life balance and personal well-being is lower in the Asian context than in Western culture (Chandra, 2012), environmental supports are needed that can facilitate employees' recovery, improving their well-being as well as their work-related outcomes.

The literature on leadership is highly relevant to individuals' environmental roles and need for support in recharging energy or replenishing personal resources (cf., Carmeli, Ben-Hador & Waldman, 2009; Lanaj, Johnson & Lee, 2016; Song et al., 2012). Leaders, because of their authority and strategic position at work, are important influences on employees' work lives and performances (Farh, Lanaj & Ilies, 2017) as they set goals, make decisions, monitor progress, evaluate processes and lead projects (Lanaj et al., 2016). Over the past several decades, scholars have explored the role of leadership in, and the effects of leaders' behaviors on, followers' affective well-being, attitudes, motivation and performance-related outcomes (Bono & Judge, 2004; Judge & Piccolo, 2004). It is paramount that researchers and organizations seek ways of increasing leadership's ability to produce organizational success by focusing on leaders' roles (cf. Hogg, van Knippenberg & Rast, 2012). Accordingly, this chapter

https://doi.org/10.1515/9783110671988-012

outlines ways of promoting Asian employees' recovery and identifies their benefits from a leadership perspective.

Occupational Stress and Recovery in the Asian Work Setting

Modern workers are increasingly faced with heavy work demands, long work hours and intense time pressures (Bakker, Demerouti & Sanz-Vergel, 2014; Christian, Eisenkraft & Kapadia, 2015; Perlow, 1999), all of which complicate the use and management of their energy (Quinn, Spreitzer & Lam, 2012). Employees in the Asian context have high levels of exposure to such unfavorable environmental conditions.

Asia's miraculous economic growth has been driven by its workers' work ethic. According to a survey of more than 26,000 Asian employees conducted by AIA and Rand Europe, across the world, Asians work the longest hours. About half of Hong Kong employees work more than 50 hours per week, and Indonesian employees reported working more than 60 hours per week. Other countries, such as the Philippines, Thailand, Vietnam, China and South Korea, are similarly overworked. One academic study of a large population (n = 5,270 managers) found that Asian employees reported lower levels of job satisfaction and higher rates of turnover intention than Anglo (e.g., British), East European (e.g., Russian), and Latin American (Brazilian) employees (Spector et al., 2007). Similarly, a recent study on employees in China and Australia found that Chinese employees reported higher levels of psychological strain and lower levels of work engagement and social support than Australian workers (Brough et al., 2013).

What's more, longer working hours do not always correspond to a high quality of work. On average, employees in Hong Kong are absent or unable to concentrate on work for a total of 77.4 days per year because they experience physical or psychological illness. Employees in other countries showed similar losses of work productivity, including 73.4 days for Malaysia, 56 days for Thailand and 48 days for Sri Lanka. Considering US employees only lose fewer than 10 days due to absenteeism and presenteeism (e.g., employees present at work but not fully engaged in work due to illness or mental disengagement; Maestas, Mullen & Rennane, 2018), this number is very detrimental for organizations in Asia. Asian employees also suffer from a lack of job control and support, whether because of their lesser levels of job security or health support or the greater demands of their work. This suggests that Asian employees' occupational stress thus might detract from their physical and psychological health, lowering the quality of their work performance. Perhaps not surprisingly, Asian organizations spend significant sums on their employees' health care and related expenses. According to the report "Asia Total Health and Choice in Benefit in 2019," corporate health costs will double in Asia over the next few years

(Mercer Marsh Benefit, n.d.). Asian employees' occupational stress is also related to their unhealthy lifestyle (e.g., lack of exercise and unhealthy eating), which could explain their pattern of chronic illness and other health-related costs. Accordingly, minimizing the negative effects of Asian employees' occupational stress (e.g., long working hours, intense work demands) could help improve their work-related outcomes and organizational success.

The Construct of Recovery

To conceptualize employees' recovery process, scholars have proposed several theories, such as conservation of resources (COR) theory (Hobfoll, 1989), effort-recovery (ER) theory (Meijman & Mulder, 1998), the ego-depletion model (Baumeister et al., 1998) and the stressor-detachment model (Sonnentag, 2012). According to COR theory (Hobfoll, 1989), individuals have limited amounts of resources (e.g., physical energy, cognitive attention) with which to meet the demands of their surroundings, and when these resources are depleted, they experience stress. From this perspective, individuals experience strain (e.g., exhaustion) when their resources are threatened with loss, are lost or are not restored. To avoid negative consequences, individuals need to cease resource expenditure or replenish their resources.

ER theory (Meijman & Mulder, 1998) highlights the importance of timing for the recovery experience, positing that the continuous expenditure of effort (e.g., on work-related tasks) may deplete individuals' resources and decrease the quality of their performance. Accordingly, avoiding the negative costs of resource depletion requires that individuals cease their effort expenditure or gain resources through appropriate experiences.

The ego-depletion model (Baumeister et al., 1998) sees an individual's central psychological resources (ego) as determining his or her capacity for self-regulation but holds that this ego is limited and drained easily by working on self-regulatory tasks. In short, any kind of self-regulation draws on the same inner resources, so that self-regulation becomes increasingly difficult and less successful (Baumeister et al., 1998; Muraven & Baumeister, 2000). It is thus important that employees maintain the personal resources needed to avoid the regulation depletion status. More important, when individuals continue their regulatory activities (e.g., concentrating on tasks, regulating emotions), their subsequent self-regulatory efforts are likely to diminish in efficacy as their resource pool is drained (Muraven & Baumeister, 2000). In this view, self-regulatory resources act like a muscle or an engine that becomes fatigued and strained when used continuously, functioning less effectively as a result. To restore self-regulatory capacity, individuals must rest and avoid regulatory activity (Muraven & Baumeister, 2000) – a theoretical proposition with application to employees' workdays (Beal et al., 2005; Meijman & Mulder, 1998; Trougakos & Hideg, 2009).

Sonnentag and colleagues (2010) introduced a stressor-detachment model to explain the importance of psychological detachment in the recovery process. Psychological detachment refers to mental absence from work during the recovery process (Sonnentag et al., 2010). According to this model, psychological detachment plays both mediating and moderating roles between job stressors and strain outcomes. In short, the degree and experience of work stressors' detrimental effects vary with individual psychological detachment experiences.

Integrating all these theories, we can conclude that employees need the opportunity to (1) cease their work-related tasks or (2) replenish resources through timely and appropriate recovery experiences. Although employees engage in various activities (e.g., low-effort activities, socializing, hobbies, personal chores), these activities do not always support the recovery process. Four types of recovery experience are identified in the literature: psychological detachment, relaxation, mastery and control (cf. Sonnentag & Geurts, 2009). Psychological detachment refers to absence from work, relaxation to low-effort activities in which employees cease effort expenditure, mastery to learning new skills and gaining personal satisfaction by overcoming positive challenges, and control to recovery over nonwork time (e.g., recovery period). The associated recovery experiences have been found to correlate with various outcomes of recovery, such as psychological well-being, job attitude and performance (cf. Binnenwies, Sonnentag & Mojza, 2009; Sonnentag, Binnenwies & Mojza, 2008). Overall, this line of research has suggested that self-selected employee activities that either halt resource expenditure or replenish spent resources can represent effective energy management strategies for reenergizing employees. Next, we review various recovery domains inside and outside the work setting.

Empirical Findings on Recovery Off the Job

Prior research on recovery has focused primarily on the benefits of engaging in the recovery process during nonwork time, such as in the evenings after work, on weekends and during vacations, for employees' psychological well-being (cf. Trougakos & Hideg, 2009), job attitudes and performance (Binnewies et al., 2009). Researchers have argued that employees' recovery experiences in various personal settings help reduce stress and replenish resources while boosting productivity. In addition to traditional cross-sectional designs, recent studies on recovery have also employed an advanced study design called the experience sampling method (ESM). ESM requires that participants give responses multiple times per day regarding their affective state, attitudes, perceptions and experiences. By analyzing within-person variation and removing between-person effects (centering), ESM provides a good baseline for comparing recovery effects. Indeed, recent ESM-based research into recovery off the job has expanded the effects of recovery process during nonwork time for various outcomes.

Sonnentag and colleagues (2012) conducted daily ESM and found a reciprocal relationship between employees' daily level of recovery and their engagement at work. They found that employees' evening recovery level predicted their work engagement the next morning, which in turn affected their recovery level at the day's end. Niks and colleagues (2016) also conducted daily ESM-based diary design among a sample of hospital employees for eight consecutive working days, recording three data points per day. Their findings provided evidence that employees' detachment experience predicted their recovery state, which in turn predicted their job resource level the next morning. More recently, Clinton and colleagues (2017) conducted a daily ESM study with church ministers, finding that ministers' detachment experience at night was associated with their sleep quality, which in turn affected their level of vigor the next morning. Beyond the night-time recovery process, a couple of recent studies have investigated the recovery experience during weekends. For example, Petrou and Bakker (2016) examined employees' weekend leisure activities. Their weekly-design ESM data indicated that employees' leisure experiences (which are similar to the construct of mastery from their measurements) predicted their psychological satisfaction on their autonomy. Rasdale and colleagues (2016) also assessed recovery effects over weekends and found that employees' experiences of psychological detachment and control over weekends were associated with self-reported burnout and engagement.

Empirical Findings on Recovery on the Job

Beyond the recovery process in nonwork settings (e.g., evenings after work, weekends and vacations), employees can recover from their work in the work setting (e.g., through work breaks, lunch hours and microbreaks). Several empirical studies of recovery have been made since 2000, and most have been conducted using an ESM design. For example, Trougakos and colleagues (2008) conducted a daily diary study with a sample of cheerleading instructors to assess the effects of fixed breaks at work. Their hierarchical linear modeling analysis found that cheerleading instructors' respite activities during fixed breaks between sessions were associated with a high level of emotional display performance as measured by trainees' observations. Examining recovery processes during the lunch hour, Trougakos and colleagues (2014) found that employees' daily social activities during lunch hour were related to a reduced level of fatigue when their autonomy was high. This study highlighted the roles of both social activities and autonomy (control) in the recovery process.

Microbreaks, another form of recovery at work, have recently gained the attention of researchers. These short respites are taken informally and voluntarily between tasks as needed (Kim et al., 2017). Zacher and colleagues (2014) conducted an ESM study for ten consecutive working days and found within-person effects of employees' microbreaks (e.g., short breaks) on vitality (positive) and fatigue (negative). Hunter and Wu (2016) also highlighted the importance of timing for employees' micro-breaks, finding that employees' engagement in preferred activities and micro-breaks before work tasks predicted increases in their resources after work, which in turn led to lower levels of somatic symptoms. More recently, Kim and colleagues (2017) conducted another ESM study, lasting ten consecutive working days, in which they defined microbreak activities as employees' momentary and voluntary participation in respite activities between discretionary tasks or during working hours. Their multilevel path analysis found that employees' relaxation and social activities buffered the relationship between daily work demands and psychological well-being (i.e., negative affectivity at the end of the workday).

Kim and colleagues also identified increases in positive effects as a productivity benefit of employees' microbreaks (Kim, Park & Headricks, 2018). During these discretionary breaks, employees can choose to engage in their preferred respite activities, including relaxation (e.g., stretching, power napping), nutrition intake (e.g., consuming beverages and snacks), socialization (e.g., calling significant others, chatting with coworkers about nonwork matters) and cognitive activities (e.g., reading a magazine for fun; Kim et al., 2017, 2018; cf. Fritz et al., 2011). Overall, recent research has largely painted a picture in which work breaks reenergize individuals, increasing their well-being, improving their performance and reducing their strain (e.g., Hunter & Wu, 2016; Kim et al., 2018; Trougakos et al., 2008; Zacher et al., 2014; Zhu et al., 2019).

By reviewing the literature on recovery, the current study has highlighted the ways in which employees' various recovery opportunities enable them to repair the costs of their occupational stress and boost their levels of health and productivity. Now we turn to the ways in which leaders can facilitate employees in recovering health and productivity.

Leadership and Recovery in an Asian Context

Leadership in Asia

Because of their authority and strategic position at work, leaders are important influences on employees' work lives and performances (Farh et al., 2017) as they set goals, make decisions, monitor progress, evaluate processes and lead projects (Lanaj et al., 2016). Evidence for leadership's role in followers' well-being, job satisfaction and performance-related outcomes is ample (cf. Derue et al., 2011; Montano et al., 2017). Moreover, an increasing body of research has shown that the quality of leadership performance varies across workdays, with its fluctuations predicting important daily follower outcomes such as stress and work engagement (e.g., Barnes et al., 2016;

Breevaart & Bakker, 2018; Diebig, Bormann & Rowold, 2016; Tims, Bakker & Xantho-poulou, 2011; Lanaj et al., 2016).

In the Asian context, cultural emphasis on power distance, paternalism, collectivism and social relations is stronger than in Western culture (Hofstede & Hofstede, 2004; Pellegrini & Scandura, 2008). What's more, social gatherings play an important role in generating, sustaining and otherwise benefiting organizations. These cultural, contextual and institutional characteristics give Asian leaders great influence on and power over employees' work lives and work-related outcomes. However, because cross-cultural similarities in leadership outnumber differences, Western findings regarding the effects of leader behaviors are appropriate for application to Asian leaders (Bass, 1997; House et al., 2004). For example, recent research has found no difference between Chinese and Western employees' power distance orientation or reactions (Kirkman et al., 2009). Organizational support systems, such as job autonomy or quality of leadership, are important job resources for employees the world over. Accordingly, a role for leadership and its influence on employees can be suggested and confirmed in the Asian context.

Leadership and Recovery

Leadership's key role in promoting policy and changing practices in the work setting (Kossek, Barber & Winters, 1999) could allow employees to minimize situational constraints that inhibit their recovery from work (Bakker, Demerouti & Euwema, 2005). In general, leaders such as CEOs, board members and managers have the power and authority to set rules, conditions and contractual obligations. Although a firm may officially espouse recovery-friendly policies, the success of their implementation depends on the degree to which leaders understand the policy and try to put its ideas into practice in the work setting (Lirio et al., 2008). Accordingly, leaders' perceptions of recovery and attitudes toward employees' recovery experiences significantly affect those recovery experiences. For example, if leaders do not support employees' recovery experiences, then employees may feel guilty or uncomfortable when engaging in such experiences. Recovery on the job in particular may raise the spectre of retaliation by leaders. Accordingly, when leaders acknowledge the importance of subordinates' recovery experiences to performance quality and support and implement recovery programs, employees can better reap the benefits of recovery experiences while reducing the negative costs of work demands.

To actively show the support of recovery, leaders could provide both tangible and intangible resources. Tangible resources include everything that employees can use to recover at both home and work. For example, leaders can offer wellness programs that promote physical activity with which to help employees recover (Society of Human Resource Management, 2017), or they can provide various resources for employee recovery opportunities at work, such as external internet access to social media platforms (e.g., Facebook, YouTube), recliners in the resting area, free coffee, vending machines, magazines and newspapers. However, the availability of tangible resources is not solely determined by leaders – top management is also influential.

Intangible resources include formal or informal policies, cultures or climates that management and leaders create to support or manage employee recovery. When management provides more tangible resources and a supportive environment rich with intangible resources, management support for microbreaks is stronger. However, leaders must go beyond providing various resources to also make them accessible to employees, such as by placing them in visible and accessible locations (e.g., by putting vending machines in the kitchen rather than the corner of the hallway) or by communicating effectively with employees through emails, or newsletters. In short, organizations may support recovery-friendly cultures, but implementation of those supports depends on employees' direct supervisors – their leaders. Specifically, leaders can encourage employee recovery by implementing two job resources: health climate and recovery autonomy.

Health climate is defined as "employee perceptions of active support from coworkers, supervisors, and upper management for the physical and psychological well-being of employees" (Zweber et al., 2016, p. 250). This multifaceted construct captures employees' perspectives about how each source supports employee health and well-being. The workgroup factor (1) addresses the ways in which norms and expectations about health and health-related behaviors are communicated and encouraged during interactions with coworkers. Moreover, because workplace climate emerges through employee interactions as well as organizational policies and procedures and supervisory practices (Schneider & Reichers, 1983), this construct includes (2) supervisory support and encouragement for employee health and (3) organizational resources for, and responsiveness to, employee health and health issues. Zweber et al. (2016) theorized that these three elements are critical parts of establishing a healthy workplace, and this health climate can be assessed as an overall latent construct.

Employees' recovery practices and their effects could vary among employees who work in different health climates. Generally, climate refers to the ways in which individuals in an organization make sense of their environment in its norms, values, attitudes and behaviors (Reichers & Schneider, 1990). Accordingly, employees' perceptions of their health climate may either promote or inhibit their replenishment of personal resources for work and health.

In a favorable health climate under supportive leadership, employees may view participation in recovery-inducing activities (e.g., not taking work home, taking frequent breaks at work) as appropriate and viable health-related behaviors, especially when their resource capacity is running low. For example, when supervisors are highly supportive of their health and well-being, employees will feel more psychological safety when receiving information about the importance of recovery after work or taking discretionary breaks as needed and deciding how to spend them. By contrast, in an unsupportive health climate, employees postpone appropriate recovery due to a lack of support and information about recovery. Further, some break activities (e.g., napping, chatting about nonwork matters, enjoying social media) may be considered counterproductive and may be frowned upon. Those working in an unsupportive health climate may be likely to refrain from recovery even when they need to repair their poor resource capacity for the sake of their health (e.g., sickness) or their work-related outcomes (e.g., low engagement).

Another aspect of leaders' support of employees' recovery process is *recovery autonomy*. Perceived control refers generally to the degree to which individuals can take actions at their discretion (Karasek & Theorell, 1990). Likewise, recovery autonomy represents individuals' perceived ability to freely choose when and how to engage in recovery (cf. Sonnentag & Fritz, 2007; Trougakos et al., 2014). Asian employees are constantly under pressure to perform work-related activities so as to achieve higher productivity and better quality. An employee who has recovery autonomy has the choice to engage in recovery experiences as needed. In short, such an employee has the discretion to balance recovery and work tasks. To promote autonomy, leaders can set clear boundaries between employees' work and personal lives, prohibit overworking at night or on weekends, or let employees decide more freely how to structure their workdays to better balance work and rest to better account for fluctuating resource levels.

Under supportive leadership that values and advocates for well-being and health, employees may develop a greater sense of autonomy over their recovery as their leaders endorse various respite activities for the sake of employees' well-being and work outcomes. COR theory also views individuals' autonomy and control as important resources that can facilitate resource-gain processes (Halbesleben et al., 2014; Hobfoll, 2011; Hobfoll et al., 2018). In short, employees who have greater autonomy in recovery may have discretion over the planning and execution of their brief respite activities, strengthening the effects of recovery. Taken together, leaders' level of support for recovery autonomy influences employees' perceived level of cognitive and behavioral control over recovery and thus predicts actual recovery.

As already noted, employee health is underprioritized in Asian work settings (Mercer Marsh Benefit, n.d.). As Asian organizations have aggressively expanded their markets and achieved rapid growth, they have often sacrificed employees' personal lives and well-being. As a result, amid longer working hours and demanding duties, employees have lacked support in recuperating from work and recharging their resources. Asian employees generally receive poor support from their leaders for their health and well-being and thus suffer high levels of work-related stress and associated effects on health and work outcomes (Olano, 2020). Leadership, then, must play a decisive role in Asian employees' recovery.

Future Research in Asian Leadership and Recovery

In this section, I suggest future research avenues that can address gaps in the research on leadership and recovery, as well as possible theoretical backgrounds for these studies. First, future research could investigate the direct effects of leaders' support for employees' recovery in Asian contexts specifically. Despite a rich body of findings concerning the recovery process and its various outcomes, previous research has focused on Western contexts (cf. Trougakos & Hideg, 2009; Sonnentag et al., 2017). The potential for cultural differences in leadership's effects on employee recovery (cf. Luo et al., 2019) calls for use of Asian samples to investigate the role of Asian leadership in the recovery process.

Second, organizational scientists could use advanced technology to investigate the role of leadership in employees' recovery. According to McKinsey (2016; 2019), Asia has fostered the use of technology (e.g., smartphones, high-speed internet, social media, artificial intelligence) and digital innovation over the past few decades. In this quickly growing and aggressive market, individuals have ready access to cutting-edge mobile and digital technologies. Future studies could employ those advanced technologies to investigate the broader relationship between leadership by testing a comprehensive model of recovery and recovery outcomes (e.g., recovery's effects on psychological, physiological and behavioral outcomes). For example, researchers could use wearable devices (e.g., Fitbit, Apple Watch) to assess participants' physiological (e.g., blood pressure, heart rate) and physical (e.g., exercise) outcomes. Furthermore, smartphone applications such as Stepz or Cue can provide objective information about individual physical activities (e.g., movements) and other types of recovery-inducing activities (e.g., stretching, breathing fresh air).

Third, the role of leader–employee relationships in leaders' support of recovery should be examined, for the quality of leaders' support of employees will not be same for every relationship. The leader–member exchange (LMX) perspective posits that a leader forms and maintains relationships of varying quality with different employees within the group (Liden & Maslyn, 1998). Specifically, a leader spends differing amounts of time and resources to develop relationships with each employee, and the quality of each employee's experienced interactions with the leader may vary depending on the degree of each relationship (cf. Bono & Yoon, 2012). Because the degree of experience or effect transferred from leaders to followers differs for each relationship, LMX may be an important boundary condition for the crossover effects of leaders' impacts on followers' perceptions and attitudes (McCauley, 2012). Specifically, relationships have great power in the Asian context, as expressed by the concepts of *guanxi* in China or *inhwa* in South Korea. Individual relationships between leaders and employees will thus affect leaders' support of their employees' recovery. In Asian workplaces, leaders selectively maintain high- or low-quality LMX with their followers, as exemplified, respectively, by high trust, interactions, support and formal/informal rewards or by low trust, interactions, support and rewards (Liden & Maslyn, 1998). Thus, leaders' degree of interest in and attention to their followers may differ based on the quality of each one-on-one relationship. Following this argument, leaders sort their followers into an in-group that enjoys higher-quality LMX or an out-group that experiences lower-quality LMX, then manifest different attitudes and behaviors toward each group (Tse, Ashkanasy & Dasborough, 2012). Future studies could assess the role of LMX in Asian leaders' support of recovery and in their employees' subsequent recovery outcomes.

Conclusion

In the context of Asia, the workplace has become globalized, and the market is getting competitive with fast-changing technology. Today's Asian leaders experience a significant amount of stress and work pressure to facilitate their followers' work performance as well as organizational success in the market. They have considerably long working hours and their positions come with high demands and expectations from various stakeholders. Considering that recovery plays an important role in reducing occupational stress and promoting one's wellbeing and work outcomes, Asian leaders should acknowledge the importance of recovery for the quality of their leadership. By experiencing the benefits of recovery from various recovery-inducing activities (e.g., relaxation, exercise, socialization), Asian leaders seek to sustain their physical and psychological resources for long-lasting effective leadership, as well as avoiding burnout or exhaustion. Sustainability is one of the important key factors in today's globalized business market, and recovery can be one of the answers for Asian leaders' sustainability.

References

Bakker, A. B., Demerouti, E. & Euwema, M. C. (2005). Job resources buffer the impact of job demands on burnout. *Journal of Occupational Health Psychology*, *10*(2), 170–180.

Bakker, A. B., Demerouti, E. & Sanz-Vergel, A. I. (2014). Burnout and work engagement: The JD-R approach. *Annual Review of Organizational Psychology and Organizational Behavior*, *1*, 389–411.

Bass, B. M. (1997). Does the transactional–transformational leadership paradigm transcend organizational and national boundaries? *American Psychologist*, *52*(2), 130–139.

Baumeister, R. F., Bratslavsky, E., Muraven, M. & Tice, D. M. (1998). Ego depletion: Is the active self a limited resource? *Journal of Personality and Social Psychology*, *74*(5), 1252–1265.

Barnes, C. M., Guarana, C. L., Nauman, S. & Kong, D. T. (2016). Too tired to inspire or be inspired: Sleep deprivation and charismatic leadership. *Journal of Applied Psychology*, *101*(8), 1191–1199.

Beal, D. J., Weiss, H. M., Barros, E. & MacDermid, S. M. (2005). An episodic process model of affective influences on performance. *Journal of Applied Psychology*, *90*, 1054–1068.

Binnewies, C., Sonnentag, S. & Mojza, E. J. (2009). Daily performance at work: Feeling recovered in the morning as a predictor of day-level job performance. *Journal of Organizational Behavior*, *30*, 67–93.

Bono, J. E. & Judge, T. A. (2004). Personality and transformational and transactional leadership: a meta-analysis. *Journal of Applied Psychology*, *89*(5), 901.

Bono, J. E. & Yoon, D. J. (2012). Positive Supervisory Relationships. In L. T. de Tormes Eby & T. D. Allen (Eds.), Personal Relationships: The Effect on Employee Attitudes, Behavior, and Well-being. Pennsylvania, PA: Taylor & Francis Group.

Breevaart, K. & Bakker, A. B. (2018). Daily job demands and employee work engagement: The role of daily transformational leadership behavior. *Journal of Occupational Health Psychology*, *23*(3), 338–349.

Brough, P., Timms, C., Siu, O. L., Kalliath, T., O'Driscoll, M. P., Sit, C. H., . . . & Lu, C. Q. (2013). Validation of the Job Demands-Resources model in cross-national samples: Cross-sectional and longitudinal predictions of psychological strain and work engagement. *Human Relations*, *66*(10), 1311–1335.

Carmeli, A., Ben-Hador, B., Waldman, D. A. & Rupp, D. E. (2009). How leaders cultivate social capital and nurture employee vigor: Implications for job performance. *Journal of Applied Psychology*, *94*(6), 1553.

Chandra, V. (2012). Work–life balance: Eastern and Western perspectives. *The International Journal of Human Resource Management*, *23*(5), 1040–1056.

Christian, M. S., Eisenkraft, N. & Kapadia, C. (2015). Dynamic associations among somatic complaints, human energy, and discretionary behaviors: Experiences with pain fluctuations at work. *Administrative Science Quarterly*, *60*(1), 66–102.

Clinton, M. E., Conway, N. & Sturges, J. (2017). "It's tough hanging-up a call": The relationships between calling and work hours, psychological detachment, sleep quality, and morning vigor. *Journal of Occupational Health Psychology*, *22*, 28–39.

Diebig, M., Bormann, K. C. & Rowold, J. (2016). A double-edged sword: Relationship between full-range leadership behaviors and followers' hair cortisol level. *The Leadership Quarterly*, *27*(4), 684–696

Derue, D. S., Nahrgang, J. D., Wellman, N. E. D. & Humphrey, S. E. (2011). Trait and behavioral theories of leadership: An integration and meta-analytic test of their relative validity. *Personnel Psychology*, *64*(1), 7–52.

Farh, C. I., Lanaj, K. & Ilies, R. (2017). Resource-based contingencies of when team–member exchange helps member performance in teams. *Academy of Management Journal*, *60*(3), 1117–1137.

Fritz, C., Lam, C. F., & Spreitzer, G. M. (2011). It's the little things that matter: An examination of knowledge workers' energy management. *Academy of Management Perspectives*, *25*, 28–39. doi: 10.5465/amp.25.3.zol28

Halbesleben, J. R., Neveu, J. P., Paustian-Underdahl, S. C. & Westman, M. (2014). Getting to the "COR": Understanding the role of resources in conservation of resources theory. *Journal of Management*, *40*, 1334–1364.

Hobfoll, S. E. (1989). Conservation of resources: A new attempt at conceptualizing stress. *American Psychologist*, *44*, 513–524. doi:10.1037/0003-066X.44.3.513.

Hobfoll, S. E. (2011). Conservation of resource caravans and engaged settings. *Journal of Occupational and Organizational Psychology*, *84*, 116–122. doi: 10.1111/j.2044-8325.2010.02016.x.

Hobfoll, S. E., Halbesleben, J., Neveu, J. P. & Westman, M. (2018). Conservation of resources in the organizational context: The reality of resources and their consequences. *Annual Review of*

Organizational Psychology and Organizational Behavior, 5, 103–128. doi: 10.1146/annurev-orgpsych-032117-104640.

Hofstede, G. & McCrae, R. R. (2004). Personality and culture revisited: Linking traits and dimensions of culture. *Cross-Cultural Research, 38*(1), 52–88.

Hogg, M. A., Van Knippenberg, D. & Rast III, D. E. (2012). Intergroup leadership in organizations: Leading across group and organizational boundaries. *Academy of Management Review, 37*(2), 232–255.

House, R. J., Hanges, P. J., Javidan, M., Dorfman, P. W. & Gupta, V. (eds), (2004) *Culture, Leadership and Organizations: The GLOBE Study of 62 Societies*, Sage Publications (Thousand Oaks, CA).

hu, Z., Kuykendall, L., & Zhang, X. (breaks on daily recovery processes: An event-based pre-/post-experience sampling study. *Journal of Occupational and Organizational Psychology, 92*, 191–211. doi: 10.1111/joop.122462019). The impact of within-day work

Hunter, E. M. & Wu, C. (2016). Give me a better break: Choosing workday break activities to maximize resource recovery. *Journal of Applied Psychology, 101*, 302–311.

Judge, T. A. & Piccolo, R. F. (2004). Transformational and transactional leadership: a meta-analytic test of their relative validity. *Journal of Applied Psychology, 89*(5), 755.

Karasek, R. & Theorell, T. (1990). *Healthy Work: Stress, Productivity, and the Reconstruction of Working Life*. Basic Books (New York, NY).

Kim, S., Park, Y. & Headrick, L. (2018). Daily microbreaks and job performance: General work engagement as a cross-level moderator. *Journal of Applied Psychology, 103*, 772–786. doi: 10.1037/apl0000308.

Kim, S., Park, Y. & Niu, Q. (2017). Micro-break activities in the workplace to recover from daily work demands. *Journal of Organizational Behavior, 38*, 28–44. doi: 10.1002/job.2109.

Kirkman, B. L., Chen, G., Farh, J. L., Chen, Z. X. & Lowe, K. B. (2009). Individual power distance orientation and follower reactions to transformational leaders: A cross-level, cross-cultural examination. *Academy of Management Journal, 52*(4), 744–764.

Kossek, E. E., Barber, A. E., & Winters, D. (1999). Using flexible schedules in the managerial world: The power of peers. *Human Resource Management: Published in Cooperation with the School of Business Administration, The University of Michigan and in alliance with the Society of Human Resources Management, 38*(1), 33–46.

Kühnel, J., Zacher, H., De Bloom, J. & Bledow, R. (2017). Take a break! Benefits of sleep and short breaks for daily work engagement. *European Journal of Work and Organizational Psychology, 26*(4), 481–491.

Lanaj, K., Johnson, R. E. & Lee, S. M. (2016). Benefits of transformational behaviors for leaders: A daily investigation of leader behaviors and need fulfillment. *Journal of Applied Psychology, 101*, 237–251.

Liden, R. C., & Maslyn, J. M. (1998). Multidimensionality of leader-member exchange: An empirical assessment through scale development. *Journal of management, 24*(1), 43–72.

Lirio, P., Lee, M. D., Williams, M. L., Haugen, L. K. & Kossek, E. E. (2008). The inclusion challenge with reduced-load professionals: The role of the manager. *Human Resource Management: Published in Cooperation with the School of Business Administration, The University of Michigan and in alliance with the Society of Human Resources Management, 47*(3), 443–461.

Luo, A., Guchait, P., Lee, L. & Madera, J. M. (2019). Transformational leadership and service recovery performance: the mediating effect of emotional labor and the influence of culture. *International Journal of Hospitality Management, 77*, 31–39.

Maestas, N. A., Mullen, K. J., & Rennane, S. (2018). Absenteeism and presenteeism among American workers. Journal of Disability Policy Studies, Retrieved from: https://www.econstor.eu/bitstream/10419/216444/1/dp13132.pdf.

McCauley, C. D. 2012. Reflection and integration: Supervisor–employee relationships. In L. Eby & T. Allen (Eds.), *Personal Relationships: The Effect on Employee Attitudes, Behavior and Well-Being* (pp. 95–105). New York, NY: Taylor & Francis.

McKinsey (2016). Digital innovation in Asia: What the world can learn. *McKinsey.com*. Retrieved on 9 January 2021, from: https://www.mckinsey.com/business-functions/mckinsey-digital/our-insights/digital-innovation-in-asia-what-the-world-can-learn.

McKinsey (2019). Winning in a world of ecosystem. *McKinsey.com*. Retrieved on 9 January 2021, from: https://www.mckinsey.com/industries/financial-services/our-insights/winning-in-a-world-of-ecosystems.

Meijman, T. F. & Mulder, G. (1998). Psychological aspects of workload. In P. J. D. Drenth, H. K. Thierry, & C. J. De Wolff (Eds.), *Handbook of Work and Organizational Psychology* (2nd ed., pp. 5–33). Psychology Press/Erlbaum (Hove, UK).

Mercer Marsh Benefit (n.d.). Asia total health and choice in benefits report. Retrieved on 9 November 2020, from: https://www.mercer.com.sg/our-thinking/health/mercer-marsh-benefits-medical-trends-survey-2019.html#.

Montano, D., Reeske, A., Franke, F. & Hüffmeier, J. (2017). Leadership, followers' mental health and job performance in organizations: A comprehensive meta-analysis from an occupational health perspective. *Journal of Organizational Behavior*, *38*(3), 327–350.

Muraven, M. & Baumeister, R. F. (2000). Self-regulation and depletion of limited resources: Does self-control resemble a muscle? *Psychological Bulletin*, *126*(2), 247–259.

Niks, I. M., Gevers, J. M., De Jonge, J. & Houtman, I. L. (2016). The relation between off-job recovery and job resources: Person-level differences and day-level dynamics. *European Journal of Work and Organizational Psychology*, *25*(2), 226–238.

Olano, G. (2020). Theres's a huge gap in support for employees' mental health – AXA Asia CEO. *Insurance Business Asia*. Retrieved on 10 November 2020, from: https://www.insurancebusinessmag.com/asia/features/interviews/theres-a-huge-gap-in-support-for-employees-mental-health–axa-asia-ceo-214577.aspx.

Pellegrini, E. K. & Scandura, T. A. (2008). Paternalistic leadership: A review and agenda for future research. *Journal of Management*, *34*(3), 566–593.

Perlow, L. A. (1999). The time famine: Toward a sociology of work time. *Administrative Science Quarterly*, *44*(1), 57–81.

Petrou, P. & Bakker, A. B. (2016). Crafting one's leisure time in response to high job strain. *Human Relations*, *69*(2), 507–529.

Quinn, R. W., Spreitzer, G. M. & Lam, C. F. (2012). Building a sustainable model of human energy in organizations: Exploring the critical role of resources. *Academy of Management Annals*, *6*(1), 337–396.

Reichers, A. E., & Schneider, B. (1990). Climate and culture: An evolution of constructs. In B. Schneider (Ed.), *Organizational climate and culture* (pp. 5–39). San Francisco, CA: Jossey-Bass.

Schneider, B. & Reichers, A. E. (1983). On the etiology of climates. *Personnel Psychology*, *36*(1), 19–39.

Sonnentag, S. (2012). Psychological detachment from work during leisure time: The benefits of mentally disengaging from work. *Current Directions in Psychological Science*, *21*, 114–118. doi:10.1177/0963721411434979

Sonnentag, S., Binnewies, C. & Mojza, E. J. (2008). "Did you have a nice evening?": A day-level study on recovery experiences, sleep, and affect. *Journal of Applied Psychology*, *93*, 674–684.

Sonnentag, S. & Fritz, C. (2007). The Recovery Experience Questionnaire: development and validation of a measure for assessing recuperation and unwinding from work. *Journal of Occupational Health Psychology*, *12*(3), 204–221.

Sonnentag, S., Mojza, E. J., Demerouti, E. & Bakker, A. B. (2012). Reciprocal relations between recovery and work engagement: the moderating role of job stressors. *Journal of Applied Psychology, 97*(4), 842–853.

Sonnentag, S., Kuttler, I. & Fritz, C. (2010). Job stressors, emotional exhaustion, and need for recovery: A multi-source study on the benefits of psychological detachment. *Journal of Vocational Behavior, 76*(3), 355–365.

Sonnentag, S. & Geurts, S. A. E. (2009). Methodological issues in recovery research. In S. Sonnentag, P. L. Perrewé, & D. C. Ganster (Eds.), *Current Perspectives on Job-Stress Recovery: Research in Occupational Stress and Well-being* (pp. 1–36). Emerald Publishing Group (Oxford, UK).

Sonnentag, S., Venz, L., & Casper, A. (2017). Advances in recovery research: What have we learned? What should be done next? *Journal of Occupational Health Psychology, 22*: 365–380. doi: 10.1037/ocp0000079

Song, J. H., Kolb, J. A., Lee, U. H. & Kim, K. H. (2012). Role of transformational leadership in effective organizational knowledge creation practices: Mediating effects of employees' work engagement. *Human Resource Development Quarterly, 23*(1), 65–101.

Spector, P. E., Allen, T. D., Poelmans, S. A., Lapierre, L. M., Cooper, C. L., Michael, O. D., . . . & Brough, P. (2007). Cross-national differences in relationships of work demands, job satisfaction, and turnover intentions with work–family conflict. *Personnel Psychology, 60*(4), 805–835.

Tims, M., Bakker, A. B. & Xanthopoulou, D. (2011). Do transformational leaders enhance their followers' daily work engagement? *Leadership Quarterly, 22*(1), 121–131.

Tse, H. H. M., Ashkanasy, N. M. & Dasborough, M. T. (2012). Relative leader–member exchange, negative affectivity and social identification: A moderated-mediation examination. *Leadership Quarterly, 23*, 354–366.

Trougakos, J. P., Beal, D. J., Green, S. G. & Weiss, H. M. (2008). Making the break count: An episodic examination of recovery activities, emotional experiences, and positive affective displays. *Academy of Management Journal, 51*, 131–146.

Trougakos, J. P. & Hideg, I. (2009). Momentary work recovery: The role of within day work breaks. In S. Sonnentag, P. L. Perrrewé, & D. C. Ganster (Eds.), *Research in Occupational* Stress *and Well-being* (Vol. 7, pp. 37–84). JAI Press (Oxford, UK).

Trougakos, J. P., Hideg, I., Cheng, B. H. & Beal, D. J. (2014). Lunch breaks unpacked: The role of autonomy as a moderator of recovery during lunch. *Academy of Management Journal, 57*, 405–421.

World Bank (n.d.). World Bank Open Data. Retrieved from: https://data.worldbank.org.

Zacher, H., Brailsford, H. A. & Parker, S. L. (2014). Microbreaks matter: A diary study on the effects of energy management strategies on occupational well-being. *Journal of Vocational Behavior, 85*, 287–297. doi:10.1016/j.jvb.2014.08.005.

Zweber, Z. M., Henning, R. A. & Magley, V. J. (2016). A practical scale for multi-faceted organizational health climate assessment. *Journal of Occupational Health Psychology, 21*(2), 250–259.

About the Editor

 **David De Cremer** is Provost Chair and Professor in Management and Organisation at NUS Business School. Before moving to NUS, he was the KPMG endowed Professor of Management Studies at Cambridge Judge Business School (CJBS) and a fellow at St. Edmunds College, University of Cambridge (UK). He is the director and founder of the Centre on AI Technology for Humankind (AiTH) at NUS Business School. Currently, his external affiliations include an honorary fellowship at CJBS, fellow at St. Edmunds College at Cambridge University and a research affiliate at the Justice Collaboratory at Yale Law School, Yale University. He received his Ph.D. from the University of Southampton, England, an M.A. from the University of Cambridge, and an M.Sc. in Psychology and B.A. in Philosophy from the University of Leuven, Belgium. He was a faculty member and (visiting) professor at London Business School (LBS), China Europe International Business School (CEIBS), Harvard University, Stanford University and Rotterdam School of Management (RSM). He has taken up several senior leadership roles including director and founder of two research centers at NUS and RSM, head of department, school leadership team and academic directorships at Cambridge University, NUS and CEIBS, and Vice-president (Internationalization) at Wenzhou College of Business.

As a best-selling author, his book *Huawei: Leadership, Culture and Connectivity* (awarded the 2018 PwC Best Business Book in Russia) has sold over 1,000,000 copies and is to date still the number one best-selling book in the Asia-Pacific region in the category "business and management." His most recent book *Leadership by Algorithm: Who Leads and Who Follows in the AI Era?* has topped the charts of the kindle version at amazon.com, has been referred to as one of the best 15 leadership books to read in 2020 by Wharton and his thought leadership in this area has been picked up by the World Economic Forum.

In 2005, he received the honor to become a fellow of the Royal Dutch Academy of Science. In 2009–2010, he was named the most influential (behavioral) economist in the Netherlands (Top 40 of economists), and then in 2016 was voted one of the Top Thought Leaders in Trust by Trust Across America (alongside the late management guru Stephen Covey; and Richard Edelman, President and CEO of Edelman, and Publisher of the annual Edelman Trust Barometer) whose annual list recognizes people for efforts "in elevating societal trust." In 2020, he was named one of the 30 Global Gurus and Speakers in management by the organization GlobalGurus, included in the World's top 2 percent of scientists, and in 2021, he was named a Thinkers50 Radar, which is an annual ranking by the organization Thinkers50 to identify 30 minds globally to watch (*The Financial Times* called it the "Oscars of Management Thinking"). He is also the recipient of many scientific awards including the British Psychology Society award for "Outstanding Ph.D. Thesis in Social Psychology," the "Jos Jaspars Early Career Award for Outstanding Contributions to Social Psychology," the "Comenius European Young Psychologist Award," and the "International Society for Justice Research Early Career Contribution Award." In 2013, he was awarded the CEIBS Research Excellence Award (Shanghai, China), and in 2015 received the mid-career award from the British Psychology Society for his contributions to the field of Social Psychology.

https://doi.org/10.1515/9783110671988-013

List of Contributors

Audrey Chia is Associate Professor at the NUS Business School, with a joint appointment at the Yong Loo Lin School of Medicine, National University of Singapore. She is also Programme Management Chair of the MSc. Environmental Management Programme, which is a collaboration by nine faculties and schools across NUS. Professor Chia's research applies leadership, change and innovation as theoretical foundations to address health, environmental and social challenges. Her work has been published in journals such as *JAMA* (*Journal of the American Medical Association*) and *Academy of Management Executive*. She has been invited as an expert on social entrepreneurship, innovative philanthropy, innovative financing and sustainable development to meetings of the United Nations, Asian Development Bank, OECD, and the Asia-Pacific Leaders' Malaria Alliance. Professor Chia has also served as consultant or expert on leadership, change and social innovation for companies such as Bridgestone, Dentsu, Deutsche Bahn-Schenker, Total, Catalyst, DHL, Jones Lang LaSalle, L'Oreal, McDonald's, Maersk, Mitsui, Panasonic, Samsung, Telenor, Royal Brunei Airlines, PT Astra, Temasek Foundation, Brunei's Ministry of Health, Singtel and Swiss Re. Professor Chia directs NUS Business School's Leadership Development Programme, which attracts participants from five continents. She also conducts Leadership Ethics at Yale-NUS College. From 2011 to 2017, she was Programme Director of the NIHA (NUS Initiative to Improve Health in Asia) Healthcare Leadership Programme for senior leaders in the public, private and NGO sectors from 15 countries across Asia.

Melody Chong is an instructor at City University of Hong Kong. Her courses focus on Asian values and managerial practices, and comparative management. She has published research papers in *Journal of World Business*, *Journal of Cross-Cultural Psychology*, *Leadership and Organization Development Journal*, *Chinese Management Studies*, and *Thinking Skills and Creativity*. Her research interests center on leadership, Asian management, cross-cultural management and creativity.

Hannah De Cremer is an enthusiastic four-year old exploring the world by asking questions, testing ideas and wondering about life's deeper meanings like the necessity to bring the entire Sylvanian family together. Early on she became interested in assisting the current research project to understand the cultural dimensions of the world that we live in with the aim to arrive at a more comprehensive view on the kind of leadership we will see in the future. Related to this ambition, she also served as an inspiration for David De Cremer's book *Leadership by Algorithm: Who Leads and Who Follows in the AI Era?*

Irene E. de Pater is Associate Professor at Curtin University's School of Management, Faculty of Business and Law. In her research, she applies theory of organizational behavior to understand how employees react to and can deal effectively with the experiences they have at work and the consequences these experiences have for both their work and personal life. Her research focuses mainly on experiences related to the work they conduct (i.e., the content of work) and the people they encounter (i.e., interpersonal interactions). Her work has been published in scholarly journals such as *Journal of Applied Psychology*, *Journal of Organizational Behavior*, *Personnel Psychology*, *Group and Organizational Management*, and *Journal of Occupational and Organizational Psychology*. She is an active reviewer for numerous scientific journals in management and psychology and currently serves as Associate Editor for the *Journal of Managerial Psychology*.

https://doi.org/10.1515/9783110671988-014

Alison R. Eyring, Ph.D., is the founder and CEO of Organisation Solutions and Adjunct Associate Professor at the NUS Business School. She is the chief architect of Produgie, a B2B SaaS solution offering premium, personalized growth leadership services as affordable, pay-as-you-go products. She has more than 30 years of experience guiding organization growth and transformation.

James D. Eyring, Ph.D., is Chief Operating Officer of Organisation Solutions. James has led global and regional HR and L&D functions in leading multinationals. As an experienced executive coach, James has worked with leaders around the world as they drive business growth and team development. He is an industrial/organizational psychologist.

Jamie L. Gloor, Ph.D., is a senior lecturer at the University of Exeter Business School and a Digital Society Initiative Research Fellow at the University of Zurich. Her research interests include gender and diversity, leadership, and humor.

Sooyeol Kim is Assistant Professor (tenure-track) in the Department of Management and Organization at National University of Singapore. He received his Ph.D. from University of Illinois at Urbana-Champaign in Human Resources Management. He also received his BA from Michigan State University in Psychology and his MA from George Mason University in Industrial and Organizational Psychology. His research interests include occupational stress and well-being, recovery process, and leader–member dyadic interactions at work. His research has been published in internationally refereed journals such as the *Journal of Applied Psychology, Journal of Organizational Behavior, Journal of Occupational Health Psychology, and Journal of Applied Social Psychology*.

Sandy Lim is Associate Professor in the Department of Management and Organisation at the NUS Business School. She is also the Director of Victim Care Unit at the Office of the Senior Deputy President and Provost in NUS. Sandy obtained her Ph.D. in Organizational Psychology from the University of Michigan. Her research focuses on incivility, mistreatment and disruptive behaviors in the workplace. She also conducts research on medical trauma teams and leadership, occupational health, work–family, and gender issues. Her work has received best paper awards from the U.S. and European Academies of Management and was recently highlighted at the U.S. National Academy of Sciences, Engineering and Medicine. Sandy has received Outstanding Educator Awards at the NUS Business School and has more than 20 years of experience working with different organizations in the public and corporate sectors, including the Singapore Committee for UN Women (UNIFEM), International Labor Organization (ILO), and regional banks and government agencies.

Lucy Liu, BSc, is a research and teaching assistant at the University of Zurich while she conducts her master's studies in banking and finance. She has also previously worked in various finance roles at Julius Baer, Raiffeisen, and Vontobel.

Ke Michael Mai conducts research that mainly focuses on both employee creativity and employee deviance and unethical behaviors. He has published multiple times in top tier journals such as *Journal of Applied Psychology, Organizational Behavior and Human Decision Processes*, and *Journal of Experimental Social Psychology*, and specialty journals such as, *Journal of Business Ethics* and *Journal of Vocational Behavior*. He was selected as one of the "18 influential under 40" Business Professors by *Singapore Business Review* in 2016, and his research has also been covered and featured in various media outlets, such as *CNNMoney, Fortune* magazine, *Huffington Post, Bloomberg Businessweek, South China Morning Post* and *Psychology Today*. He obtained his Ph.D. in Management from University of Arizona, and MA in HRM from Rutgers University.

Malika Richards is Professor of Management at the Pennsylvania State University, Penn State Berks. She has published in journals such as the *Journal of International Management*, *International Business Review*, *Journal of Cross-Cultural Psychology*, and the *Journal of World Business*. Her research interests are the impact of culture on international management and multinational firm strategy.

Prem Shamdasani is Associate Professor of Marketing at the NUS Business School. He is the Academic Director, NUS Executive MBA; Program Co-Director, Stanford-NUS Executive Program in International Management; and Program Director, Marketing Strategy in a Digital World. He is active in teaching marketing strategy, customer-centricity, and branding to senior executives in the executive MBA programs and in open and customized executive education programs. He has worked with more than 110 companies globally in designing, orchestrating and delivering executive programs, workshops, strategy retreats and consulting. He received his Ph.D. in Marketing in 1990 from the University of Southern California, Los Angeles, USA. He has co-authored *Focus Groups: Theory and Practice* for Sage Publications, USA and published articles in the *Journal of Consumer Research*, *Journal of Advertising*, *Journal of Advertising Research*, *Journal of Business Research*, *Journal of Retailing and Consumer Services*, *Asia Pacific Journal of Management*, *Asian Case Research Journal* and *Journal of Leadership Studies*.

Zhaoli Song is Associate Professor of Management and Organization at NUS Business School, National University of Singapore. He has research interests in job search, newcomer socialization, leadership, work emotion, entrepreneurship, cross-culture management, and behavioral genetics. He has published articles in *Academic of Management Journal*, *Journal of Applied Psychology*, *Leadership Quarterly*, *Journal of Business Venturing*, *Human Relations*, *Journal of Vocational Behavior*, *Journal of Organizational Behavior*, *Human Performance*, and *Applied Psychology: An International Review*. Currently, he is the PI of a large project on cross-culture innovation with an Asia-centric perspective.

Gareth S. X. Ting studied at the Department of Psychology, Faculty of Arts and Social Sciences at the National University of Singapore and worked as research assistant at the National University of Singapore Business School, Department of Management and Organisation. He is currently a human resources executive at a global logistics company, where he supports the implementation of evidence-based organization development and culture-building initiatives.

Dean Tjosvold (Ph.D., University of Minnesota) is Emeritus Professor of Management at Lingnan University. In 2005 he was elected to the Academy of Management Board of Governors. He has published over 200 articles, 30 book chapters, and 100 conference papers on managing conflict, cooperation and competition, and other management issues.

Lim Yee Wei is a physician and health systems researcher with two areas of interest. The first area is the design and evaluation of integrated health and social care systems. Recent projects include evaluations of Alexandra Hospital's transitional and community-based programs; co-design of home-based healthcare solutions with patients; development and evaluation of robot nurse assistants; and a case study of a multi-sector integrated care system in the Philippines to improve primary care in impoverished communities. The second area of work explores the role of social innovation in health. Recent projects include the evaluation of social enterprises in Singapore and in Southeast Asia providing community-based healthcare through use of technologies and community empowerment; a systematic review of social ventures in obesity prevention; and the examination of the impact of philanthropic innovations in health. Professor Lim has served as a program implementation and evaluation expert for the Finnish National Institute for Health and

Welfare, ADB, the Asia-Pacific Leaders' Malaria Alliance and Singapore's Ministry of Health. From 2011 to 2017, he was Programme Director of the NIHA (NUS Initiative to Improve Health in Asia) Healthcare Leadership Program for senior leaders in the public, private and NGO sectors. Before joining NUS, he worked as a health policy researcher at the RAND Corporation, USA. His research has been published in journals such as *Nature*, *JAMA* and *Annals of Internal Medicine*.

Alfred Wong (Ph.D., Sheffield Hallam) is Associate Professor of Management at Lingnan University, Hong Kong. He has research interests in the areas of leadership, cooperation and competition, conflict management, and supply chain management. He has published research articles in a variety of international journals.

Kai Chi (Sam) Yam is Associate Professor and Dean's Chair at the National University of Singapore Business School. Sam's research focuses primarily on behavioral ethics, leadership, humor, and the future of work. His work has been published in premier journals such as *Proceedings of the National Academy of Sciences*, *Academy of Management Journal*, *Academy of Management Review*, *British Medical Journal*, *Journal of Applied Psychology*, *Journal of Personality and Social Psychology*, *Organizational Behavioral and Human Decision Processes*, and *Personnel Psychology*. In 2016, Sam was named by Poets and Quants as one of the "Best 40 under 40 Business Professors" in the world.

Jingxian Yao received his Ph.D. in Management at the National University of Singapore Business School. He is currently Assistant Professor at Católica Lisbon School of Business and Economics. Jingxian's research interests include extra-role behaviors, workplace interpersonal relationships, work–family interfaces, and information technology use. Jingxian received the Best Paper Award (Organizational Behaviour Division) at the 2019 Asia Academy of Management Conference and the Kwok Leung Memorial Dissertation Award by the International Association for Chinese Management Research.

Ma Yu is a Ph.D. student in the Organization and Human Resources Department at the Business School, Renmin University, China. Her research interests include servant leadership, human resource management, cross-culture management, organizational behavior, and informal learning. She has published articles in *Human Resources Development of China*. She was a visiting Ph.D. student at the NUS Business School, National University of Singapore from 2019 to 2020.

Jess Zhang currently heads business development (China) for NUS Business School Executive Education. She holds an MBA from CEIBS (China Europe International Business School), Bachelor of Arts from Nanjing University, and a diploma in Post-Production Computer Animation from the Academy of Design (Toronto). Jess has worked and lived in six countries. Prior to joining NUS, she held various corporate relations development positions with Cambridge Judge Business School, University of Cambridge, HULT, and CEIBS. She co-founded CEIBS Centre on China Innovation while she worked as Strategic Planning Manager for the Dean of CEIBS. Jess has a scholarly interest and has published in *Harvard Business Review*, *The Financial Times* and *The European Business Review*. She also translated two bestseller books, *Legionnaire: Five Years in the French Foreign Legion* (over 2 million copies sold worldwide) for Sir Simon Murray, CBE, and *Huawei: Leadership, Culture, and Connectivity* (over 1 million copies globally). Jess loves poetry, painting, graphic design, photography, and video production.

www.ingramcontent.com/pod-product-compliance
Lightning Source LLC
Chambersburg PA
CBHW061815210326
41599CB00034B/7009